Pius XII:
The Hound of Hitler

Gerard Noel read history at Oxford University before being called to the Bar, after which he made writing his career. He is the author of some twenty books, including *The Anatomy of the Catholic Church*.

He was editor of the *Catholic Herald* between 1971 and 1982, and the translator of volume one of the official documents relating to the Holy See in the Second World War.

He is a Vice-President of the Council of Christians and Jews, a Fellow of the Royal Society of Literature and a Freeman of the City of London.

Pius XII:
The Hound of Hitler

GERARD NOEL

continuum

CONTINUUM

The Tower Building 80 Maiden Lane
11 York Road   Suite 704
London   New York
SE1 7NX   NY 10038

www.continuumbooks.com

First published 2008

British Library Cataloguing-in-Publication Data
A catalogue record for this book is available from the British Library.

ISBN 9781847063557

Typeset by YHT Ltd, London
Printed and bound by Cromwell Press, Trowbridge, Wiltshire

Contents

Introduction

The title of this book was carefully chosen. A quest for Eugenio Pacelli has developed during the half-century since Pope Pius XII died in 1958. This particular quest for Pacelli, however, comes to quite different conclusions about Pius XII. Furthermore it is based, in part, on very different and more personal sources from those on which other authors have relied. Below is a brief explanation of why the present study is different from any previous book about this controversial figure, leading to a discovery of the man I have called 'the hound of Hitler'.

In 1948, due to a curious and accidental set of circumstances, I had the fortunate experience of attending, with my mother, a private audience with Pope Pius XII. My interest in this extraordinary man began with that meeting. The audience resulted from a casual remark made to Monsignor David Cashman, secretary to Archbishop William Godfrey, then Apostolic Delegate to Great Britain. Both men were good friends of our family.

Monsignor Cashman, on hearing that we would shortly be visiting Rome, said he would prepare a letter for Archbishop Godfrey to sign. We could present this letter at the Vatican; it would contain a request for an audience with the Pope. Such an audience, we presumed, would involve attending one of the weekly public appearances held by him or would, at most, include us in a 'semi-private' audience where the Pope, moving around one of the ante-chambers of the apostolic palace, would stop at random, chatting to some individuals and then imparting his blessing upon all present.

Our visit to Rome was set for July. By then the Pope had departed for his summer residence at Castel Gandolfo on the shores of Lake Albano, about 15 miles from Rome. We duly presented our letter and subsequently received a note requesting our presence at Castel Gandolfo, a few days later. On arrival, we were directed to sit with a group of people waiting in a large ante-chamber. Eventually a French Monsignor came up to us and, having ascertained our names, asked us to follow him.

We still didn't realize what was happening. The truth suddenly dawned on us when the Monsignor, in answer to my question in halting Italian, stated that we were, of course, to be 'alone with the Holy Father'.

At the end of a long corridor, the Monsignor threw open a door and ushered us into the Pope's study. There was Pius XII sitting bolt upright at his large desk. We were shown to chairs in front of the desk and the Monsignor withdrew.

1

Having until the last minute been unprepared for this bombshell we, perhaps foolishly, had not prepared anything in particular to talk to the Pope about. I told him I had just left Oxford, to which he said, 'Very fine!' (a favourite English phrase of his). He went on to say that the Complete Oxford Dictionary constituted an important item in his library. This, also, he found 'very fine'.

After a slightly awkward pause, my mother mentioned the names of some friends and cousins in America who, she knew, had met the pontiff during his visit there. Pope Pius seemed interested and this topic eked out the remaining minutes of our audience, interspersed with occasional interjections by the Holy Father, mostly to describe something as 'very fine'.

The French Monsignor returned about fifteen minutes later and, after the Pope had given each of us a rosary – wrapped in square white-and-blue envelopes, engraved in gold with the papal coat of arms – we respectfully took our leave. We made our way to our hired car and sank down on the back seat, absolutely stunned, still barely able to believe what had just happened. When we returned to London, I asked Monsignor Cashman what on earth he had put in the Delegate's introductory letter to the Maestro di Camera's office at the Vatican. He later brought a copy of the letter for me to read over lunch. It stated that my father had been a privy chamberlain to Pope Pius XI, who had given First Holy Communion to my sister in his private chapel. It also mentioned that our family was collaterally descended from saints Thomas More, John Fisher and Blessed Margaret Clitherowe. The letter also declared that my father's family (Noel-Gainsborough) was a distinguished 'old Catholic family' (which was not entirely true). The waggish David Cashman and I enjoyed a good chuckle.

However, the experience of our unexpected private audience with Pope Pius XII provided a memory which has never faded. To look across the papal desk into the deep-set, dark, expressive eyes of this awe-inspiring Pope was a supremely evocative experience. From that encounter I began to take an active interest in the life and character of Pius XII, Eugenio Pacelli. This interest was pursued fitfully at first, but increased considerably as time went on. Rolf Hochhuth's provocative play *The Representative* (1963) set in motion a process of intense speculation, associated ever since with the quest for Pacelli.

Many people helped me in my personal quest. The most important was Malachi Martin, a charming and highly articulate American of Irish origin who for several years, as a Jesuit, had been private secretary to Cardinal Augustine Bea SJ, confidant and confessor to Pope Pius XII. Without ever breaking the seal of confession, Bea told Malachi, whom I got to know well after he had left the Society of Jesus, much about Pacelli of which most people, including myself, were ignorant. These were eye-opening revelations.

Having left the Jesuits, Malachi went to live in New York and made many visits to London. I was editing the *Catholic Herald* at the time and met him often, in both cities. He knew of my interest in Pacelli and my translation of the official documents relating to the Holy See and World War Two. This I had found to be a laborious yet ultimately enlightening and rewarding task, giving me valuable insights into the workings of the Vatican and the mind of Pius XII

2

from 1939 to 1940. I had also translated a book by Cardinal Bea, *The Way to Unity after the Council*. This proved a topic of mutual interest when we met.

My debt to Malachi was, and is, considerable. Sadly he died some years ago. His plan to write his own book about Pacelli did not, unfortunately, see the light of day. I never discovered what happened to the large collection of notes and books in his apartment on the Upper East Side of New York.

From our first encounter in 1948, my enduring fascination with Pacelli has thus spanned well over half a century. I found out a great deal about him during my years as a theological student in Rome, from 1953–55. In 1954, many others shared my interest: the Pope entered an intriguing new phase in his life, and Rome was positively vibrant with stories and theories about him.

One reason for previously withholding publication of this book was in order not to upset various people who have helped me and would not necessarily agree with some of my findings. Another reason was my fear of apparent disloyalty to Pius XII. On reflection however, in view of the harm done to him, as much by the well-meant but ill-conceived apologies for his career as by the attacks against him, I realized that it would be more disloyal not to reveal the whole truth about him. Only thus can justice be done.

My quest is therefore rather personal. The political and most controversial part of Pacelli's life, when he was Secretary of State and subsequently Pope, is fully described here, but not narrated in detail. Such minutiae are readily available elsewhere. My quest is for Pacelli the man and Pius the Pope, an attempt to unlock some of the mystery of an extraordinary life. This close-up examination of the psychology of Pacelli will, I hope, provide more clues to the man than yet another account of the outward facts of his life and pontificate.

For instance, this book reveals how Pius's life was saved and prolonged by the cellular rejuvenation treatment of Dr Paul Niehans, who is never mentioned in official histories of this Pope and is rarely mentioned in other accounts. However, this is a fascinating story. Dr Niehans, living in the Vatican and at Castel Gandolfo, administered three courses of treatment, the most important in 1954 when Pacelli had been given up for dead: he made a full recovery and lived for another four years.

Side-effects of the treatment, however, compounded by insomnia and a meagre diet, included the increasingly frequent hallucinations from which the Pope suffered in his last years. These years were also plagued by horrific nightmares. Pacelli's blood-curdling screams could be heard throughout the papal apartments. During waking hours, following such terrible convulsions, his feelings of hatred for Hitler – or rather for Hitler's enormous sins against humanity – surfaced with increased vigour. Pacelli was convinced that Hitler was diabolically possessed. Indeed he conducted solitary nocturnal exercises of exorcism to drive the devil from Hitler's soul. All of this he described in detail (though not under seal of confession) to Cardinal Bea. The latter took a notably enlightened attitude toward the Jews, and the Pope was painfully aware of Bea's views on this matter. Pacelli's decision to stay silent in public about the fate of the Jews caused him acute distress. His silence was motivated by his sense of duty toward the Church, and the fear that such an action would fatally compromise his 'Great Design'.

It was only in 1945, when Hitler was dead, that Pope Pius XII finally issued a condemnation of Nazism as a blasphemous aberration. The inner conflict caused by abstaining from making an earlier statement of his true belief contributed to the depressions and nervous collapses of Pacelli's twilight years. All of this is clear from what he himself said, as recounted later by Bea to Malachi Martin.

The reported visions of Pacelli's later life are impossible to distinguish from his hallucinations. Among these 'visions' were sightings of the Fátima phenomenon in the Vatican gardens, and a long conversation reputedly with Our Lord Himself. Pacelli later recounted how Our Lord had appeared to him in his bedroom. (Vatican wags expressed the hope that Sister Pasqualina had been careful to produce an extra cup of coffee.)

Undoubtedly there are pitfalls in considering Pacelli's mental condition in his latter years. Out of discreetness, most accounts barely allude to his mental difficulties. One must not, however, imply that Pacelli became mentally unbalanced in any ordinary sense; the true situation was much more delicate and complicated. However, an understanding of Pacelli's general mental state is essential if we are to unravel some of the baffling puzzles of his life and career.

No quest for Pacelli would be complete without a considerably more detailed account of the part played in his life by his housekeeper, muse and lifelong companion, Sister Pasqualina. Theirs was one of the great love stories of all time, no less so for being wholly platonic.

Unrecognized by the world, excised from official Vatican accounts, and unfairly ignored by most commentators, Pasqualina was the most powerful woman in papal history. She was also by far the most important person in Pacelli's life. They lived under the same roof, in innocent intimacy, for more than 40 years. Without the missing 'Pasqualina dimension', the true Pacelli is, quite simply, undiscoverable.

Chapter 1

The Quest Begins

Eugenio Pacelli, the third of four children, was born in Rome on 2 March 1876. During his pontificate, from 1939 to 1958, he was routinely described as a member of the 'Black Nobility'. This description applied to that small group of well-born Roman families who had remained staunchly loyal to the popes during the bitter struggle to convert Italy into a united secular state. The struggle, which saw the dismemberment of the Papal States – previously cutting an extensive swathe across central Italy – culminated in the establishment of Rome as the capital of the new nation.

Though Eugenio Pacelli was invariably referred to as an aristocrat, his family was not, strictly speaking, aristocratic. Its members owed their distinction not to nobility or wealth but to being part of that caste of Vatican lay lawyers in the service of the Holy See. In 1861, Eugenio's grandfather, Marcantonio Pacelli, helped found *L'Osservatore Romano*, the influential Vatican daily newspaper. He remained its editor until his death in 1902. The family retained close links with the Vatican. From the 1930s onwards, Eugenio's brother, Francesco, and three nephews were ennobled, in recognition of their legal and business services to the papacy and to Italy. It was thus that the Pacellis came to be considered members of the Roman 'aristocracy', even though they were much humbler than such mighty Roman families as the Orsinis and the Colonnas.

Back in the 1870s, when Pacelli's parents married, Vatican lay lawyers were poorly paid. Even in the agonizingly cold Roman winters, the Pacellis' apartment was heated only by a small brazier, around which parents and children would huddle to warm their hands. Their ethos was one of genteel poverty, allied with pious devotion to their dispossessed Catholic Church. Pacelli's younger sister, Elisabetta, noted the 'great rectitude' of their parents: 'Anything less than delicate expressions never passed their lips.'[1]

As this is not a conventional biography of Pacelli, only such facts about his life will be stressed as throw light upon his character and career. Our choice of facts will also, however, be dictated by the need to describe the atmosphere and attitudes in the Roman Catholic Church of a century and a half ago. This Church, which deeply influenced Pacelli's personality and life, differed so fundamentally from the Church of today as to have been an almost totally distinct entity.

The baby Eugenio was christened, two days after his birth, in the tiny parish church of SS Celso e Giuliano. This was round the corner from his place of birth in the Via degli Orsini. His mother was not well enough to be present. When the newly born baby was brought back from the Church and entrusted to her arms, she allowed herself to kiss him for the first time. No such intimate contact had been permitted before the child was baptized, as his body was believed to have still been inhabited by the devil, due to original sin. The devil was considered to have been expelled by the purifying waters of baptism.

Such was the intensely pious atmosphere of nineteenth-century Catholicism, into which Eugenio Pacelli was born. Also important was the political climate of the Italy in which he came to be brought up. The turning point had come in 1870, six years before Eugenio was born. The doctrine of papal infallibility was proclaimed as the climax of the First Vatican Council, according the Pope a position, at least theoretically, of unprecedented power and prestige. As this great decision was being made, a storm broke over the dome of St Peter's and a tremendous thunderclap, amplified within the basilica's cavernous interior, shattered a pane of glass in one of the tall windows. According to *The Times*, the 'infallibilists', some of them not very confident in the first place, saw the event as a portent of divine disapproval.

Be that as it may, within a matter of weeks Rome had fallen to Italian troops and was lost forever to the papacy. The effect on the once proud papal notables was traumatic. They retired into a sulky state of non-participation in the life of the newly united country. The Pacellis in particular remained faithful to a rejection of the 'usurpation' of the new King, Vittorio Emmanuele.

Henceforth it became the custom among the loyal papal bourgeoisie to wear only one glove, to place a chair facing the wall in the principal room of their residence, and to keep the shutters permanently closed. Modest though their apartment was, though housed in a block termed a *palazzo*, the Pacellis adhered strictly to these practices. Thus was the young Pacelli raised in the atmosphere of a religious life, threatened on all sides. When he became Pope, he raised the Church to a summit of triumphalism such as it had not seen for many years, and was never, after his death, to see again.

Connected with Eugenio's birth – or rather his birthplace – was a certain event which had formerly occurred periodically in Rome's Via Monte Giordano, the street (by its previous name) in which he was born. In this street, for many centuries, it had been the custom for new popes to perform an anti-Jewish ceremony during their processional journey to the basilica of St John Lateran.

The pontiff would halt to receive a copy of the Pentateuch from the hands of Rome's chief rabbi, with members of his flock in attendance. The Pope, having held for a moment the text sacred to the Jews, would return it, upside down, with 20 pieces of gold, proclaiming that while he respected the Law of Moses, he disapproved of the hard hearts of the Jewish race. This was in accord with the view traditionally held by Catholic theologians that, if the Jews would only listen with open hearts to the arguments for the Christian faith, they would instantly see the errors of their ways and convert.

That the Jews did not react in this desired manner had long infuriated official Catholicism. Their refusal to convert led to that special and peculiarly Catholic form of anti-Judaism which, in the time of Pope Pius XII, was still deeply imbued in the minds and hearts of members of the Church. The influence of this anti-Judaism on Pacelli and the whole general Catholic position was considerable, though not in the manner described by many commentators. The true situation was much more complicated and subtle, and will be discussed below at some length. Catholic anti-Judaism was, in many ways, worse than is generally supposed.

Young Eugenio became gradually conscious of all this, while being thoroughly absorbed in the intensely pious Catholic atmosphere of his earliest days. With this was combined a scholarly bent, which had the effect of making him a solitary and withdrawn participant in the events around him. From the age of six or seven onwards, he invariably appeared at table with a book, in which he would absorb himself throughout the meal. He did this, however, only after asking the permission of not only his parents but also of his siblings, Giuseppina, Francesco and Elizabetta. His beguilingly natural manner in making his request dissolved any appearance of priggishness.

Eugenio's piety and scholarly leanings continued to determine his life, both at school and at home. He made daily visits to the Chiesa Nuova near his home – St Philip Neri's Oratory – as well as to the Jesuit Church of the Gesù. Both of these churches, in the Via del Plebiscito, are spectacular monuments to the baroque architectural period of sixteenth-century Rome. At the Gesù, Eugenio poured out his heart to Our Blessed Lady, before her portrait near the tomb of St Ignatius Loyola. She is here pictured as the Madonna della Strada – our Lady of the Street – appearing as an attractive young girl with an abundance of dark hair, unveiled, such as you might come upon, face to face, around any corner in modern Rome. Eugenio made a habit of 'telling everything', including his desire to be a priest when he grew up. In his bedroom, he enacted a celebration of the Mass. His mother encouraged him; some damask, which she gave to him, was his vestment.

Eugenio's earliest education came from a kindergarten run by nuns, and then at a private Catholic elementary school near the Piazza Venezia. This had a clever but autocratic headmaster, Signor Giuseppe Marchi, who gave speeches from his high desk about the 'hard-heartedness' of the Jews.[2] One of Pacelli's contemporary biographers, Nazareno Padellaro, comments, without irony, that 'he [Marchi] knew that the impressions gained by small children are never lost'.[3]

Eugenio was then transferred to the Liceo Qurini Visconti, a state school with a pronounced anti-Catholic, anti-clerical bias. Filippo Pacelli evidently believed that his sons would benefit from first-hand exposure to the views of their secularist 'enemies'. He was probably correct. Certainly members of the Liceo's academic staff were reluctantly impressed by young Eugenio's stubborn and stout defence of traditional Catholic attitudes.

Almost all descriptions of Eugenio mention his 'delicacy' of both mind and body, and his remarkable photographic memory. Among his youthful essays, one, written when he was 15, reveals what seems to have been a rare adolescent setback. It is composed in the third person and describes someone who is 'blind with vain and erroneous ideas and doubts'. Who, he wonders, 'will give him wings' so that he can 'rise from this miserable earth to the highest sphere and tear apart this evil veil that surrounds him, always and everywhere?' He goes on to talk of this person (obviously himself) 'tearing at his hair' and wishing 'he had never been born'. He finishes with a prayer: 'My Lord enlighten him.'[4]

This appears to be a one-off dark episode that never recurred as such. There are, however, curious and striking echoes of it at times in his later life, when he appeared to be surrounded by an 'evil veil'. These were very significant signposts in his life; they have seldom, if ever, been fully recognized.

In another essay, written in Eugenio's teens in the early 1890s, he refers to an 'evil of cowardly silence'.[5] Had he but known it, the evil of (supposedly) cowardly silence was a theme that would reverberate through the career of Cardinal Pacelli, Secretary of State, and of Pope Pius XII, throughout the 1930s, 1940s and 1950s.

An early love which persisted throughout Eugenio's life and was, indirectly, to have decisive consequences, was that of music; he particularly liked Beethoven, Bach, Mozart and Mendelssohn. He was also interested in the history of music. His habit, many years later, of listening to music on the radio during fits of insomnia was to have dramatic and crucial side-effects. His favourite spiritual reading was the *Imitation of Christ*, by Thomas à Kempis, the 15th-century Dutch monastic recluse. The advice in the *Imitation* to show charity to all – with particular regard for those whom we like least – would later have a very special connotation for Eugenio. Also to become relevant later was his devotion to the *Spiritual Exercises* of St Ignatius Loyola.

Eugenio had long nurtured an ambition to study for the priesthood. As Elisabetta succinctly put it, many years later: 'As far as we were concerned, he had been born a priest.'[6] In 1894, he was admitted into the Collegio Capranica which was, and still is, famous as a nursery for Vatican 'high-flyers'. The college was founded in 1457 and named after possibly the most outstanding Renaissance Church figure to be cheated by death from being elected Pope. At the time Eugenio entered the seminary, the Pope was Leo XIII, the inspirer of a new Catholic intellectual renaissance, to be rooted firmly in the medieval teachings of St Thomas Aquinas.

Such 'neo-Thomism' – as it came to be called – lasted well into Eugenio's time as Pope Pius XII. It began to fade rapidly under his successor, Pope John XXIII, in the course of the Second Vatican Council. Pope Leo's ambition to rediscover the lost treasures of Aquinas's inheritance – the marriage of reason and revelation – seemed an inspired answer to the eighteenth- and nineteenth-century period of secular 'enlightenment'. However, during the pontificate of Pope Pius X (1903–1914), it became the blueprint for an excessively narrow approach to theology, which was a factor in the notorious witch-hunt against 'Modernism'. This overshadowed the period of Eugenio's formative early years in the priesthood.

Quite soon however, Eugenio's priestly education received an abrupt setback which caused a profound change. In the summer of 1895, he withdrew from both the Capranica and the Gregorian University for health reasons. According to Elisabetta, the food at the Capanica was to blame. He already suffered from the 'fastidious' stomach which would affect him all his life. It was a principal symptom of his excessively nervous, highly-strung constitution – a constitution that would be crucial to historic events later in his career.

Fortunately (or perhaps unfortunately) this setback did not prove a fatal obstacle to the priesthood. With their loyal service to the Church, the Pacellis had influence at the Vatican. Eugenio's father managed to obtain permission for him to live at home while continuing his studies. He returned to his loving mother's care and remained in it for the next 23 years. After that, he was to find a substitute mother figure in the person of Sister Pasqualina Lehnert. Pasqualina was to become the most important person in his life; she has been described as the most powerful woman in papal history. They lived under the same roof for 41 years.

In later years, Eugenio Pacelli, as Pope Pius XII, was viewed as ascetic and dispassionate, a man almost incapable of earthly emotions and desires. The truth was very different. He was a man filled with such enormity of emotion that he feared to express it – particularly to himself. His mother and Pasqualina gave him an abundance of selfless love. But in the final summer before Eugenio was due to take his vows for the priesthood, he met a beautiful young girl named Lucia, in the mountain village of Onano. Laying aside his childhood dream of the Church, Eugenio proposed to her. She turned him down, thus creating a local saying: 'If Lucia had said yes, he [Eugenio] would never have become Pope.'[7] Had Lucia but known it, on her decision would rest not only the future of the papacy but also the fate of millions.

Eugenio's status as a 'day-boy' seminarian, during which he continued to wear clerical garb, lasted until his ordination on 2 April, Easter Sunday, 1899. Once again he found himself in isolation from his fellow seminarians, whose priestly ordination, along with that of all other candidates from the Rome diocese, took place in the basilica of St John Lateran. Eugenio was ordained in the private oratory of the auxiliary bishop of Rome. It was yet another of the special treatments which singled him out from his fellow ordinands, and was symptomatic of his perennial aura of isolation. Equally, he never lost his devotion to his mother. When he became Pope, he decorated his pectoral cross with her jewels. Significantly, almost every night of his life for nearly 40 years was spent under his mother's roof.

The young priest continued his studies. He specialized in languages and, having obtained a doctorate in theology, embarked upon a postgraduate course on matters of ecclesiastical authority and canon law. These subjects were to dominate his subsequent life and to bring vital influence into his career, especially when channelled into the rarefied world of 'concordat law'.

At around this time he came under the influence of the Jesuits, who published a periodical known as *Civiltà Catholica*. This was strongly anti-Semitic. Eugenio's last years of priestly training coincided with the notorious unfolding in France of the Dreyfus case. Alfred Dreyfus was an army officer wrongly accused of treason, found guilty and imprisoned.

However, even after he was exonerated and pardoned, *Civiltà Catholica* continued to proclaim Dreyfus's guilt. Over the years, it became notorious for its frequent expression of anti-Semitic views.

Decades later, when this author was translating the first volume of the Vatican's official documents concerning World War Two, the Jesuits were still editing *Civiltà Catholica*. They were also in charge of the publication of the Vatican documents. I worked closely with one of their editors, the American Fr Robert Graham, a fervent admirer of Pope Pius XII. Though Fr Graham did not openly express any anti-Semitic views, he made certain remarks and statements about the subject which revealed his general line of thought and also, indirectly, that of his hero, Pope Pius.

Apart from his post-ordination studies, the young priest Eugenio did some part-time work in the field of pastoral care – the care of souls. He was spiritual counsellor to the pupils of the Cenacle Convent in Rome, as well as being a regular visitor to the Convent of the Assumption, near the Villa Borghese. Such activities involved the hearing of confessions of young people and nuns, and serving as celebrant for the chapel liturgies.

These duties constituted the only pastoral work that he performed during his entire career in the Church. This meant that his personal contact with others at a human level, and the moral cares of the ordinary world, never fully penetrated his consciousness. His approach to such matters was based purely on academic study and abstract knowledge. He was a firm supporter, as will later be seen, of an important maxim of the Church at that time: that no human disaster, however horrible, could be as ultimately evil as a single venial (minor) sin.

Nonetheless, a desire to work 'as a pastor of souls' was Eugenio's first ambition; he said so when, late one evening in early 1901, he received an unexpected visitor at home.[8] It was none other than Monsignor Pietro Gasparri, the recently appointed undersecretary at the Department of Extraordinary Affairs, the Vatican's equivalent of the Foreign Office.

Eugenio was playing the violin, accompanied by his sister Elisabetta on the mandolin. The Monsignor's arrival was announced by an insistent rapping at the door. The then 53-year-old Gasparri was one of the stars at the Curia. A portly man, of peasant stock, he was famous in international circles for his brilliance as a canon lawyer. For the previous 18 years, he had held the chair in canon law at the *Institut Catholique* in Paris. He wasted little time in coming to the purpose of his visit. Would young Pacelli join him at the Secretariat of State?

According to Elisabetta, Eugenio could not disguise his amazement. He was still artlessly unaware that his family possessed considerable influence and prestige at the Holy See, and that his own talents had not gone unnoticed. His first reaction to the undersecretary's proposal was to reaffirm his ambition to carry out pastoral duties as a priest. The Monsignor's shrewd reply was to point out the necessity of defending the Church from the onslaught of secularism and liberalism throughout Europe. At this, Eugenio relented.

No two men could have been socially or physically more different from each other than Gasparri and Pacelli. For the next 30 years, however, they worked together in close and harmonious tandem. Their single-minded application to canon law and, as it came to be called, 'concordat law', was to contribute hugely to the twentieth-century development of papal power. It was the forerunner to an even more important period when Pacelli succeeded Gasparri as Cardinal Secretary of State in 1930. He retained this position until he became Supreme Pontiff in 1939.

Thus, from 1901 onwards, Eugenio's professional energies were expended almost exclusively on Curial work. He seldom, if ever, heard confessions or engaged in any other pastoral tasks. His first job in the Secretariat of State was as an *apprendista*, an apprentice, in Gasparri's department. From the very first, he was singled out as a favourite due to his obvious intellectual gifts. From the onset, he was on a 'fast track' to promotion on the clerical ladder. He continued to receive special treatment. Soon he attracted the watchful eye of the ageing Holy Father, Pope Leo XIII. By papal appointment, he was chosen to carry a letter of condolence to London, for presentation at the Court of St James to King Edward VIII, on the death of Queen Victoria. He was still only 25.

Eugenio combined his early work at the secretariat with research for a doctorate at the prestigious Academy for Nobles and Ecclesiastics. The theme for his doctoral thesis was the nature of concordats and the history and principles of negotiating treaties between the Holy See and nation states, monarchies and empires.

The composition of this doctoral thesis was a significant turning point in Eugenio's life. Unspectacular in itself, it formed a vital basis for the most important part of his career, the Great Design of Pope Pius XII, namely to establish a newly strengthened and centralized One True Church as the most powerful body in human society. God's law, as interpreted by this body, would be understood and accepted as never before. It was little less than a revolutionary concept, in that it envisaged the establishment of a virtual world theocracy. Such a notion had never previously been conceived in so systematic a form, nor was it something that is anywhere spoken of in sacred scripture.

As a primary means for bringing into being the triumphalist dream of Pope Pius XII, concordats assumed a position of unprecedented importance in the Church. No less than 25 of them were concluded between 1914 and 1958 (the year Pius XII died.) Pacelli never appeared to regret the first of these – with Serbia, in 1914 – although the pope of the day, Pius X, expired soon after its conclusion. He was said to have died of a broken heart, knowing that the Serbian concordat was an important contributory cause of the outbreak of war. Even more disastrous were the consequences of the 1933 concordat with Nazi Germany, which Pacelli, its principal author, hailed at the time as a masterstroke.

Part of the young Eugenio's aim in producing a thesis on the subject was to refute the view of many Catholic theologians that concordats should play no part in the life of the Church. This institution was seen to possess, by definition, a natural superiority over all purely humanly constructed organizations. Political nationhood, moreover, had only recently, and very reluctantly, been recognized by the Church. She, it was persistently maintained, exercised a unique supra-national position of sovereign power over the whole world. No compromise with an individual political state – which every concordat, to some extent, had to be – was, on this view, either necessary or desirable.

Eugenio countered this view by a powerful argument in favour of the Church's right and duty, by quasi-political means, to be recognized as the supreme law-making authority in the world. The views of Pope Pius XII were echoed by Robert Graham SJ in his 1959 work, *Vatican Diplomacy.*

As mentioned previously, it was Fr Graham with whom the author worked on the translation of the Vatican's wartime documents, of which he was one of the editors. He was an unquestioning admirer of Pius XII who, it must be observed, was himself more interested and accomplished in canon law, politics and diplomacy, than in theology.

Something else happened in the early part of Eugenio's life, which had seemingly little to do – at least directly – with his studies or his incipient career. Yet the events involved throw light on another aspect of his character, to which justice has never been fully accorded.

Maria Teresa Pacelli was the daughter of Eugenio's uncle, Ernesto, another family member possessing 'a certain influence with the Holy See'.[9] Maria Teresa's parents had separated, for reasons unrecorded; consequently, from the age of five she lived almost entirely with the nuns of the Convent of the Assumption. In the year 1901 or thereabouts, Maria Teresa, then aged 13, was plunged into a *silenzio sepolcrale* – a sepulchral silence, or depression – as a result of a quarrel between her mother and one of the nuns. During a lesson, the nun had made disparaging remarks about the King of Italy. Maria Teresa's mother took grave exception. There was a terrible row, which proved extremely upsetting to Maria Teresa. The poignant importance of what followed cannot be overestimated; it also throws light on the complex psychological make-up of Pacelli. No one without personal knowledge of such a tribulation can imagine the agonies suffered by Maria Teresa at her impressionable age. The situation was very similar to what used to happen in upper-class English families.

Maria Teresa was evidently extremely fond of the nun with whom her mother quarrelled. Their quarrel wounded her deeply. The convent school had, after all, been her home for the previous eight years. It is almost certain that she would have formed deeper emotional ties with the nun at school than with her own mother. It was akin to the relationships established in former times between children, their nannies and their mother, the latter of whom they would normally only see for about half an hour each day. This was usually (in England, at least) after tea in the evening. If there was a quarrel between the nanny and the mother – and there often was – it could be deeply unsettling for the child. When the nanny finally left, the sense of loss for the child was almost unbearable.

Grown-ups rarely, if ever, realized what agonies their children suffered in these circumstances. The only solace might lie with an understanding person, to whom the suffering youngster could pour out his or her heart. It was in such circumstances that Maria Teresa Pacelli suffered a nervous breakdown. Her father, although remaining estranged from his wife, realized that his grievously suffering daughter needed someone in whom she could confide. He arranged for her to have regular meetings with her young priest cousin, Eugenio. Even though no 'cure' was effected, at least in the short term, it was an inspired choice on the part of Ernesto.

Did he have an instinctive awareness that Eugenio possessed a degree of imaginative sympathy appropriate for listening to his daughter's woes? The question is interesting, though any answer can only be speculative; but there is enough circumstantial evidence to suggest a plausible scenario.

We must also consider what lasting effects on Eugenio's psyche there may have been from the incident, already described, when, in his middle teens, he wrote of an imaginary person's 'wishing he had never been born'. The absence of a detailed account of the effects of this incident on Pacelli does not mean there were no effects. There obviously were – and evidence from Pacelli's later life suggests that they were traumatic. In one way or another, they had recurring consequences for the rest of his life.

Was the event which occurred when he was 15 the cause – or, perhaps, result – of the first of his many (known) nervous collapses? Such an eventuality is very possible; if so, it is probable that Ernesto Pacelli was aware of it. It is difficult otherwise to account for the pains he took to arrange the regular meetings between Eugenio and his troubled daughter. He must have known that Eugenio was particularly well equipped to help her.

No one is more likely to sympathize with the torments of a psychologically disturbed person than someone who has personally suffered similar problems. The cause of the problems does not matter.

They differ in every case, but the result is always the same: acute depression in the form of an impenetrable black cloud, hanging over the afflicted person during every waking moment. Theoretical expertise, as demonstrated by psychiatrists, often does more harm than good. The same can be said of much modern medication, in the form of anti-depressants and tranquillizers. There were, in any event, no such things in Pacelli's day. Nothing can replace the patient and understanding attention of a sensitive companion who is prepared to listen. Such a person, in the case of Maria Teresa Pacelli, between 1901 and 1906, was her cousin Eugenio. True, the attention and care he gave Maria Teresa regularly for those five years did not effect a cure, for no such cure is easily possible, unless something is provided by nature itself.

The opportunity, however, to confide in an understanding person can offer immense, albeit temporary, relief. Thus it was that, once a week for five traumatic years, Eugenio and Maria Teresa met every Tuesday for at least two hours. They walked and talked and sat in the vestibule of the convent chapel. Maria Teresa never forgot the experience. She spoke of it after Pacelli was dead. At the tribunal, considering his possible beatification, she stated: 'he opened me up . . . our two souls came together, bound by God'.[10] There is more than a hint that Maria Teresa was aware that her cousin was also prone to pangs of depression, so acutely sensitive was he to the symptoms of her own malaise.

In describing the development of their friendship, Maria Teresa went even further: 'Our two souls came together, bound by God', she declared. In Eugenio, she found 'another Christ'. Their conversations were protected by the seal of confession. Clearly, however, it was not a one-way affair. Eugenio obviously revealed important things about himself in the course of the 'discretion and secrecy' of their exchanges.

It is a touching story. Sadly, their friendship ended with distressing abruptness. Despite his originally sound instinct, Ernesto Pacelli failed to show such understanding later on. When Maria Teresa reached the age of 18, he put an end to the relationship. It had produced an intimacy which he could not understand, and of which he became suspicious. 'My father', Maria Teresa recorded, 'did not comprehend the discretion and secrecy, nor did he understand the noble integrity of Don Eugenio.' She goes on to describe how she 'mournfully accepted this humiliation and lost a unique support and moral and spiritual guidance'.[11]

Indeed it is easy to see how, from a purely conventional and worldly point of view, Ernesto could have misunderstood this unusual kind of relationship and become fearful that it might, if allowed to continue, have undesirable consequences. Looking forward, however, to the relationship – again unique, but in a different way – that existed for over 40 years between Pius XII and Sister Pasqualina, we can learn much from this earlier incident. In neither case was there any conventionally romantic element; the relationship was all the stronger for its absence. Such a thing can happen, though in rare cases, between people of opposite sexes.

In our quest for Pacelli, it can thus be seen that clues begin to accumulate, even in his early life: a devout, pious family, highly professional and respected, yet relatively impoverished; strong and abiding Church links; a desire to restore a dispossessed Vatican to its rightful place in the world; continuing insider influence on the young Eugenio's behalf; the Thomas à Kempis duty to show charity to all, *especially those whom we love least*; the anti-Semitism of Signor Marchi and of *Civiltà Catholica*; a quasi-mystical devotion to the Blessed Virgin Mary; a strong dependence on a mother figure; the desire to do simple pastoral work overridden by the Church's demand that Eugenio become a legal professional in its service; and finally, the use of the Pacellis' special interest in canon law to solve the Vatican's problems of dispossession by creating a new and all-encompassing Church order.

When combined with fresh evidence now available, these factors begin to throw new light on the personality and career of Eugenio Pacelli, the idealistic young man who would, one day, become Pope Pius XII. The interaction of these factors is the key to understanding the seemingly paradoxical nature of Pius XII. He emerges as an intellectually brilliant but psychologically fragile vessel, confronting ruthlessly powerful men, devoid of any scruple whatsoever, at the darkest hour in history.

Chapter 2

The Design Unfolds

Pacelli received his doctorate in concordat law in 1904. He had already made his mark at the secretariat and was soon promoted to the rank of *minutante*. His job involved digesting reports that were despatched to the secretariat from all over the world. In the same year, he was made a papal chamberlain with the title of *Monsignor*, and the following year a *domestic prelate*. He was meanwhile immersing himself more deeply than ever in the subject which was to be the basis of his work with Gasparri, namely the colossal task of revising and reforming the Church's Code of Canon Law.

Two years after embarking on this task, he made another trip to London. This was more elaborate than his earlier one, for it was in the nature of a 'state' visit, on which he accompanied the Holy See's Secretary of State. This was the formidable figure of Cardinal Rafael Merry del Val, right-hand man to Pope Pius X in the anti-Modernist campaign, often referred to as a 'witch-hunt'.

Merry del Val was no stranger to London, where his brother had been Spanish Ambassador. He was half-Irish, and spoke fluent English. The principal task of Merry del Val and Pacelli was to attend, representing the Pope, the first Eucharistic Congress to be held in Great Britain. They processed in great state through Westminster's streets. Merry del Val was received by English Catholics with a fervent enthusiasm which might not have been shared by their Anglican fellow-countrymen had they known something of his earlier accomplishments. For Monsignor (as he then was) Merry del Val had composed the first draft of a document later promulgated as a Bull by Pope Leo XIII, entitled *Apostolicae Curae*. This papal document solemnly, but not infallibly, pronounced Anglican clerical orders to be 'absolutely null and utterly void'. Such a pronouncement had a stunning effect on English Anglicans, but not in the way Pope Leo had been led to expect.

Nearly 20 years earlier, Cardinal Herbert Vaughn had been Archbishop of Westminster. He had set his heart on the 'conversion of England' which, in his eyes, could only come about by the unqualified 'return' of the Church of England to its allegiance to Rome and the Pope. He was convinced that, if England's Anglicans could be persuaded by a solemn dictum from the Holy Father that their ministers, including bishops, had never been validly ordained to the priesthood, they would embark on a stampede to be 'received back' into the 'one, true Church of Rome'.

Cardinal Vaughn was greatly disappointed when the opposite happened; there was a pronounced hardening of Anglican feeling against Rome. English Catholics today mostly believe that Pope Leo's Bull, whose original scholarship was suspect, has long since been overtaken by events and opinions and is now a dead letter. Unfortunately, however, there is little chance that Leo's Bull will be officially overturned. Such is not the way of the Holy See.

The 'Anglican orders' Pope, Leo XIII, had been replaced in 1903 by a man of very different stamp in Giuseppe Sarto, who reigned as Pope Pius X. The favourite for the papacy had been the erstwhile Secretary of State, Cardinal Rampolla; but his election was thwarted by the last case of outside secular interference with a papal conclave, in the form of an imperial 'veto' from the emperor of Austria.

Sarto, Pius X, was the antithesis of his aloof and aristocratic predecessor: the peasant son of a postman and seamstress, he had no inside knowledge of Church affairs but was chosen because of the supposed need for the papal guidance of a good and simple parish churchman.

The anti-Modernist campaign has already been referred to as a 'witch-hunt', which it undoubtedly was. By keeping a low profile, Pacelli escaped any form of discipline or censure, though many of his fellow Curialists suffered unjustly and grievously. Pacelli never voiced any positive approval for the policy of Pius X, still less the tactics by which it was executed, which included a successful espionage system. However, when he became Pope Pius XII he canonized Pius X, who was thus the first pope to be declared a saint since Pius V (1566–72). The latter, allowing for a difference of methods, had pursued very similar aims to those of Pius X. Both were determined to stamp out, as far as possible, all traces of dangerous heterodoxy.

More will be said later about the canonization (in 1954) of Pius X, for it provides an illuminating insight into Pacelli as Pope, and the way his mind was working toward the end of his pontificate. Suffice to note, for the moment, that the anti-Modernist witch-hunt was finally brought to an end only by the advent of a new pontiff, in Benedict XV, formerly Giacomo della Chiesa. When the latter sat down at his desk for the first time as Pope he found, among the papers, a list of those to be investigated as suspected Modernists. His own name was at the top of the list, which he immediately tore up.

What is relevant, however, is the pronounced effect that Pius X's harsh policy and tactics had on Pacelli. They taught him to be consummately nimble and sure-footed when climbing the slippery Vatican ladder. So many clerics, seminarians, teachers, administrators, parish priests, even bishops, were being spied upon and (often unjustly) condemned, that no one was safe. But Pacelli came through unscathed. He was lucky to specialize in canon law and to be only peripherally concerned with theological matters.

Years later, Pius XII forgave the excommunicated Romolo Murri, the heroic anti-Fascist. At heart, however, Pacelli favoured Pius's approach, unlike his boss, Cardinal Gasparri. The most important thing to happen to Pacelli as a result of the anti-Modernist persecution was the acquisition of impeccable skills in veiled language. He weighed every word he wrote or uttered with extreme caution. His utterances were masterpieces of circumspection, couched in a cocoon of elegantly ambiguous circumlocution. He never lost either the skill or the habit.

Apart from his association with anti-Modernism, Pius X was also responsible, though less well remembered, for one of the most important projects in the twentieth-century history of the Roman Church. It has already been referred to: the reform and updating of the Code of Canon Law. The project began in strict secrecy, as if a 'new order' was being imposed on the universal Church by some sort of conspiracy. In a sense, this was true. The text, as it slowly evolved, of the new Law Code was combined with the anti-Modernist oath, which all priests had to take, to establish a Church based on papal authority that would 'rule the world' with greater power than ever before. This was a stupendous objective.

Though inspired by Pius X, the massive new project was to have Gasparri and Pacelli, its principal architects, using the new weapons being forged to secure the support, on an unprecedented scale, of the world's 2,000 theological scholars and 700 bishops.

Canon Law had been developing in haphazard fashion for centuries. It had become a bewildering jungle of decrees, rules and regulations. Its organization – or rather disorganization – was based on date rather than theme or topic. Above all it was rich in local diversity, a principal defect as the reformers now saw it, which had to be eliminated in favour of universality and suitability for centralized control. Earlier attempts at this general objective, notably by Pope Pius IX in 1864, had had to be abandoned; subsequent events, particularly the Franco-Prussian war, had caused further postponement.

The Franco-Prussian war, moreover, saw the rise of intense anti-Catholic persecution in Germany, with Bismarck's *Kulturkampf*. It was the Church's courageous reaction to *Kulturkampf* which spurred the Catholics of Germany in the 1930s to show such spirited resistance to Nazism when it first appeared. The supreme irony was that this resistance gradually withered and died as a result of the policy of the Holy See itself, masterminded in the 1930s by none other than Pacelli.

Unlike all previous attempts at reform, work on the proposed new body of canon law was motivated by one primary objective. The aim now was for complete codification, not merely a new compilation. Any local considerations were to be replaced by universalism, based on purely abstract principles. What would emerge were complete and tightly controlled conformity, centralization and discipline: the crucially necessary weapons for the main plank of Pacelli's dream and Great Design. This was the raising of the Church to a position of unchallenged and unprecedented greatness in the world, by virtue of power exercised exclusively from the centre, or the apex if you will, of a mighty pyramid. At this apex stood the Pope, whose supremacy was described in the proposed new Canon 218 as 'the supreme and most complete jurisdiction throughout the Church, both in matters of faith and morals, and in those that affect discipline and Church government throughout the world'.[1] It was the most extreme claim, in explicit official form, of absolute Church power to have been made since Boniface VIII had declared that, in order to be saved, every human being must owe obedience to the Bishop of Rome.

A crucial extension was given to papal power by Canon 1323. There was now to be a blurring of the distinction between the 'ordinary' and the 'solemn' teaching authority of the Pope. Thus was created a confusion that the fathers of the First Vatican had tried so hard to avoid. This meant that there was now scope for papal encyclicals to be regarded in practice as having the same authority as an *ex cathedra* dogma. The phenomenon came to be known as 'creeping infallibility'. The net for ensnaring heterodoxy was subtly widened. Heresy and error were conflated by the terms of Canon 1324 with the statement that 'It is not enough to avoid heresy.'[2] This provision went on to declare that 'one must also carefully shun all errors that more or less approach it; hence all must observe the constitutions and decrees by which the Holy See has proscribed and forbidden opinions of that sort'.

Clearly Pacelli had absorbed the all-encompassing spirit of Pius X's anti-Modernism crusade. And it was Pacelli who did the lion's share of the work in compiling the new code. A vital new ruling was an exact definition of what comprised those 'constitutions and decrees' which had to be obeyed without question. They included 'all doctrines and decrees of the Holy See, even though they be not infallibly proposed and even though they come from the Sacred Congregations with the approval of the Holy Father'.[3] A concession of sorts was appended, in that such decrees were not strictly binding articles of faith. They merited, however, 'genuine internal and intellectual assent and loyal obedience'.[4] Thus was Pius X's anti-Modernist oath absorbed into the Code of Canon Law.

A severe blow was dealt to the possibility of meaningful ecumenical discussion. Catholics, it was stated in Canon 1325, 'are to avoid disputations or conferences about matters of faith with non-Catholics, especially in public, unless the Holy See ... has given permission'.[5] The Holy Office (formerly the Inquisition) was given a monopoly – by Canon 246 – of all judgements as to theological orthodoxy. A spate of ancillary rules grew up regarding censorship, control, supervision, correction, etc., in order to bolster and back up the main directives of the new code.

Finally and crucially, the same right to nominate bishops was given exclusively to the Pope. An instinct for the need to soften in practice the impact of this last requirement prompted the fathers of the Second Vatican Council to give their attention to 'collegiality'. This was a method of ensuring that the Pope's teaching power was to be shared with the college of bishops. In practice however, the originally desired effect was not changed, as all bishops were chosen by the Pope, according to his own views. Nevertheless, as we shall see, the practical extent of the Pope's power to nominate all bishops came into question during the negotiations for various concordats. This was a factor in the extremely difficult task of 'tidying up' concordat law and was to be of particular importance in the Holy See's dealings with Nazi Germany, masterminded by Pacelli. The monumental task of Gasparri and Pacelli, taking more than a dozen years, resulted in the code's being promulgated in May, 1917.

Thus was the mighty pyramidal structure built up at the beginning of the twentieth century. Before the code was even published, the Holy See's new thought-processes were already being tested in the Church's relations with France. This country had, of late, simultaneously exhibited virulent forms of both anti-clericalism and anti-Semitism. The Church had to accept the French ideal of a complete separation between church and state. The withdrawal of Catholics from political activity, however, was favoured by the Church as, crucially, it would be later in Nazi Germany. Catholic exclusion from politics and the self-destruction of the Centre (Catholic) Party – on the orders of the Holy See – was the price demanded by Hitler for his agreement to the concordat of 1933. It was thus that Hitler was given absolute power by the Enabling Act, a sinister turning point in modern history.

Gasparri and Pacelli's Code of Canon Law would regulate activity within the Church; concordats (legal agreements between the Church and temporal governments) would regulate activity externally. Canon law and concordats would thus form an integrated mechanism for implementing the Great Design. Unfortunately, concordats had enjoyed a chequered history. Cardinal Consalvi (1757–1824), Secretary of State under Pope Pius VII (1740–1823), had achieved a restoration of the Papal States via the Council of Vienna in 1815. Pius and Consalvi then began a series of concordats with European states. These signed contracts governed areas such as freedom of worship, the autonomy of local churchmen, teaching and schooling. The relevant nuncios monitored execution. Certainly these concordats secured benefits, yet they failed to save the Vatican from losing its temporal possessions in 1870. Concordats, as purely legal documents, had proved a poor substitute for the traditional spiritual power wielded by popes over governments and governed alike. Nevertheless to Pacelli, the canon lawyer, concordats were crucial to advancing the political power of the Church.

The first of the new concordats – with Serbia – occurred before the publishing of the 1917 Code of Canon Law. Pacelli was the chief negotiator on the part of the Holy See. That this concordat had disastrous results – in being a contributory cause of the Great War – did not, amazingly, ever seem to occur to Pacelli. Rather was it a vital cornerstone of what was to become his Great Design. One of his cherished aims was to extend the influence of Western and Latin Christianity (Roman Catholicism) into areas of Europe dominated by Orthodoxy. A friendly agreement with Serbia, a predominantly Orthodox country, would, it was thought, be a valuable first step toward this objective.

The fact that grave offence would be given to the neighbouring Austro-Hungarian Empire – together with a relinquishment of the latter's protectionist rights over Serbia – was not, unbelievably, taken into consideration. Rather was it Pacelli's prime objective to establish a Catholic 'foothold' in Orthodox territory. The Catholic population of Serbia was still small but had increased, by its recent expansion into Macedonia, Epirus and northern Albania, as a result of the 1912 war with Turkey. The actual numbers involved do not sound particularly impressive; but, relatively speaking, they were at the time. With the added territories, the number of Catholics in greater Serbia increased from about 7,000

19

to 40,000. The mostly Orthodox Serbia considered it would be advantageous to make friends with them.

On the other hand, Austria's protectorate rights over Serbia looked as if they were about to be swept away. This was viewed with great concern in Vienna. However, the Holy See appeared indifferent. The rights in question, though largely symbolic, had been jealously guarded for more than a century. They carried the authority to nominate bishops and to educate Balkan priests of the Latin rite in seminaries in Austria and Hungary. Even assumed was a right on the part of the Austro-Hungarian Empire to invade Serbian regions if Catholic communities were deemed to be under threat. The Austro-Hungarians prized such rights highly. They were nevertheless destroyed by the 1914 concordat, with a minimum of direct discussion with the Empire.

Conversely, Serbia had everything to gain by the concordat. The country was a patchwork of conflicting elements. The concordat removed doubt about its fierce sectarian partisanship of Orthodox Christianity. Also favoured were its imperialistic ambitions to be a focus of unity within the patchwork of peoples of both Latin and Orthodox background in the region.

The Holy See too had much to gain. An end was signalled to the centuries of antagonism after the original 'schism' between Rome and Orthodoxy. The prospect was opened up of Catholic, Latin and Eastern (Catholic) Rite evangelization toward Russia and Greece. The papacy, moreover – and herein lay Pacelli's greatest dream – would be endowed with vital elements of authority, such as the appointment of bishops and prelates. These were later to be incorporated in the 1917 Code of Canon Law, to which, of course, Pacelli was ever looking forward. Such rights, until now, had been enjoyed by the Austrian Emperor via ancient usage. Pacelli was exalted by it all. The first plank in his Great Design seemed about to fall into place.

Conversely, Austria-Hungary was deeply troubled. She had most to lose by the proposed arrangements, on which she was barely being consulted. Most of all, she dreaded an increase of Serbian, pan-Slavic influence along her southern borders. The great empire, for so long a major bulwark of Catholic prestige in Europe, seemed about to be humiliated – by the Holy See.

Was Pacelli unaware of such considerations? Or was he indifferent to them? His eyes, as on later occasions, were fixed firmly on the future and the welfare of his Great Design. The whole affair tended to portray him as a tactician rather than a strategist, a diplomat rather than a prophet, a politician rather than a statesman.

The greatest short-term act of blindness was, in other words, the ignoring of the effect of the concordat on Austria. Was the 1914 concordat, then, a significant contributory cause of the Great War? Unquestionably it was. Nevertheless Pacelli, the Vatican's chief negotiator throughout, hurried the project to a conclusion despite all warnings, including solemn cautionary advice from the papal nuncio in Vienna.

In the latter capital, news of the concordat provoked outrage. The press was up in arms. Headlines blazed with indignation at the proposed treaty. Austria sent an imperious ultimatum to Serbia. It contained terms to which Serbia could not possibly agree. From then on, war was inevitable. Looking back on it all, with the inevitable accumulation of hindsight, it is ironic and rather awe-inspiring to contemplate that, among the immediate causes of both the Great War and the rise of Hitler to supreme power, were the policies of the Holy See. In each case, the single most important person directing the Holy See's actions was Eugenio Pacelli.

The Serbian concordat presents us, for the first time, with a close-up view of Pacelli's methods and mentality. Such methods were to be repeated on crucial occasions in the future, notably over the negotiations for the concordat with the Third Reich. The most striking characteristic of such methods was single-mindedness, coupled with constant reference to the Great Design. Pacelli was thus determined, regardless of what pleadings came from Vienna, to end the Austrian protectorate over Serbian ecclesiastical affairs for the sake of his treasured centrist papal policies.

Any local benefit that might accrue for Serbian Catholics took distinctly second place. As a gesture, though a somewhat empty one, to the Austrians, Pacelli was prepared to promote the idea of *patronatus* rights. These consisted of such 'purely honorific rights as are compatible with canon law'.[6]

We here see Pacelli acting in his favourite role of meticulous canonist. The scheme would involve the Austrians in the intricacies of canon law, on the pretext of preserving something of their protectionist role in Serbia. As Pacelli himself well knew, however, the proud and mighty, classically Catholic Austro-Hungarian Empire would, in practice, retain nothing in the way of their long-treasured 'honorific rights'.

Pacelli would not be moved. He received the backing, moreover, of the formidable Secretary of State, Cardinal Merry del Val. The latter advanced cogent reasons of his own in favour of the Serbian concordat and remarked that 'If we say that we cannot trust the Serbs, all the more reason for pinning them down with a concordat.' Herein lay an ominous foreshadowing of the argument employed by Pacelli to justify the Reich Concordat. As previously mentioned, the fallacious reasoning lay in the implication that a mere piece of paper was needed to justify the exercise of papal power.

Even more ominous were the words of Cardinal Gasparri, just before the concordat with Serbia was signed. Gasparri alone seemed to understand the dangerous net into which the Holy See was being drawn. The Curia imagined that the opportunity was being created to exert direct control over Catholics in the Balkans, leading to the glittering prospects of missionary success in the (Orthodox) East. Serbia, however, was shrewdly luring the Vatican into the notorious quicksands of Balkan politics, without its realizing the inevitable tensions in the region to which this might lead. Nevertheless, the first major step of Pacelli's Great Design had been successfully taken. There could be no turning back. The concordat was signed on 24 June 1914. On 28 June the Austrian Emperor, Archduke Franz Ferdinand, was gunned down in Sarajevo by a pro-Serbian terrorist. The most terrible war, until then, of modern times was declared on 4 August. On 20 August, Pope Pius X died – it was said of a broken heart.

In the midst of these tumultuous events, Pacelli's career was going from strength to strength. He was soon to become undersecretary at the Sacred Congregation for Extraordinary Ecclesiastical Affairs. Pius X was succeeded by the very different and more gentle figure of Giacomo della Chiesa, as Pope Benedict XV. It was this pope who was to nominate Pacelli Archbishop of Sardi [Sardes] on 13 May 1917.

On the very same day, at Fátima in Portugal, three children claimed to have seen an apparition of Pacelli's childhood icon, the Blessed Virgin Mary, surrounded by dazzling light. Subsequently, the spinning sun of Fátima was allegedly witnessed by thousands. In 1928, the first great Secret of Fátima was revealed. It dealt with the twin perils of Pacelli's life – war and communism. Forty years afterwards, at the end of his life, Pacelli would himself witness, in the Vatican gardens, the apparent phenomenon of the spinning sun. And the child who gave the first great Secret of Fátima to the world? She bore the name Lucia – that of Pacelli's lost love.

Chapter 3

The First Breakdown: Enter Pasqualina

Josefine Lehnert was born on 25 August 1894, the seventh of 12 children, on a small farm near the country village of Ebersberg in Bavaria, about 25 miles from Munich. As with the young Eugenio Pacelli, some 16 years previously, she was a serious, pious child. Yet where he was introverted she was extroverted, fearless and bold and possessed of an instinctive sense of leadership which he would always lack. In the words of her mother Maria, 'Josefine was a lady at seven, the year that she received her First Holy Communion.'[1] Her bemused family celebrated her general bossiness with the teasing nickname 'Mother Superior'. Her disapproval of anything that seemed silly or wrong was conveyed by a swift, merciless 'No!' Decades hence, her swift, merciless 'No!' would puncture the bombast of the most powerful cardinals in the Vatican.

The Pacellis had been professionals, albeit relatively impoverished. By contrast, the Lehnerts were peasant subsistence farmers, rising at dawn for 15-hour days of unremitting toil. The faces of both parents were etched with the pain of lives of struggle, simply to put food on the table for 14 people. In the kitchen, the one room in the house big enough for all of them, the whole family would get down on their knees on the bare boards to pray together at the beginning of each day. More than 80 years later, a *grande dame*, once named Josefine, would remember the cracks in those bare boards and the soil beneath.

Almost from the outset, it was obvious that Josefine was spectacularly different from the rest of her family. Were her father and mother parents to her, or was she the parent to them? At the age of five, she delighted them by asking that the family said an extra prayer ... then another. At the age of seven, she horrified them by volunteering to get up at four-thirty in the morning to work in the fields. This time it was her mother who exclaimed: 'No, Josefine! Absolutely not!'[2]

Yet it quickly became apparent that, while Josefine was only too willing to say 'No!', she was equally unwilling to accept it. A few days later, she sidled up to her mother and, with honeyed tongue, murmured: 'Mama, why is it wrong for a girl to work in the fields?' Before her stunned mother could answer, she followed her first question with another, the verbal equivalent of a knockout punch: 'When did Jesus say that women and girls should not be in the fields?'[3]

A century later we feel a stab of pity for poor, tired Maria, confronted with a daughter old beyond her years. When Josefine asked, 'Is it wrong for me to want to do different things?' Maria must have instinctively known that her cherished child would go far beyond the little farm at Ebersberg.

So Josefine joyfully chose what her horrified family regarded as drudgery. Tiny Josefine worked in the fields. Tiny Josefine milked huge cows. Tiny Josefine turned out for work in a starched white blouse and pleated chequered skirt that she had pressed herself. Years later, she noted: 'There's no reason why people working at hard labour cannot dress cleanly and neatly. Discipline is the answer. If one learns discipline during childhood, all things are possible.'[4] In Josefine's life, so many, many things would be possible. And yet those things which remained resolutely impossible would plunge her into an abyss of pain.

Meanwhile her childhood continued apace, as her indomitable 'Mother Superior' persona remorselessly dominated the family. 'I hate clutter!' she admonished untidy brothers twice her age. Boys taking baths in the kitchen in full view of the family? 'It's not right!' she insisted, and banished them to a makeshift bathing place she created in the barn. 'What nonsense', her father scoffed. 'I've bathed in the kitchen all my 50 years and I'm not changing now. No daughter is going to tell me what to do!'[5] Soon afterwards, he too ended up in the barn.

As Josefine grew, so also did her unshakeable self-confidence. She was a leader in her family and a leader at school. Her solitary daily journey of several miles, from home to school, gave her precious time to herself. She practised French and Italian, perhaps unconsciously accepting that the farm at Ebersberg would have to be left, sooner or later.

Hard work on the farm; hard work at school. Like Pacelli, Josefine was an exemplary student, getting straight A's. Whereas she lacked his intellectual brilliance, she compensated with her experience of the rough and tumble of everyday life which he would never encounter directly. The Lenherts were a pious family, no less than the Pacellis. But if, with the Pacelli parents, 'Anything less than delicate expressions never passed their lips', it is highly likely that strikingly indelicate expressions passed the lips of Josefine's father and six brothers when they stubbed toes or missed a nail and hammered a thumb instead. It is equally likely that she promptly admonished them.

On Josefine's 11th birthday, she received a kitten. While she was bathing it in the sink, three of her brothers threw in a snake. That evening, when they were bathing in the barn, she threw in three snakes, one for each of them. If Pacelli had thrown a few snakes around in his childhood, he might have been better prepared to deal, later on, with certain politicians – the greatest snakes of all.

When she was 13, her 21-year-old brother John, a part-time mechanic, appeared with a wondrous new invention which terrified the family – a motorcycle. Josefine jumped up and down in excitement, begging him to take her for a spin. To Maria's horror, they roared off in a blur of speed. Josefine, the 'good girl', the relentless perfectionist, had discovered an addictive, lifelong excitement. In later years she would cry, '*Più presto! Più presto!*' ('Faster! Faster!'), exhorting the papal driver to put his foot down hard on the accelerator.[6] And one day, she would even drive a motorcycle herself. In its sidecar would sit a most distinguished passenger – Eugenio Pacelli.

As the young Eugenio had done more than a decade earlier, Josefine turned her tiny attic bedroom into a private shrine to Jesus and the Blessed Mother. There she prayed. For all of their lives they would share a desire for the joy of private prayer and meditation, and their private rooms would be characterized by Spartan simplicity. The young Josefine's rosary beads hung from a nail by the door of her bedroom.

As she grew into her teens however, Josefine realized the hopelessness of her situation, a peasant girl trapped in a web of poverty and ceaseless toil. Surely life must hold more than this? Would her childhood élan tarnish into dull mediocrity?

In 1910, at the age of 15, she attended the Passion Play at Oberammergau. She witnessed the enactment of Jesus's suffering, His supreme gift of His life for humanity, His plea that others would follow.

Her parents were outraged when she told them of her decision to leave home to become a nun. Their devotion to Catholicism was one thing; losing their favourite child was quite another. But reasoning was futile. For perhaps the first time in her life, Josefine encountered an argument which she could not possibly win.

And so, at 15, she left home. She went out into the world with barely any possessions as, nearly 50 years later, she would go out into the world once again, from the Vatican, with barely any possessions. There were then no friends for refuge, no welcoming community to embrace her.

Worst of all, she had to leave home without even saying goodbye to her parents and her 11 brothers and sisters. And such was the strength of her father's disapproval, she knew that once having left, she could never return.

It is well-nigh impossible for us to imagine the harshness of convent life 100 years ago. The Teaching Sisters of the Holy Cross at Altötting, near Munich, whom Josefine joined, were ruled by a draconian Mother Superior. Extreme privation and constant, unquestioning obedience were the watchwords of a hermetically enclosed community. Bells clanged viciously at four-thirty each morning, to rouse nuns and postulants from the fleeting sanctuary of oblivion. The Mother Superior's piercing whistle meant, 'Do this ... Do that ... Immediately!' Eyes must be lowered; hands must be kept out of sight. For most of the time, speech, the most human form of expression, was prohibited. Sign language was curt, unforgiving. A snap of a nun's fingers meant 'Stand up!' Two snaps meant 'Turn around!'

Of her own free will, Josefine had chosen her fate. As trial succeeded trial, her resolve was constantly questioned, then strengthened: losing her lovely golden hair, her symbol of womanhood; living off a wretched diet of bread and water for day after day; keeping a humiliating record of trivial errors.

'All for Jesus!' For the four years of her life, from 15 to 19, Josefine was not allowed to leave the Mother House even once. Her faith in her decision was enshrined in her simple mantra. The thousands of hours of silent prayer and meditation nourished her. The ceremony of Holy Mass nourished her. The soaring voices of the choir nourished her. 'All for Jesus!'[7]

After four years of gruelling hardship, Josefine had been transformed into the

25

Mother Superior's template of a nun. Domestic and nursing skills were honed to a fine art. Blind obedience was instinctive. Whereas Josefine had once viewed her stern, unyielding Mother Superior as lacking in understanding and compassion, now 'I could easily see the wisdom of her words and actions ... I wanted to become so much like her ... It is impossible to describe the serenity and courage one receives when in constant communion with Almighty God.'[8]

'With the taking of my vows, I gave myself to Jesus for all eternity, and he was my Lord and Saviour for all time as well.'[9] Josefine had renounced her family for God. When she embraced her lifelong vows of poverty, chastity and obedience, there was no loving parent or sibling present. Even her name Josefine, the last relic of her former life, was discarded. She took the name Pasqualina, from Paschal, meaning Easter, Christ's resurrection, symbol of a new life.

Almost immediately, Pasqualina was sent to the Stella Maris retreat at Rorschach in the Swiss Alps. Here members of the clergy came to recover from illnesses of body and mind. For the next four years, she worked from five o'clock in the morning until midnight, nursing priests back to health. Then, in November 1918, when she had just turned 24, a reserved, withdrawn Italian bishop came to Rorschach, bitterly wounded in spirit. An awed rumour quickly spread throughout the nursing home that he was a man of great importance in the Church, a close adviser to none other than Pope Benedict himself. His name was Eugenio Pacelli.

Pacelli's Serbian concordat, the first step of his Great Design, had played its part in plunging Europe into the horror of World War One. It may also have precipitated the death of Pope Pius X. On 3 September 1914 Pius was succeeded by Giacomo Della Chiesa, as Pope Benedict XV. Chiesa, nicknamed *picoletto* (tiny one), was an aristocrat from Genoa, a much more tolerant and personable man than the severe Pius, under whom he had been demoted and viewed with suspicion.

Benedict's reign mercifully signalled the beginning of a new and more enlightened era in papal history. He swiftly dismissed Merry del Val as Secretary of State and suspended the papal spy network for the witch-hunting of 'Modernists'. Yet the anti-Modernist oath and the censorship of books written by clergymen would remain in place for many decades, as would the strictures of Gasparri and Pacelli's emergent Code of Canon Law. Thus would papal obedience, however formidable, be enforced throughout the Church.

Benedict promoted Gasparri to Secretary of State, in effect Foreign Secretary. Pacelli too was promoted, to secretary in the Department of Extraordinary Affairs. Here he worked on behalf of prisoners of war, on both sides of the conflict. In every diocese with POW camps, bishops were tasked to ensure that priests with relevant language skills aided communication between prisoners and their families. As may be imagined, this required administrative skills of a high order. Pacelli demonstrated impressive competence. In liaison with the Swiss government and the Red Cross, he negotiated exchanges of wounded prisoners. It is estimated that, through his agency, some 65,000 prisoners were repatriated.

Inevitably Pacelli's department was flooded with enquiries about soldiers missing and killed in action. He also oversaw the Holy See's funding of food and medicine, without which many more fatalities would have occurred. In effect, he managed what we would now consider to be a vast programme of humanitarian aid. It is said that, for the first three years of World War One, Pacelli did not take even a single day's respite from his toils. In addition to his more than full-time job, he continued working on the Code of Canon Law, now nearing completion. In 1916, rumours circulated in the Vatican that he was to be appointed papal nuncio in Munich. But the post went to Archbishop Giuseppe Aversa instead. It was rumoured that Gasparri would not hear of Pacelli's leaving Rome until the code was finally published.

Archbishop Aversa, however, died from appendicitis on 3 April 1917. Pope Benedict decided that Pacelli would be the obvious replacement. Benedict was desperate to bring an end to what had become the greatest war in history. Pacelli was a key to his plan.

On 13 May 1917, the day of Fátima, Benedict personally consecrated Pacelli in a private ceremony in the Sistine Chapel. With Benedict were Gasparri and Pacelli's colleague and friend, Achille Ratti, the future Pope Pius XI. Much of the power of the Church was concentrated in these four men. Pacelli's father had died several months previously, but his beloved mother and his brother Francesco were present to witness the papal blessing. What a contrast to Pasqualina's bleak, friendless taking of her vows, a few years previously.

Pacelli's train journey from Rome to Munich was one of spectacular elaborateness. The train contained a compartment for Pacelli's private use. A separate carriage contained a large quantity of food for his 'fastidious stomach'. This included 60 cases of groceries. The food bill came to some 8,000 lire. No less than four Italian government ministries had to be called in to facilitate the arrangements. The foreign ministry issued special passports, and the finance ministry had to give special permission for the huge quantity of precious food to leave Italy.

The following day Baron Carlo Monti, an Italian diplomat, saw fit to inform the Pope of his protégé's unusual behaviour. Benedict was shocked. He commented that, had be been despatched to Munich, he would have wished to live like everyone else in war-ravaged Bavaria. For all his aristocratic origins, Benedict was a man who conducted himself with disarming simplicity. Earlier, he had been horrified to discover that a chicken which had reached the papal dining table had cost the princely sum of 20 lire. Pacelli was making off with the equivalent of 400 overpriced chickens. But Benedict was no Pius X – or Pius XI (Achille Ratti). While he deplored Pacelli's extravagance, his nuncio to Munich was being entrusted with a delicate and sacred mission.

The business of Pacelli's food is an interesting example of his seemingly paradoxical nature. Here is someone who, as a child, routinely suffered from cold in his own home. (Similarly in World War Two, as Pope, he would voluntarily go without adequate heating.) Here is someone doing two supremely demanding jobs at the same time – saving tens of thousands of prisoners, while making the most scholarly, meticulous compilation of canon law. Here is a man who will not take a single day's respite, a man pushing body and mind to their limits. And yet he remains in thrall to the 'fastidious stomach' which made him quit the seminary and could easily have terminated his career in the Church before it had even begun.

From personally distributing food parcels, Pacelli well knew the conditions under which people had to live. Yet on his journey to Munich, he behaved like an emperor. In later years, he would justify the pomp of his papal coronation to a shocked, disapproving Pasqualina with the comment that it was for the Church, not for him. Did he regard a food bill of 8,000 lire as a small price to keep a key papal executive operating at maximum effectiveness? Certainly it was a far cry from Pasqualina's many dreary days of bread and water.

On 25 May 1917 Pacelli was installed, in some style, as papal nuncio in Munich. The nunciature was a neo-classical palace on the Brennerstrasse, opposite what would later become the Brown House, where so much Nazi hatred would be fomented. An *uditore*, assistant, Monsignor Schioppa, presided over the lay staff. A limousine, with doors adorned by papal crests, stood awaiting the wishes of the new nuncio.

Meanwhile Pope Benedict was becoming increasingly preoccupied with formulating a plan for peace, in hopes of 'seeing ended at the earliest moment the terrible struggle that appears increasingly a useless carnage ... Shall, then, the civilised world be nought but a field of death? And shall Europe, so glorious and flourishing, rush, as though driven by universal madness, towards the abyss, and lend her hand to her own suicide?'[10]

Benedict's plan for a 'just and lasting peace' involved ending hostilities by a process of arbitration, backed up by sanctions if need be.[11] Conscription would be abolished. There would be staged disarmament. Occupied territories would be returned. Disputed territories would be arbitrated, in line with the wishes of their inhabitants. Poland would be reunited, and the independence of Belgium would be guaranteed.

Pacelli lost no time in meeting with King Ludwig III of Bavaria and his foreign minister. Following this initial contact, he went to Berlin to meet Matthias Erzberger, a leader of the Centre Party and a man with whom he would have crucial dealings in the 1930s. By this stage in the war, the German Chancellor Bethmann-Hollweg was not adverse to suing for peace. He courteously remonstrated with Pacelli about the anti-German invective of French bishops. This breach, by the latter, of Church neutrality is interesting, given the Pacelli-inspired muzzling of clerics in World War Two.

Reporting back to his superior, Gasparri, Pacelli noted that a head of the Christian Workers' Union had been invited to a banquet held in his honour, 'an indication that the government actually intends encouraging workers' parties'.[12] To the reactionary Pacelli with his *idée fixe* of autocratic, centralized rule, such grassroots participation must have seemed a terrible error.

On 28 June, Pacelli left Berlin for a meeting with the Kaiser. A 'sumptuous special imperial railway wagon' took him to a castle at Kreuznach, where an 'elegant apartment' had been made ready for him.[13] By contrast, the Kaiser met him in an austere room, with maps of the conflict adorning the walls.

Despite the Kaiser's finding Pacelli 'a distinguished, likeable man, of high intelligence and excellent manners', he treated his Vatican visitor to a wide-ranging rant of the evils perpetrated upon a seemingly innocent Germany.[14] The versions of the meeting given by both men differ significantly in places. On the key question of the Pope's role in mediation, Pacelli and his assistant, Monsignor Schioppa, pointed out that there were still no diplomatic relations between the Vatican and the Italian government. This would make it difficult, if not impossible, for the Pope to promote peace directly between Austria and Italy.

Indeed the startled Schioppa, perhaps fearing that Pacelli was getting out of his depth, went even further. The Italian government was entirely capable of mobilizing 'the *piazza*', i.e. a popular reaction, even an attack on the Vatican and the Pope himself. The Kaiser's account states that he insisted the Pope had a unique opportunity to promote world peace, regardless of personal cost. Furthermore, 'if the Pope did nothing ... there was danger of peace being forced upon the world by the socialists, which would mean the end of the power of the Pope and the Roman Church'. [15]

At this, according to the Kaiser, Pacelli was swayed. But the frightened Schioppa again intervened, pointing out the danger of 'the *piazza*'. The Kaiser replied acidly that Jesus Christ had never feared 'the *piazza*'.[16] The Kaiser recalls that an emotionally overcome Pacelli gripped his hand and affirmed, '*You are absolutely right! It is the duty of the Pope; he must act; it is through him that the world must be won back to peace*' [Italics added].[17] If the Kaiser is to be believed, Pacelli was implicitly declaring the Pope's unique role in mediating the destiny of nations at war.

Yet despite Pacelli's best efforts, Benedict's peace plan died stillborn, amid a climate of distrust and political opportunism. US President Woodrow Wilson publicly doubted the integrity of Germany. The French and British governments tried to use the Vatican discussions as a way of eliciting German intentions. Conversely, Germany was trying to assess the Allied position. Both sides held fast to the hope that they could win the war. Millions of dead were sacrificed for the gilded lure of political advantage.

Both sides were annoyed with Benedict; both sides tried to use the Vatican for their own advantage. Allegedly Clemenceau, the French Prime Minister, sneeringly referred to Benedict as the 'Boche Pope'.[18] The Germans took issue with the condemnation of the sinking of *The Lusitania*, while the British implored the Pope to denounce German atrocities in Belgium. The attempts, by both sides, to ensnare the papacy in their own propaganda may well have made Pacelli extremely wary when he had to deal with the same belligerents, twenty-five years later, in World War Two.

In October 1917, Pacelli made a brief visit to Rome to confer with Benedict and Gasparri. All three had to concede defeat. Ironically, their plan was very similar to those enumerated in the famous 14 points put forward subsequently by President Wilson in the post-war negotiations. When Pacelli returned to Munich, it was to plunge once again into the turmoil of relieving the sufferings of war victims.

For the fourth and final year of World War One, 'the war to end all wars', Pacelli criss-crossed Germany, bringing food and clothing to the suffering. One account sees him received with adulation in a prisoner-of-war camp: 'He [Pacelli] correct and dignified, calm and serene, casts his sympathetic gaze, clouded with sadness, over this crowd of men whose inmost hearts he has touched.'[19] In a letter to Gasparri, Pacelli noted that after one prison camp visit, the 'compassionate and inexhaustible charity of the Holy Father had carried a soothing balm of faith and love into their terrible suffering.'[20]

While Pacelli gave aid to those 'of all religions', an incident with a Dr Werner, rabbi of Munich, gives pause for thought.[21] Dr Werner contacted the nuncio to beg a favour, namely that the Pope might intercede with the Italian government to stop the blockage of a consignment of palm fronds (to celebrate the Feast of Tabernacles). Pacelli vetoed the request. Shamelessly, he fobbed off poor Dr Werner with a practised bureaucrat's sleight-of-hand. He wrote thus to Gasparri: 'Professor Werner was perfectly convinced of the reasons I had given him and thanked me warmly for all that I had done on his behalf.'[22] The whole episode has a bad odour to it. Pacelli showed, at the very least, little sympathy for German Jews. He also demonstrated a lack of simple humanity; those harmless palm fronds would have given comfort to a great many people. And the bureaucratic sleight-of-hand is disturbing. As in the meeting with the Kaiser, the old canard was trotted out that the Vatican had no diplomatic relations with the Italian government. If the Vatican could not call in a few discreet favours in the spirit of humanity, did it really have a credible role in mediating the destinies of nations?

In the wake of the Russian revolution, Germany, ravaged by war, had became widely infested with militant communist groups, bent on fomenting disturbance and furthering the cause of the revolution beyond Russian territory. This development greatly alarmed Pacelli, for whom the threat of atheistic communism posed the greatest danger imaginable to Christian civilization. Indeed, its defeat was very much a plank of his Great Design.

Moreover, his first year in Munich marked the first time in his life when he had to confront the world beyond Rome. Apart from brief visits abroad, he had never worked outside the comparatively cloistered corridors of the Vatican. Apart from this he had, until he was 38, spent almost every night of his life at home, in the somewhat oppressive and over-protective care of his mother. It was well known that he was a 'mother's boy'. This was one of the causes of the numerous and somewhat eccentric examples of the hypochondria that was to afflict his later life.

Pacelli's most consistent phobia concerned flies, and he always carried a swatter attached to the belt under his robes for use whenever necessary. Among his imaginary illnesses were a chronic toothache of mysterious origins, an irregular pulse, a suspected heart condition, bilious attacks or liver disorder, and anaemia. He genuinely suffered from an inflamed colon and chronic gastritis, but one of his doctors considered the latter to have been brought on by hypochondria.

Pacelli cleaned his teeth many times a day, in a long and complicated ritual – first brushing with toothpaste made especially for him by a chemist, then washing out his mouth with a strong astringent, then finally massaging his gums with sterilized cotton swabs that he dipped in a disinfecting solution. Convinced that his gums were bad, and listening to none of the advice from competent Vatican doctors, he later found a Roman dentist who prescribed a 'remedy' for his 'bad gums'.

Unfortunately the supposed remedy was chromic acid – a strong preparation also used to tan hides. Not only did this cause his gums to become increasingly sensitive but, over the years, the chromic acid gradually worked upon him like a slow poison, causing stomach disorders, spasms of the diaphragm, and his famous attacks of hiccups.

The strain of the first year in Munich had imposed heavy burdens on his notoriously fragile nervous make-up. His first exposure to the world since leaving Rome had seen him engaging in new struggles and facing new dangers. The situation in Germany as the war lurched to its end was extremely unpropitious. The position immediately after the signing of the Armistice in November 1918 got steadily worse, particularly from the point of view of the Church in general and the nunciature in Munich in particular. Militant communist groups were active in Bavaria. Foreign embassies came under immediate danger: they were constantly being invaded and their contents requisitioned. The local militias, temporarily assuming power, effectively cut off all communications between the Munich nunciature and the Vatican.

In one of the last ciphered messages that got through, Pacelli asked if it would not be advisable to leave Munich altogether, for the time being. Gasparri replied that Benedict had granted permission for him to move the nunciature. However, he was instructed first of all to seek the advice of the Archbishop, Faulhaber of Munich. This was sound counsel, for Faulhaber had spotted something of great concern. Pacelli was exhausted from his many years of revising the Code of Canon Law, the death of his father, the failure of Benedict's peace plan, and the four years of administering a huge relief programme throughout World War One, including his many personal visits to the suffering. Bruised in spirit, he had succumbed to a nervous breakdown – the first of several in his long career.

Faulhaber advised Pacelli to leave the nunciature and recuperate at a discreet clinic designed for clergy in need of a 'rest'. It was directed by a Professor Jochner and run by nuns in the Swiss Alps – at a place named Rorschach.

Chapter 4

The Attack at the Nunciature

The Italian priests who normally came to Rorschach were easy-going characters, fully intending to enjoy their 'rest' with plenty of good food and congenial conversation. Archbishop Pacelli could not have been more different. His body was emaciated, his face gaunt, his dark, lustrous eyes piercing with the intensity of a mystic. His manners were impeccable yet his persona was detached, aloof. It was as though he had gathered an invisible cloak around him. The other nuns were intimidated by his aura and by the plethora of rumours that quickly circulated about his proximity to the Pope. But fear had never stopped Pasqualina. She saw him for what he was – a broken man. It was her sworn duty to help him.

Pacelli was a perfectionist, accustomed to his slightest whim being obeyed instantly. Pasqualina was equally a perfectionist. From her earliest days with the Mother Superior, she was conditioned to a life of service. Even before, at the little farm at Ebersberg, hard work and discipline had been her solutions to life's problems. 'Discipline is the answer. If one learns discipline during childhood, all things are possible.' Her mantra, her *raison d'être*, was, as we have seen, 'All for Jesus!' The emaciated, haggard Pacelli might have been the embodiment of Jesus.

His recovery began with a *rapport* with Pasqualina. He expected his clothes to be washed and ironed to perfection. Very well then, they would be; it didn't matter if she had to stay up half the night to make sure they were ready. He expected his quarters to be spotless; they were. He expected instant attention from her; no matter that she had so many other clergy in her care. He must never know the competing demands upon her time. It must be as though she existed solely for his welfare.

Rapport established, she made demands on him. Realizing how careless he was of his personal health (despite his neuroticism), she insisted that he take regular meals, that he stick to his regime of medicine, that he go to bed on time. While he slept she slipped in, at all hours, watching over him protectively. By degrees he began to get better, although on bad days he seemed to be relapsing into an alarming state of renewed depression. Clearly, his physical and mental health could never be taken for granted.

Pasqualina, still only 24, gave the middle-aged Pacelli exactly the sort of care and attention he needed at this time. She understood that certain types of sympathetic and understanding therapy are far more effective than medication or more complicated forms of treatment. She realized, above all, that he needed to talk, to get off his mind things that deeply troubled him. She listened attentively and intelligently for long periods to his increasingly candid and prolonged discourses. Quite soon, he began to show marked improvement.

Pasqualina knew that Pacelli, no less than she, was driven to work, to expend himself in the service of Our Lord. The easy life would never be for him. His very identity depended upon work, upon service. On Pasqualina's advice, and under her care, he began to spend part of almost every day dealing with his official duties. A stream of communications flowed between Rorschach and Munich, as Pacelli's decisions were conveyed to the nunciature. This activity acted as a highly effective form of therapy. It also served to camouflage from the outside world the fact that the papal nuncio to Bavaria was spending three months in a Swiss nursing home, undergoing a nervous breakdown.

By the end of his three months, Pacelli had put on weight and regained much of his strength and vitality. He was a changed man from the gaunt, emaciated figure who had arrived at Rorschach. For the first time, he started to smile – even, occasionally, to laugh.

And then, one morning, he was gone, as suddenly as he had arrived. He took his leave of the Mother Superior and the Prioress. But there was nothing for Pasqualina, not even a note from the patient whom she had nursed back to life. Such seeming ingratitude ... Pasqualina, as with legions of later commentators on Eugenio Pacelli, then believed the stern, ascetic Churchman to be a creature of intellect, devoid of emotion. She would come to learn the truth – that Pacelli was a man overflowing with emotion.

At the end of February 1919 Pacelli thus returned, invigorated, to Munich. Conversely, the nunciature was in a state of domestic rebellion, with members of staff quarrelling amongst themselves. Nothing could have been worse for his nerves than this situation, had it been allowed to continue. Thus, he made arguably the best decision of his entire life, a decision which would profoundly influence his career for the next 40 years.

Three months after her patient had left, without a word of thanks, Pasqualina was passing the office of the Prioress one day when she heard a familiar voice, which she had never expected to hear again. 'Have you a sister who is capable of keeping house for me at the nuncio's office in Munich?' The question was being asked by Mgr Pacelli.

'I could give you Sister Pasqualina,' came the measured response. 'She has been trained as a nurse and teacher, and is very competent. Perhaps you would give her a trial, Your Excellency?'

'If you so recommend the good sister, I shall be delighted,' Pacelli gravely replied.[1]

The prelate and the Prioress spoke as though both were entirely unaware of a message, some days earlier, from the Vatican to Rorschach, authorizing Pasqualina's transfer to Munich. Pacelli had pulled strings at the highest level. The Teaching Sisters of the Holy Cross had treated Josefine as a mere chattel. Pasqualina's transfer had come from Pope Benedict himself.

When their distinguished visitor had departed and Pasqualina was summoned to the Prioress to be notified of her transfer, her convent training schooled her impassive acceptance. Yet inside, her heart was singing. By nightfall, she had packed and gone.

To Pasqualina, born and bred a Bavarian, Munich was the city of her dreams, replete with museums and art galleries. But the nunciature was a mess, and chronically overstaffed to boot. In addition to Monsignor Schioppa, Pacelli's aide, there was a cook, a butler, a valet and a chauffeur, together with two elderly nuns to do the cleaning. To Pasqualina's practised eye, the whole place needed cleaning, dusting and polishing. And with Pacelli absent on business for much of the time, surely he had no need of anyone but herself? A life of idleness had given the staff too much time for causing trouble.

Pasqualina had arrived thinking herself mistress of the house; yet, to the other staff members, she was an unwanted chit of a girl. They carried on as they pleased, wilfully ignoring her with 'their shameful, callous manner'.[2] When freezing her out didn't work, one of the nuns went to Pacelli, one of the most senior men in the Church, and gave him a blunt ultimatum: 'Your Excellency, she leaves or we leave!'[3] So much for the vow of obedience ... Pacelli, ever the diplomat, poured oil upon troubled waters, blithely assuring them that all would be well. He would talk with Sister Pasqualina.

'Your Excellency, I was trained to be efficient,' she told him, choking with emotion. 'Either I must live up to my training to do things right, or else I must return to the Mother House.' But instead of giving him a counter-ultimatum, she offered a compromise. 'I beg your Excellency to let me do all their work. Let them sit idly by until they are shamed enough,' she told him.[4] Pacelli refused at first but, as would happen so many times in his life, he eventually gave in to her.

For the next few weeks, Pasqualina worked from dawn to late at night, like a robot, cleaning the nunciature from top to bottom. Floor after floor was scrubbed. Furniture was polished. Hundreds of dishes and glasses were washed. Vestments were taken from closet after closet, cleaned, and immaculately ironed. She cooked every meal. Slowly the nunciature was transformed; the exhausted Pasqualina revealed its potential as a mansion of distinction, a proud symbol of the glory of the Church.

When Pacelli returned from his travels, he was amazed by what she had achieved. She had demonstrated a passion for order equal to his own. He never thanked her, never admonished the other staff. Shamefacedly, they returned to work but only merited his coldness. As he passed Pasqualina on the stairs, he smiled in approval. For her, it was enough. All her efforts had been worthwhile. However perilous the world, at least the papal nuncio to Munich could find peace in the sanctuary of his home.

But soon Pacelli was away again, pushing mind and body to their limits once more. Hoping to put moral pressure on the Allies, he bluntly denounced their blockade as genocide, wantonly perpetrated on the starving population of Germany. He pleaded with the bureaucrats of the Swiss government, the Red Cross, and indeed the Vatican, to push through vital supplies of food and medicine before thousands more died. Whatever Eugenio Pacelli's frailties, in both world wars he saved many thousands of lives.

Invariably, hordes of starving people found their way to the back door of the nunciature, begging for food and clothing. The easy life of the overstaffed building had vanished. Nevertheless, it was largely left to Pasqualina to minister to the afflicted. Once more, she was locked in an inexorable battle with exhaustion, putting together parcel after parcel of food, striving to raise people's spirits, even as her own were flagging. 'Jesus will not let you down!' she told them with assurance, forcing yet another smile, knowing that it was only her iron faith that kept her on her feet.[5]

In the midst of her struggle, Pacelli came back after one mission in a frighteningly weak condition. She sent him to bed for three days and gave him the same round-the-clock care she had administered at Rorschach. Accustomed by now to his petulance, she was nevertheless aware of his deep, underlying gratitude for her efforts in keeping him alive.

When the guns had finally fallen silent on 11 November 1918, Germany was plunged into the despair of the defeated. The Kaiser fled to safety in Holland, leaving for his former subjects a power vacuum and a deep sense of betrayal. Millions of soldiers trudged back through winter cold and rain to their despoiled homeland. Poverty and hunger awaited them. Conditions were ripe for revolution.

Revolutions need demagogues. A Berlin journalist, Kurt Eisner, toppled the 700-year-old Wittelsbach dynasty and created the first republic in Bavarian history. The so-called Free Corps had very pronounced notions of freedom, which did not appear to include religious toleration. Anti-Semitism within the Free Corps killed Eisner's career. He was denounced as an ambitious Jew offering radical democracy, rather than the fabled nirvana of socialism. Within a few months, his government was overthrown and he was assassinated.

Czarist Russia had fallen to the Bolsheviks, who were aiming at nothing less than world revolution. By Spring 1919, after bitter street fighting, they had taken Munich. The red flag flew over the city and the communist Soviet Republic of Bavaria came into being.

Munich was reduced to a charnel house. The diplomatic elite lost no time in getting out and seeking sanctuary in Berlin or their native countries. With great courage, Pacelli insisted on remaining at his post. He ordered the household staff to leave, for their own safety. Pasqualina refused. Pacelli's secretary, valet and chauffeur also refused.

Pacelli and Pasqualina continued their tiny relief operation, ignoring the peril on every side. To the communists, Pacelli's pectoral cross was a potent symbol of what they most loathed. For them, the gratitude of the people of Munich towards Pacelli was a 'hearts and minds' threat, which was growing increasingly dangerous.

Ever the professional, Pacelli managed to get a long report through to Gasparri of a visit by his secretary, Monsignor Schioppa, to the local communist leader, Max Levien, to insist that the diplomatic immunity of the nunciature be respected. Pacelli's report reads as follows (Levien's headquarters being in part of the former royal palace):

> The scene that presented itself at the palace was indescribable. The confusion totally chaotic, the filth completely nauseating; soldiers and armed workers coming and going; the building, once the home of a King, resounding with screams, vile language, profanities. Absolute hell. An army of employees were dashing to and fro, giving out orders, waving bits of paper, and in the midst of all this, a gang of young women, of dubious appearance, Jews like all the rest of them, hanging around in all the offices with lecherous demeanour and suggestive smiles. The boss of this female rabble was Levien's mistress, a young Russian woman, a Jew and a divorcée, who was in charge. And it was to her that the nunciature was obliged to pay homage in order to proceed.
>
> This Levien is a young man, of about 30 or 35, also Russian and a Jew. Pale, dirty, with drugged eyes, hoarse voice, vulgar, repulsive, with a face that is both intelligent and sly. He deigned to receive the Monsignor Uditore in the corridor, surrounded by an armed escort, one of whom was an armed hunchback, his faithful bodyguard. With a hat on his head and smoking a cigarette, he listened to what Monsignor Schioppa told him, whining repeatedly that he was in a hurry and had most important things to do.[6]

It will be noticed that Pacelli constantly harped on the Jewishness of this party of would-be usurpers of power. It was a reflection not only of his own views, but also of those prevalent among Germans, that the Jews were among the principal instigators of the Bolshevik revolution. Indeed their principal aim, it was widely perceived, was the destruction of Christian civilization

Pacelli's words, however, also reflect his instinctive dislike of Jews, a dislike amounting to repugnance, extremely prevalent throughout the Catholic world of that time, but also containing a paradoxical element.

Pacelli did not hate the Jews; he 'loved' them in a way that was typical of the anomalous sense of the expression, in a Catholic context. The Church was not anti-Semitic in the usual sense of the term. It had, however, been engaged in no less than 19 centuries of anti-Judaic activity, officially denouncing all Jews for all time as murderers of Jesus Christ and therefore guilty of the hideous sin of 'Deicide'. As such, they were accursed in God's eyes and were rightly condemned to live forever in a state of exile. They could never again have a home of their own. The old Israel had been supplanted by the 'new Israel', the latter, of course, being the Catholic Church. Jews were forever condemned to live in a state of 'Diaspora'. They could never again acquire nationhood. The consequent persecutions they received, wherever they went, were directly attributable to the relentless condemnation of them, pronounced officially by the Church.

We have seen, however, that Pacelli had great devotion to the writings of Thomas à Kempis, notably his classic work the *Imitation of Christ*. In this book, Thomas à Kempis says that it is not possible to like all our fellow humans but that we have a Christian duty to *love* them. It was in this sense that Pacelli loved all Jews, even though he certainly did not like them. We will see later to what extent his paradoxical attitude toward Jews in general affected his career and some of the major decisions he had to make.

Soon after Schioppa's visit to Levien, Pacelli was the victim of a face-to-face confrontation with the Red Mob when they invaded the nunciature. The incident that followed has endlessly been cited as an illustration of his impassive courage, allied to his deep hatred of communism.

The official version of the incident portrays Pacelli as confronting the intruders of his nunciature with an air of lofty calmness and dignified authority. They put their rifle to his breast and shouted that they would not leave without taking possession of his car. According to Pasqualina, the garage was then opened up and the revolutionaries departed in his limousine. There are, however, other versions of the same story. That of Pacelli himself has since become available in the Vatican archives. Under the date of 30 April 1919, writing to Gasparri, Pacelli reported that the commandant of the Red Brigade, a man called Seyler, invaded his nunciature with an accomplice called Brongratz and other soldiers, armed with rifles, revolvers and hand grenades. They pushed their way past the butler who had opened the door, and declared that they were intending to impound the papal limousine, which Pacelli described as 'a splendid carriage, with pontifical coat of arms'.

Pacelli's account continues: 'I presented myself and made it clear to the commandant that this violent entry into the nunciature and the request for the car was a flagrant violation of the international rights of all civilized peoples and I showed him the certificate of extraterritoriality that had been released by the Commissioner of the People for Foreign Affairs.'

'An accomplice pressed his rifle against my breast and the commander, a horrible type of delinquent, having given the order to his satellites to hold ready their hand grenades, told me insolently that talk was pointless and he must have the car immediately.'[7] The party was thus conducted to the garage but it appeared that the nunciature's chauffeur, anticipating such an eventuality, had immobilized the vehicle. The commandant then telephoned the Ministry of Military Affairs saying that, if the car was not immediately put into service, they would blow the whole place up and 'the whole nunciature gang' would be arrested. Not however being able then and there to take possession of the car, the invaders left. Pacelli ends his report by noting: 'All returned to peace at the nunciature, but not for long.'[8]

What happened next was extremely alarming; accounts of it have entered very few books about Pacelli. He suffered an immediate collapse.

Pasqualina and the remaining staff helped him into the downstairs reception room. A telephone call was promptly put through to his doctor. Within the hour, he was on his way back to the nursing home at Rorschach, suffering from a relapse of his nervous breakdown.

The next day the communist mob returned at nine o'clock in the morning with a document of requisition from Herr Egelhofer, supreme head of the Red Brigade. Pacelli was safely absent, not only during this intrusion but on all subsequent visits by the communists. In describing the situation to Gasparri, Pacelli later noted: 'I was at the clinic of Professor Jochner, having recently had a strong attack of influenza and suffering from a bad stomach, for which I was undergoing a special treatment.'[9]

This euphemistic description of one of his many nervous collapses became the conventional formula to describe subsequent attacks. To the outside world, Pacelli had appeared an imperturbable hero. A carefully fostered image become permanently established of a haughty and dignified prince of the Church confronting an unruly mob, within the very precincts of the papal nunciature, regaled in his full canonical robes consisting of a *feriola* (a long, flowing, ecclesiastical-style cloak), *zucchetto* (skullcap) and purple *cincture* (belt).

This incident fixed in the public consciousness an enduring image of Pacelli the fearless churchman, facing down a menacing gang of intruding thugs with imperturbable calmness and courage. Outwardly, this is correct. Inwardly, however, Pacelli received a mortal psychological wound from which he never fully recovered. He experienced a terrible churning in his stomach that rose in his body so as almost to choke him. This was the initial sign of an abrupt nervous collapse.

It was the first of many such attacks in his life – but there was something special about this one. It pierced so deeply into his subconscious being as never completely to depart. It left him, forever, 'a man afraid'. He developed a per-manent condition of profound apprehension, at moments of danger. A steel-like terror gripped the innermost part of his being, although his iron will never allowed it to show. The extreme tension set up in his nervous system by this conflict was the cause of recurring breakdowns. Even the contemplation of possible danger, as occasioned by an extremely difficult decision, was liable to bring on an attack.

So deep was the wound in Pacelli's psyche caused by his confrontation with the communist thugs in Munich that it gave him blood-curdling nightmares which started soon afterwards. These nightmares never left him; indeed, in later life, they grew worse. As he confided to his doctors, as well as to Pasqualina, he suffered from them even in his final years as Pope. His terrifying cries filled the night and could be heard all over the papal apartments. As his graphic accounts made clear, such nightmares were directly traceable either to the traumatic incident in Munich in 1919 or to a particularly unnerving interview he had with Weizsäcker, the German Ambassador to the Holy See, in 1943. Vivid images of each occasion came back to him in his dreams. He gave a graphic account of the latter to Cardinal Bea, which was recounted to me by Malachi Martin.

Naturally, no public attention was ever given to Pacelli's proneness to nervous breakdowns. It was kept a closely guarded secret. Nevertheless, at various times it was a potent motivating force for his actions. The very effort of forcing the demon into the lowest depths of his conscious mind, and trying to crush its head under his heel, was the main cause of the trouble. The snake's venom could never be entirely dispelled.

After the first attack on his nunciature, Pacelli made no less than three visits to Rorschach, in rapid succession. During a subsequent attack, the gangsters sprayed the upper storey of the building with bullets. Having seen a light being put on, they imagined that they were about to be fired upon. Pacelli was safely absent during these hostile and hate-filled visits and his deputy, the luckless Monsignor Schioppa, was invariably left to face the miscreants.

By instinct, Pacelli was anything but a coward; his very being rebelled against any such weakness. His fear was an involuntary prompting of nature, against which he endlessly fought, but which never left him in peace. From the onset, no one understood this better than Pasqualina. She was, providentially, always at his side to help him stave off the horror. Future decisions and actions were often unconsciously influenced by this submerged fear in Pacelli's make-up, combined, contrarily, with a stubborn determination not to be deterred from his Grand Design.

As it happened, the communist Soviet Republic of Bavaria was destined to be short-lived. Within weeks, the Free Corps and their allies brutally counter-attacked, in another revolutionary outburst of bloody street fighting. Anybody thought to be a communist was slaughtered. By early May, the red flag had been torn down.

The Free Corps collaborated in the formation of an interim socialist-democratic government. General Ludendorff, the former German chief of staff, was put in charge. Ludendorff lost no time in turning up, unannounced, at the nunciature and demanding Pacelli's help in tracking down communists in hiding. To Ludendorff's astonishment, Pacelli refused to have any part in the persecution of his former tormentors. The Church, he sternly told Ludendorff, must be strictly neutral with regard to politics. Ludendorff rounded on him. 'This isn't Christian behaviour! It's just a dirty trick!' He furiously stormed out.[10]

Many years later, when Pacelli spoke up for Ludendorff, saving him from an Allied trial for alleged war crimes, the German general would have occasion to ponder the churchman's magnanimity.

In a Germany humiliated by defeat and downtrodden by the Treaty of Versailles, beset by internal strife and the spectre of communism, one man saw the possibility of rebirth on a grandiose scale. In the Munich of 1919, seething with political unrest, he awaited his chance.

Late one night, there came a knock at the door of the nunciature. The staff had gone to bed; only Pasqualina remained awake. The caller was a young man who bore a letter of introduction from Ludendorff, commending him for bravery while a corporal, under the general's command. He requested a meeting with Pacelli. A suspicious Pasqualina took him to the sitting room to await the nuncio.

Their unexpected visitor – who happened to be a Catholic – told Pacelli that he was determined to stop the spread of atheistic communism, not only in Munich but throughout Germany. A still suspicious Pasqualina, hovering outside the room, heard Pacelli reply: 'Munich has been good to me, so has Germany. I pray Almighty God that this land remain a holy land, in the hands of Our Lord and free of communism.'[11] (Pasqualina was an inveterate eavesdropper.)

Despite his assurances to Ludendorff of Church neutrality, Pacelli was a mortal enemy of communism, due to its avowed aim of exterminating Catholicism. Pasqualina saw Pacelli give a considerable sum of Church funds to his visitor for his anti-communist struggle. 'Go, quell the devil's works,' Pacelli told him. 'Help spread the love of Almighty God!'

'For the love of Almighty God!' their visitor replied.[12]

The young man had grave need of funds for his fledgling political party, which would be dedicated to much more than a struggle with communism. It would one day become known as the party of National Socialism – the Nazi Party. The young man was Adolf Hitler.

Chapter 5

The Best-Informed Diplomat in Germany

In 1870, six years before Pacelli's birth, the doctrine of papal infallibility had been proclaimed as the climax of the Vatican Council. Theoretically, the Pope was awarded a position of unprecedented power and prestige. In reality, this edict was swiftly followed by the collapse of the secular power of the Church in Italy. The Papal States were annexed; all that remained was the tiny enclave of the Vatican.

In Germany, further catastrophe was to follow. Two years later, Bismarck loftily pronounced, 'I do not believe that, after the recently expressed and publicly promulgated dogmas of the Catholic Church, it is possible for a secular power to arrive at a concordat without that power, to some degree or in some manner, losing face. This the German Reich cannot accept at all.'[1]

The Reich legation to the Holy See was dissolved, leaving the Vatican with no means of political representation with Germany or Prussia. Bismarck was free to promote his savage *Kulturkampf* persecutions of Catholics. Yet Catholicism proved too strong for Bismarck; it astonished the whole world with its courage and its desire to remain strong and independent. In 1882, as *Kulturkampf* ebbed in power, a Prussian legation to the Vatican was re-established. But for almost the next 50 years, there was no Reich representation in Rome.

World War One had markedly changed the public perception of Catholics in Europe. In France, some 30,000 clergy fought in the trenches; over 4,000 died. Similarly in Germany, Catholics had given their lives for their country with the same obedience as their Protestant counterparts. In the bitter aftermath of war, Catholics were suffering just as much as Protestants. For decades they had been branded *Reichsfeinde* (enemies of the Fatherland). Surely it was time to lay this slur to rest?

In 1919, a third of the German population was Catholic. Ironically, *Kulturkampf* had caused the Catholics to become organized at a grassroots level, the better to survive. There were Catholic schools, colleges, youth groups, trade unions, newspapers, publishers. At a national level, the Catholic Centre Party was second only to the Social Democrats. In the 1919 election the Centre Party took 91 seats with six million votes, whereas the Social Democrats took 163 seats with over 11 million votes. Politically, the Centre Party was emerging as a key power sharer in a series of Weimar coalition governments. From 1919 to the suspension of democracy in 1933, five chancellors would be drawn from the Centre Party.

Max Scheler was Germany's foremost Catholic philosopher and political scientist at the time. He saw Christianity as a social religion. He believed that Christian principles should be advanced by democratic societies, communities and of course individuals, who could co-operate in the furtherance of enlightened social and political objectives. Scheler was a profound anti-communist; he believed that the greatest obstacle to communism could be provided by a courageous form of Christian democracy.

Scheler had powerful allies in regarding the Centre Party as vital for the best of Catholic and democratic ideals in a tolerant, pluralist society where minorities (e.g. Jews) would be made welcome. One such ally was Matthias Erzberger, the Catholic Centre Party leader, whom Pacelli had met while trying to promote Pope Benedict's peace plan in 1917. Erzberger represented Germany in signing the Treaty of Versailles. In some quarters, he was thereby vilified as a traitor, a 'November criminal', who would eventually be assassinated. Erzberger at Versailles – a patriot, making a pragmatic but unpalatable political decision, with terminal personal consequences – is strongly reminiscent of the Irish rebel leader, Michael Collins.

Back in 1917, Erzberger had told Archbishop von Faulhaber of Bavaria that 'a great Catholic renaissance' was going to come about, *regardless of whether Germany won the war*.[2] As the 1919 election showed, he was entirely correct. Erzberger and many of his fellow politicians were convinced that an entirely new type of pragmatism was essential for Catholics in post-war Germany. It was time for Catholics to enter more fully into the life of the nation. They must be allowed due representation in the upper echelons of the professions. It was time to join with Protestants in a pluralist, tolerant society.

It was supremely ironic that an historic Vatican initiative was taking shape, which was about to subvert the entire enlightened progress as outlined by such men as Scheler and Erzberger. For it so happened that an important anniversary for the Catholic Church in Germany was approaching: 10 December 1920 would be the 400th anniversary of the burning, at the instruction of Luther, by his students, of the corpus of canon law. Luther had made deadly criticisms of the Church, some of which were no less valid at the end of the second decade of the twentieth century. To him, compendia of canon law 'say nothing about Christ'. He had noted that the Vatican 'exalts its own ordinances above the commands of God'[3] – and he had thereby broken away from the Church.

Rather than hail the 400th anniversary as an occasion for proclaiming the necessity of reconciliation and friendship between Protestants and Catholics, the Holy See decided instead to celebrate the anniversary of the former insult to canon law by proclaiming the 1917 Code of Canon Law as ripe for imposition upon the Catholics of not only Germany but, indeed, all the world. By this means, it was intended to concentrate Church authority purely in the person of the Pope. Rigorous centralization was to be the guiding light for the future. Nothing could have been in stronger contrast to the 'political' Catholicism being urged by Scheler and Erzberger.

Thus began the Church's 13-year path to achieving its concordat policy in Germany. Negotiations were conducted on behalf of the Pope by Pacelli alone.

In most cases, these negotiations were carried out over the heads of not only the faithful, but also the clergy and the bishops of Germany. Therein lay a profound danger. The purpose of these concordats was the proclamation of the new Code of Canon Law and the imposition of an obligatory consensus, whereby the lives of priests and faithful were to be regulated from the top downward by reference to this selfsame canon law. The papacy would henceforth be able, without consultation with local hierarchies and Catholic communities, to enforce its will and impose a virtual theocracy on the world.

This form and degree of papal control was something which, as already mentioned, had never been envisaged in scripture and had never before been attempted in such a systematic and grandiloquent fashion. Even such men as Pope Innocent III and some of the immensely powerful popes of the Middle Ages had not contemplated any such position of worldwide power. Abdication from Scheler/Erzberger 'political Catholicism' was a necessary condition of this type of papal fiat. Pacelli's Great Design – a worldwide pyramid of Catholic hierarchy, with power centralized with the Pope at the apex – would be achieved via concordats and subsequent absolute obedience to canon law. Pacelli was inspired throughout by a quasi-messianic belief that the Church could only survive in the modern world by this unprecedented strengthening of papal authority. The blueprint had been envisaged as far back as the time of Pope Pius IX. Now Pacelli was putting it into practice.

With the Serbian concordat Pacelli had won advantage to the Holy See, yet incurred horrendous political consequences which contributed to the outbreak of World War One. Similarly Pacelli's German concordat policy, while furthering his Grand Design, would incur even more horrendous political consequences, contributing to the outbreak of World War Two. Pacelli's vision of papal autocracy simply took no heed of prevailing political imperatives for parties other than the Holy See. True, Pacelli the diplomat was a consummate political fixer. But for Pacelli the absolutist, the position of the Church was ultimately all that mattered. As we shall see, the latter refused, as Pope, an invitation to preside over an international Christian conference to avoid war, on the grounds that to attend would be to imply equality between the one and only Roman and apostolic Church and other Christian churches. Pacelli's absolutism came at a high price.

Catholic Bavaria, with Pacelli's power base of Munich, was the obvious candidate for the first German concordat. Ironically however, the first challenge to the Church's canon law authority came from Protestant Prussia. On 11 November 1919, Archbishop von Hartmann of Cologne died. Local tradition, confirmed by an 1821 papal bull, dictated that the new archbishop be locally elected. The 1917 Code of Canon Law stipulated that the new appointment be decided by Rome. A diplomatic impasse promptly ensued between Prussia and the Vatican, with enciphered cables being hastily exchanged between Pacelli and Gasparri. The first test case of the 1917 code was occurring with a formidable opponent. It was resolved in a masterly fashion, illustrating the calibre of Vatican diplomacy.

Within a month of von Hartmann's death Luigi Maglione, the papal nuncio in Switzerland, learned from Diego von Bergen, Prussian minister at the Holy See, that Monsignor Schulte, Bishop of Paderborn, was the preferred choice of the canons of Cologne, the German bishops, and the Prussian government. Maglione wrote thus to Gasparri: 'If perhaps he was also acceptable to the Holy Father, as I think it to be the case, then filling this most important vacancy would proceed with the great satisfaction of everyone in Germany.'[4] An indication that Schulte would be made a (German) cardinal in the next consistory would seal the deal.

Another enciphered cable passed between Gasparri and Pacelli. Shortly afterwards, Pacelli arrived in Cologne and informed the canons that, *on this occasion only*, they could elect an archbishop according to their tradition. Schulte was duly appointed and rebellion was circumvented. Pacelli, of course, was angling to get into a position where rebellion would be downright impossible.

Also in 1919, it was announced that the Prussian legation in Rome was to be upgraded to the status of a German embassy to the Holy See. Diego von Bergen, who had proved so helpful in resolving the Cologne impasse, was to be the first ambassador. As well as Prussia, he would represent the entire Reich. Erzberger, the new *Reichsminister*, looked forward to a Reich concordat, to formalize relations between Germany and the Vatican. But whereas the Vatican was a distinct negotiative body, the same could not be said of Germany, which was beset by traditional rivalries of religion and territory. Munich and Catholic Bavaria were often opposed by Berlin and Protestant Prussia. Upgrading the Prussian legation in Rome to embassy status would, it was assumed, involve closure of the existing Bavarian legation.

Such thinking was not to Pacelli's liking. Ever the wily diplomat, he saw his chance to play divide-and-rule with Germany. He stipulated 'a Reich embassy to the Vatican, with a papal nunciature for German affairs (excluding Bavaria) in Berlin, and a Bavarian legation to the Vatican in Rome, with a papal nunciature in Munich'.[5] And, crucially, he made this stipulation a key condition for mutual diplomatic representation between the Reich and the Holy See.

In thus engaging in political brinksmanship between Germany and the Vatican, Pacelli was playing for high stakes. Before World War One, the Vatican had received more financial donations from Germany than from all the other countries in the world put together. A friendless and ruined post-war Germany had desperate need of an international political ally such as the Vatican. And a Vatican depleted of German funds needed a revitalized German economy. In jockeying for increased political power, Pacelli was putting this mutual benefit in peril.

Germany gave in. There would be a Reich embassy (also representing Prussia) at the Holy See. Pacelli would be the nuncio to the Reich in Berlin. He would also remain as the Bavarian nuncio in Munich. Only two years previously, Erzberger had confidently stated that a Bavarian nuncio could never be accredited to the Reich or Prussia; it would imply political demotion for the Reich *vis à vis* Bavaria. But Pacelli proved him wrong. German political need outweighed diplomatic protocol. And Pacelli as 'double nuncio' could exploit the Prussian/ Bavarian rivalries. On the face of it, Pacelli had achieved a diplomatic coup for the Vatican. But in so doing, he delayed a concordat with the Reich. Had the Reich concordat been negotiated in the early 1920s, Catholic democracy in Germany would not have been compromised and Hitler's National Socialist party would have faced fierce political opposition. Delaying the Reich concordat until 1933 gave Hitler the almost unbelievable advantage of having his most dangerous political enemies voluntarily disband – at Pacelli's behest.

Under the new Weimar government, Pacelli became the first diplomat to the Reich and the most senior diplomat in Berlin. He stated: 'For my part, I will devote my entire strength to cultivating and strengthening the relations between the Holy See and Germany.'[6] (In 1933, Hitler would ominously utter the same words as he used the Holy See to secure the dictatorship of Germany.)[7]

Pacelli's opening sally for a Bavarian concordat staggered the Germans with its audacity. The management of Catholic schools was of prime importance for the Church. While Pacelli wanted the state to assume the financial burden for schools, he insisted that the local bishop (controlled by Rome, via his Grand Design) would have power of veto over teachers of religion. If, for instance, the bishop so demanded, the state would have to terminate the employment of such a teacher.

In Munich, such 'excessive demands' gave rise to pronounced 'ill feeling'. A senior Foreign Office civil servant in Berlin caustically noted: 'The most striking thing about Pacelli is that he seems to have little awareness of what is possible in Germany and that he negotiates as if he were dealing with Italians.'[8] Pacelli the autocrat, chasing his vision of the greater good, was sublimely untroubled by grassroots concern for Vatican policies. As with the double nunciature issue, he linked his demands to greater political imperatives. No control of schools would mean no concordat; no concordat would mean no help from the Holy See in Germany's disputes regarding territories removed by the Allies after the war.

As before, Pacelli won his case; his demands over schools were met in a draft concordat in November 1920. Irrespective of bad feeling among Catholics (and dismay from German Protestants), he had his way. With a Bavarian concordat looking likely, he pursued simultaneous negotiations with Prussia and the Reich. Divide-and-rule appeared to be working very well indeed for Pacelli in Germany. Such appearances would ultimately prove deceptive.

Among the territories occupied by the Allies was the Rhineland. In 1920, Pacelli received notification that black French troops were raping German women and children. He notified Gasparri and recommended Vatican pressure on the French government to remove these troops. A German government inquiry supported allegations of rape and other crimes; conversely, the French ambassador to the Holy See denounced the allegations as 'odious propaganda' from Berlin.[9] The incident, known as the 'Black Shame', became an international cause célèbre. Although a US House of Representatives investigation appeared to disprove the German inquiry, Pacelli was not convinced. In 1921, he again wrote to Gasparri, urging Vatican pressure on the French. Nothing happened. Until the Rhineland was finally re-occupied, there were continued allegations of the 'Black Shame'.

A quarter of a century later, as the Allies prepared to enter Rome at the end of World War Two, Pacelli requested the British ambassador to the Holy See to ask the Foreign Office that 'no Allied coloured troops would be among the small number that might be garrisoned at Rome after the occupation'.[10]

In 1921, the Reich government was pushing hard for a concordat. Upper Silesia had been claimed by Poland; Germany wanted the political assistance of the Holy See. Pacelli prevaricated, possibly due to his disapproval of the left-wing chancellor. When finally asked for an agenda, Pacelli gave what amounted to a draft of the Bavarian concordat, with the same schools stipulation. In Bavaria this had caused 'ill feeling'; to Prussia, it was explosive. As before, he linked the schools issue to a concordat and resulting political intervention regarding disputed territories. Under duress, however, Prussia backed down.

Discussing his latest diplomatic coup with Cardinal Bertram, Pacelli stressed that it was not due to his ability, but to God. Bertram and Archbishop Schulte, the leading Churchmen in Germany, were horrified. To Schulte, there was 'a most extraordinary risk' of encouraging French adventurism in disputed territories.[11] Bertram urged Pacelli to be cautious, fearing mutual damage both to Germany and the Holy See. German ministers had noted Pacelli's lack of concern for grassroots political considerations, so obsessed was he with implementing his concordat policy. Unfortunately this obsession would prove fatal when it came to dealing with his erstwhile visitor in Munich – Adolf Hitler.

Pacelli's beloved mother Virginia died in 1921, plunging him into a deep depression, where he could neither eat nor sleep. As before, Pasqualina nursed him. From then on, her role as mother substitute would become even more important. Early in the following year, 1922, Pacelli's mentor, Pope Benedict XV, also died. Again he was plunged into depression. His friend, Achille Ratti, was elected Pope Pius XI. The first unofficial act of his papacy was to send a sympathetic letter to Pacelli. Pasqualina came into his room, waving it in front of him, imploring him to rise from his depression and resume his vital role. Gasparri was to continue as Secretary of State and the concordat policy would proceed as before. Pacelli and Ratti were united in their hatred of communism. As ever, the Great Design of canon law, implemented through concordats, seemed the best bulwark against communism and the best means of securing the Holy See's pre-eminence.

Archbishop Schulte's fears of French adventurism bore fruit when French and Belgian troops invaded the Ruhr in January 1923. Berlin encouraged passive resistance. Strikes and terrorist attacks on industry followed. Harsh discipline was meted out, leading to widespread civil unrest. The value of the mark collapsed, bringing further ruin to Germany's economy. Beleagured Western countries were prime targets for Russian takeover. Pacelli was concerned about a possible communist coup in the Ruhr. He was also concerned lest political instability scupper his concordat policy. When Achille Ratti wrote an open letter in *L'Osservatore Romano* criticizing the French occupation, French fury was met with German delight. Pacelli's diplomacy brought the warring factions together and outright enmity was swapped for a climate of distrust. But, crucially, political disaster had been averted.

In March 1924, after five years of preparation, the Bavarian concordat was finally signed. The concordat ensured that the new Code of Canon Law would be recognized by Bavaria as the basis for the appointing of all bishops and higher clergy. Pacelli achieved all the powers he had been looking for in the running of religious schools, and for religious education in general. Recognition, protection and advancement of the Catholic Church were achieved on all fronts and in every part of Bavaria. The Church was forced to make only minor concessions including the reasonable one that, because Bavaria was paying the salaries of all the clergy, only those of German citizenship should be employed as teachers in Catholic schools.

For Pacelli, the Bavarian concordat was yet another diplomatic success. If anything, his sense of hubris was heightened. The Reich concordat was now top of his agenda for control of Catholic Germany. At this point, the Prussian government made it clear that Prussia must have its own concordat, not a rehash of the Bavarian one; and a Reich concordat must be subject to their approval.

Soon after this, Pacelli was promoted to the office of papal nuncio for the whole of Germany. In 1925, he moved officially to Berlin and was ensconced in a luxurious residence in Rauchstrasse 21, in the elegant Teirgarten quarter. He soon became a familiar sight in social and diplomatic circles, in the country's capital. He would arrive in his ornate robes, complete with flowing purple silk cloak, his limousine sweeping him to formal receptions and private houses in all parts of Berlin.

He threw glittering receptions and gave superb dinner parties at the nunciature. In fact Pacelli, with the subtle assistance of Pasqualina, began to enjoy himself and to relax. For the sake of greater diplomatic success, he discarded much of his normal austerity and spared no efforts in his planning, again with the help of the ever-adaptable Pasqualina. There were excellent gourmet meals, with the finest wine and after-dinner brandy. The only luxury the nuncio did not lavish on his guests was the serving of cigars, since he had a great dislike of tobacco in any form. Curiously, Pacelli's detestation of smoking was shared by Adolf Hitler: an odd association between two such differing personalities.

Pacelli was described by the American writer Dorothy Thompson as 'the best-informed diplomat in Germany'.[12] He made friends in all quarters. One of these supplied him, in an estate in the outskirts of Berlin, with an electrically powered mechanical horse on which he could exercise. This he did, wearing specially made jodhpurs and a hacking jacket.

Pacelli was visibly elated by his fame and success. When he came back to the nunciature after a walk one morning, he reported to Pasqualina with undisguised delight that a small boy had approached him and asked him if he was God.

When the last of the guests had departed after a dinner or function, Pacelli, the suave, affable diplomat, often reverted to a cold, emotionless, introverted state. He did not wish to speak or be spoken to. He did not want to be bothered by anybody or anything. He was hypersensitive to noise. All he wanted was to be left alone. Pasqualina had always found his abrupt mood changes trying. She worked to accommodate him, insisting that he move his private quarters to the third floor of the nunciature, away from the staff, asking everyone to keep their voice down and wear felt slippers to reduce noise. Woe betide any offender.

> Archbishop Pacelli had the mind of a mystic, who drew strength from prayer and meditation. It was essential for him to have a certain amount of solitude each day. He was happiest when in solitary communion with Jesus. If he had his way, he would have withdrawn into a world of asceticism, largely away from people.[13]

This was the judgement of Pacelli from Pasqualina, the person who undoubtedly knew him best. A quarter of a century before, he had told Gasparri that he aspired to be no more than 'a pastor of souls'. Gasparri had pointed out the necessity of defending the Church from the onslaught of secularism and liberalism. Pacelli, the glittering diplomat, had risen admirably to that defence. More, much more, was to come.

For some years, negotiations had been going on in Rome for the conclusion of an even more important concordat than those of Germany. The aim of this particular agreement was to bring to an end the long estrangement that had existed between the Holy See and the Italian state. Ever since the latter had come into being in 1870, the Holy See and Italy had not been on speaking terms. The Vatican refused to recognize the new state. The Pope of the time, Pius IX, never left his palace thereafter, defiantly declaring himself to be 'a prisoner in the Vatican'. This started a tradition of popes and secretaries of state remaining in self-exile within the Vatican precincts – a dangerously isolationist policy.

This isolationist policy was continued at lower levels. As a mark of its disapproval and non-recognition of the new Italy, the Church forbade its subjects from taking any active part in politics. This was a serious mistake. It had counterproductive results inasmuch as a vacuum was left, of which secular parties took full advantage, and the Church correspondingly lost a voice in affairs and forfeited its power to influence events in Italy. In this respect, and in many others, the Lateran Treaty – the concordat between Italy and the Holy See – was a foreshadowing of the pact which Pacelli piloted through, between the Holy See and Hitler, in 1933.

Unknown to the world in general however, then and even now, the Lateran Treaty was necessitated for quite different reasons. In the mid-1920s, the relationship between Pacelli and Pasqualina was deepening and becoming ever more platonically intimate. In effect, Pasqualina served as a trusted *consigliere*, an adviser to this adviser of popes, who continued to insist that he was without personal ambition in the Church. 'His heart's desire was to dedicate himself to the care of souls', Pasqualina noted. Nevertheless she reminded him, as had Gasparri, of his duty to put his talents to best use. Soon the aged Gasparri would retire. Pasqualina the king-maker worked to stiffen Pacelli's ever-wavering resolve. Taking over from Gasparri, becoming Secretary of State, would bring him just one step away from the greatest prize in the Catholic Church.

One evening, during one of the long and free-ranging conversations that began to take place between them, Pacelli let slip to Pasqualina a matter of the highest confidentiality. A fact only known to very few high-ranking ecclesiastics was that the Catholic Church was in extremely dangerous financial straits. Insolvency could be avoided only by some drastic remedy. To Pasqualina, it seemed incredible that the greatest religion in the world, nearly 2,000 years old, with more than 300 million members, could be penniless. But Pacelli assured her that for decades, the Church had been at the 'most awful mercy' of anti-Catholic forces in Italy, inspired, he claimed, by the devil. By degrees, the temporal strength of the Church had been depleted. Even that formerly 'good Catholic', Benito Mussolini, had become a 'terrible man'.[14]

It was the fear of stark bankruptcy that induced the Holy See to put out feelers for a settlement with the Italian state, hopefully yielding desperately needed financial benefits. It was essential, however, that Mussolini did not learn of the Church's near-destitution. For his part, Mussolini wished to promote Rome as an upmarket tourist attraction, bringing untold wealth to Church and state.

Pasqualina remained unconvinced. 'A man like Mussolini can never be trusted! Why should such an enemy of the Church give up so much and ask so little in return?'[15] Yet Pacelli insisted that the Italian dictator be given his chance.

Shortly afterwards, an agreement came into being and the Church was saved from bankruptcy. Naturally it was presented to the world as a settlement of a very different nature, including as merely a minor detail the fact that the Church received 92.1 million dollars, a very considerable sum in those days, as a contribution from the Italian government. The official reason for this lump sum was to compensate the Church for property taken over by the new state, when Italy had been unified and created in 1870.

On 11 February 1929, in the Vatican's Lateran Palace, the so-called Lateran Treaty was signed between the Pope and Mussolini. The Vatican portrayed it as the greatest event in modern Church history – which it undoubtedly was, albeit for different reasons from those given to the public. The terms allowed for the sole recognition by the state of Catholicism as its official religion. A vital condition of the agreement was that the Holy See acquired the right to impose its new Code of Canon Law throughout Italy. An extremely important article of this code – Article 34 – provided for state recognition of the validity of marriages performed in church. The papacy acquired sovereignty over the tiny territory of 108.7 acres within Rome that came to be called Vatican City. This would have its own flag, currency and citizenship, even its own police force and guards. In addition to receiving territorial rights over a considerable number of buildings and churches in Rome, the Church acquired the summer palace of Castel Gandolfo, where the Pope could reside in the hottest months. This property, which comprised the estate of Castel Gandolfo, was nearly 30 acres larger than Vatican City.

All this came at a heavy price. The Catholic clergy were now legally required to swear oaths of loyalty to the Fascist government. No cardinal, bishop or priest could be appointed for service in Italy without the approval of Mussolini. Clergymen refusing to obey Fascist strictures could be fined and imprisoned. To Pasqualina, though trained in blind obedience to the Church, the fabulous Lateran Treaty was nothing more than a sell-out. Confronting Pacelli, she received the bland rejoinder that 'concordats generally result in surrender of certain Church privileges ... The Holy Father himself has said that he would negotiate with the devil if the good of souls required it.'[16] Ever the diplomat, Pacelli saw communism as a worse evil for the Church than Fascism. With Fascism, some kind of political accommodation was possible; with communism, there was none. For Pacelli, Mussolini, the suppressor of communism, was an enemy's enemy.

But the Church's surrender to the state went deeper, with an agreement to withdraw from political activity. This agreement meant the dismemberment of the very powerful democratic Catholic popular party, the *Partito Populare*, similar to the Centre Party in Germany. With its disbandment its leader, Don Liugi Sturzo, was exiled. The Lateran Treaty thus gave a clear victory to the Fascists. From then on, they thrived as the sole organ of power in the Italian state. After 1933, the Nazis were to benefit in a similar way from their concordat with the Holy See. In the latter case Pacelli put his faith in Hitler, just as, after the Lateran Treaty, Pope Pius XI spoke of Mussolini as 'a man sent by Providence'.[17]

After the Lateran Treaty, the only form of political activity permissible to Catholics in Italy was through a movement known as Catholic Action. This was an extremely ineffective means of keeping the Catholic flag flying, and was entirely dominated by the clergy. Pius XI described it as 'the organised participation of the laity in the hierarchical apostolate of the Church, transcending party politics'.[18] In other words, the Church was setting its face against party politics in Italy just as it was in other countries, particularly Germany. The Church's fear was that such parties would form alliances with left-wing groups and thus produce coalition governments, tending toward socialism.

The Church had a distinct aversion to socialism, even though this fell far short of communism. Indeed, when it came to sacrificing the Centre Party in Germany, the fact that this party had been on friendly terms with the Social Democrats was a major factor in making the Church determined that it should be shut down. Catholic Action, the Church decreed, could only be developed as an activity 'outside every political party and in direct dependence upon the Church hierarchy for the dissemination and implementation of Catholic principles'.[19]

No one was more interested in eliminating Catholic participation in politics than Pacelli himself. He had developed this distaste during the days of Pius X, and was now beginning to see it as an essential condition for his concordat policy and his ultimate objective – the Great Design – for bringing the whole world under the effective 'government' of the Church, by means of canon law. The Lateran Treaty, which was negotiated by Pacelli's elder brother Francisco, thus conformed exactly: its measures were designed to cripple political and social Catholicism, the condition which Pacelli desired to bring about in Germany by means of a Reich concordat.

It seems that Pacelli remained unaware, or at least indifferent, to one very ominous development. A certain person was delighted by the Lateran Treaty for quite separate reasons from those of the Church. A few days after the signing of the treaty, Adolf Hitler wrote an article for the *Völkischer Beobachter*, warmly welcoming the agreement. His article was published on 22 February 1929. In it, Hitler confidently asserted: 'The fact that the Curia is now making its peace with Fascism shows that the Vatican trusts the new political realities far more than did the former Liberal democracy, with which it could not come to terms.' Hitler went on to rebuke the leadership of the Centre Party for continuing to attach itself to democratic politics. 'By trying to preach that democracy is still in the best interests of German Catholics', he continued, 'the Centre Party ... is placing itself in stark contradiction to the spirit of the treaty signed today by the Holy See.'[20]

Hitler went on to say certain things which were even more ominous, although they were not at the time given sufficient attention, particularly by the Church. 'The fact that the Catholic Church has come to an agreement with Fascist Italy', he continued, 'proves beyond doubt that the Fascist world of ideas is closer to Christianity [and now came the most ominous section of all] than those of Jewish Liberalism or even atheistic Marxism to which the so called Catholic Centre Party sees itself so closely bound, to the detriment of Christianity today and our German people.'[21]

Even in the late 1920s, Hitler was showing signs of his later wily policy, the most important feature of which was his covert desire to attack the Jews and completely eliminate them. He was, at the same time, boasting that the Holy See was casting favourable glances toward the Nazi party. The supreme irony was that one of the greatest forces in Germany which was opposing (and was well placed to continue to oppose) Nazism was none other than the local Catholic Church.

Hitler had already acknowledged, when writing *Mein Kampf*, that confrontation with the Catholic Church in Germany would prove disastrous. This left him with an indirect strategy for undermining the power and prestige of the Church. With the unwitting help of Pacelli, he was to bring this strategy to its triumphant conclusion.

Chapter 6

Secretary of State

Throughout the drafting of the Lateran Treaty, Pacelli had continued with his plans for a Prussian concordat. He encountered stiff resistance. Centralized Catholic autocracy was ranged against decentralized Protestant pluralism. Pacelli played upon anxieties about the future of Catholic schools, meanwhile working relentlessly for Church control over those same schools. The harder he pushed, the harder the Prussians pushed back. Finally, Pacelli had to give way over schools and over clerical appointments. The Prussian concordat was signed on 14 June 1929.

Four months later, in October 1929, came the Wall Street crash. The US economy went into freefall as the nation entered a decade of economic depression. The German economy was dependent upon the US for finance and trade. Existing loans were promptly stopped; new ones were called in. Trade slumped. Soon German exports were unable to pay for imports. Banks failed. Businesses died. Unemployment soared.

In November 1929, late at night, a telephone call came through, from Gasparri at the Vatican to Pacelli at the German nunciature. At nearly 80, Gasparri was finally retiring. Pacelli was to be named as his successor. A delighted Pasqualina saw Pacelli's face take on a strange look of exhilarated awe. It was, she said, as though a saint was being told to seat himself at the right hand of God. 'I am being transferred to Rome. The Holy Father needs me', an excited Pacelli told her as he put down the telephone.[1]

Interestingly, Pasqualina's account is markedly at variance with that of Cardinal Bea, then a priest. Bea wrote:

> In 1929, passing through Berlin, I made a point of calling on the Apostolic nuncio, Archbishop Pacelli, whom I already knew for ten years almost. I said to him half jokingly, 'Your Excellency, they are saying in Rome that you are preparing to leave.' He answered me seriously, 'Yes, it's true. It's been said often already, and it was not true. But this time it's true. My wish was to have a large diocese and I asked the Holy Father to give me one, for my ideal would be to preach, to confirm, to do pastoral visitation. But the Holy Father did not want that, and I have to obey and go to Rome.'[2]

The two accounts may not be irreconcilable. Throughout his life, Pacelli seems to have 'blown hot and cold', especially where major decisions were concerned. A recurring theme is initial enthusiasm followed by self-doubt. Interestingly, the caveat about his promotion echoes his initial reservations to Gasparri, back in

1901. And as we shall see, his elevation to the papacy ten years later would trigger a paroxysm of self-doubt. Did Pacelli really yearn after pastoral work? Or were such declarations modesty taken to extremes? Or were they merely a focus for self-doubt? In 1939, Winston Churchill was to remark of impending Russian action: 'It is a riddle, wrapped in a mystery, inside an enigma.' The same description applies to Pacelli.

Back at the nunciature Pacelli's promotion, whether welcome or not, spelled disaster for Pasqualina. Shortly after the announcement, he shattered her dream by telling her that, for the time being, she would not be coming with him. Rome was not Berlin or Munich. In the political snake-pit of the Vatican, he well knew that he could afford not even a hint of impropriety to attach itself to him. Typically, he lacked the courage to tell her outright that she was now redundant to him. A crushed Pasqualina fled from the room. 'You will need me yet! You will see!' she warned.[3]

In fact, as Pacelli was well aware, there were precedents for popes to have 'women at the Vatican'. Pope Pius X had a German nun called Teresa Bong, founder of the Sisters of St Anne. Bong had acted as a gatekeeper to the Pope, thereby earning the malicious nickname 'the Cardinal' in the Vatican.[4]

Achille Ratti, Pius XI, had his former housekeeper, Teodolinda Banfi, actually resident in the papal apartments, on site for her duties. Her presence threw Vatican protocol into some disarray. The inventive title of 'Mistress of the Wardrobe' was dreamed up to accommodate her presence.[5] However, much to the delight of traditionialists, Banfi proved to be too much of a despot even for Ratti.

Obviously both of these situations were entirely proper. But Pacelli would have viewed women at the Vatican as perks for popes, not mere cardinals, even though as Secretary of State he was now the second most powerful man in the Church. Then again, he was fully aware that secretaries of state rarely attained the top position. If despite his protestations he yearned after the papacy, he would have known better than to give ammunition to inevitable political enemies. The presence of a young and good-looking German nun at the Vatican would have sent the rumour machine into overdrive.

Without Pacelli, Berlin held nothing for Pasqualina. Occasional letters failed to assuage her loneliness. A skiing trip to the Alps was interrupted before it had properly begun with another Vatican message for Pacelli, calling him back to Rome at once. Pasqualina could have screamed. But a rapt Pacelli stared at the message, which informed him that he was to be made a cardinal. Mussolini's $92.1 million Lateran Treaty donation had saved the Church from bankruptcy. Pacelli, in the background as chief architect of the treaty, was being rewarded by a grateful Pope.

When Pacelli finally left Berlin, tens of thousands of Germans, Protestant and Catholic alike, turned out in vast crowds to give him a hugely emotional send-off. The normally reserved Germans had taken this odd Italian cleric to their hearts. And in truth, he had been a great friend to Germany for many years and in many guises – struggling in vain with the Allies for Benedict's peace plan, easing the sufferings of war prisoners, denouncing the savagery of the Treaty of Versailles, saving the lives of the starving in post-war Munich, drafting the Bavarian and Prussian concordats, and remaining relatively untainted by the base self-interest of the Lateran Treaty. Pacelli had stood with Pasqualina in the freezing, ruined post-war streets of Munich giving money, food and medicine to people with next to nothing. As nuncio to Munich and Berlin, he had played the glittering diplomat. He had criss-crossed Germany, time and time again, on the most delicate and sensitive of missions. He had done so much good for a country which had lost its way and was in desperate need of friends. How could anyone have imagined that Pacelli's relationship with Germany would result in the greatest evil ever to overtake the world?

On 19 December 1929, in the Sistine Chapel, Eugenio Pacelli was made Cardinal. On 10 February 1930 he was made Secretary of State, second only to the Pope himself.

As the world entered the 1930s, the Great Depression deepened. In the US, 13 million people were unemployed – more than 25 per cent of the workforce. The European economies of Britain, Germany and Italy followed suit. It was a time of deep, paralysing fear. 'The human spirit ... is in chains', Pacelli adjudged. 'The world is imprisoned financially, politically and spiritually.'[6] In Germany and Italy, nationalism begat anti-Semitism. Somebody had to take the blame for this economic misery, and 'Jewish financiers' were a convenient scapegoat. Thus were the fires of Fascism fanned.

Ironically, at the same time that finance seemed to be ruining the world, it was assuming a very different role for the formerly impoverished Church. The bulk of Mussolini's $92.1 million had been entrusted to Bernardino Nogara, a mysterious financier. Nogara had total control over investing the funds. His remit was to use money to make money, irrespective of whether this involved 'ethical investment'. For instance, though the Church denounced artificial birth control, Nogara used Church funds to buy a controlling interest in Italy's largest manufacturer of birth control products. The Church preached peace, but Nogara used Church funds to buy shares in armament manufacturers. The Church prayed for stability, but Nogara used Church funds for currency speculation. Like a talented few before and after him, Nogara knew how to turn economic depression and the threat of war into rich opportunities for making money. Yet to Pasqualina, Nogara's financial amorality constituted a mockery of Church values. If the Lateran Treaty had been deceitfully portrayed to the world, the use of Lateran-derived funds was downright hypocritical. To her, the Church had double standards.

When Pacelli arrived in Rome, he stayed temporarily with his brother Francesco on the Via Boezio, pending taking an apartment at the Vatican as Secretary of State. Just before his appointment, he asked his sister Elisabetta to manage his new household. As a wife and mother she had other obligations; nevertheless, Pacelli insisted. As he knew only too well, a soundly run establishment was crucial to his well-being.

Shortly afterwards, Pasqualina left Germany without the permission of either

Pacelli, her employer, or her order. She arrived in Rome and begged Elisabetta for help, citing poverty and lack of ability in Italian. (Interestingly though, she had studied Italian at Ebersberg, some 30 years previously.) Once Elisabetta took her in, Pasqualina of course quickly reverted to type, assuming control over everything. An exasperated Elisabetta shut up the apartment and went to Lourdes, simply to get rid of Pasqualina. The 'extremely cunning' (*scaltrissima*) Pasqualina was undeterred.[7] She moved into Pacelli's new Vatican apartment, under the guise of getting it decorated and furnished. She then moved her two assistants, nuns from the same order, from Germany to Rome, and presented Pacelli with the *fait accompli* of a supremely well-run household, as before.

Back in 1919, Pasqualina had come to the nunciature in Munich for a trial period of a few months only. With her *snellezza*, her mental agility, and her steely devotion to Pacelli, she had extended her trial period indefinitely.[8] She was to remain with Pacelli, on an increasingly intimate but never improper basis, until the end of his life. She even accompanied him on all his trips abroad, and made herself in every way indispensable to his needs. For instance, for over a decade Pacelli had found it necessary to return to the Rorschach nursing home at least twice a year. As his nurse, Pasqualina invariably accompanied him on these visits, during which Pacelli became a different person. Occasionally they went off on skiing trips together.

When Pasqualina had first arrived at the Munich nunciature, such was the jealousy of the rest of the staff that they spread a malicious rumour that Pacelli had cast more than merely innocent eyes on the young nun. This had infuriated Pacelli. He had insisted upon a thorough investigation of this '*orribile calunnia*' (horrible slander).[9] The enquiry took place at the highest levels of the Vatican; unsurprisingly, the distraught Pacelli was completely cleared of any impropriety. However greatly Church staff in Munich, Berlin or Rome detested Pasqualina, a formal charge of impropriety was a card that could only be played once at the Vatican.

Associates of Pacelli such as the very able Jesuit, Father Robert Leiber, who worked with him for many years, learned to live with Pasqualina's presence. Leiber, who greatly admired Pacelli but not Pasqualina, once commented that the then nuncio 'should send her packing, but he doesn't want to, because she knows the domestic economy of the house extremely well'.[10] Returning to Rome had given Pacelli an opportunity to distance himself from Pasqualina. But, like many another churchman, he had failed to appreciate her steely determination. Her life was one of unremitting service to Eugenio Pacelli, and to Jesus Christ Himself.

> Political parties have nothing to do with religious problems, as long as these are not alien to the nation, undermining the morals and ethics of the race; just as religion cannot be amalgamated with the scheming of political parties.[11]

Thus wrote Hitler, with words that might have been borrowed from Pacelli. Both men were autocrats, striving for a total world view. Pacelli had his Great Design; Hitler had his Third Reich. The first was conceived for the glory of God;

the second glorified a warped vision of a master race. Hitler's plan, little less than a diabolical one, involved the elimination of Catholicism and, indeed, all forms of religion.

The ironic and, in the light of future events, tragic reality was that after the 1920s, Catholicism was in an immensely powerful position. If properly encouraged, it would undoubtedly have been able to present such opposition to Nazism as would ultimately have proved a successful bulwark against its assumption of power. Thanks to the strength of the Centre Party, which the Holy See was shortly to destroy, there had been an unprecedented growth of Catholic life in the period immediately after the war. This permeated both religious and cultural circles. During the 1920s, Catholic clergy numbers rose from 19,000 to 21,000. The number of members of religious orders doubled from 7,000 to 14,000. Male monastic foundations increased from 366 to 640. By 1930 the Catholic population in Germany was 23 million people. This was about one-third of the nation, a rise of two-and-a-half million since the start of the Great War.

In accordance with the vision inspired by Scheler and Erzberger, Catholicism was making a vital contribution to national life in the Weimar Republic through its writers, journalists, artists, poets and academics. Men like Romano Guardini and Peter Lippert gave the Catholic Church a deserved reputation for original thought and energetic action. Professorial chairs in Catholic ideas were endowed in several universities, while Catholic professional and academic clubs flourished, arranging frequent conferences and seminars on Catholic topics in every part of Germany. Certainly there were fewer Catholics than Protestants. But Catholic youth movements, involving one and a-half million young people, helped Catholicism to remain, until 1933, the largest single social institution in the country.

Looking back upon this period, with inevitable hindsight, it is a profound tragedy to consider that all this was thrown away by the Church itself.

Another example of Catholic vitality in Germany, in the immediate pre-Nazi period, was its vigorous activity in the realm of publishing. By the end of the 1920s there were no less than 400 daily Catholic newspapers. This represented approximately one-sixth of national daily circulation. There were also over 400 Catholic periodicals in Germany, at least 30 of which had circulations of about 100,000. There were two Catholic news and feature services which syndicated material throughout the nation, and there was even a cinema review, *Film-Rundschau*, which was both an expression of and a further impulse to an expanding German cinema industry, which owed more to Catholic influence than in most other countries.

The Catholic youth movements – which later suffered greatly from, and ultimately were taken over by, the Nazis – were very active with apostolic work. Rallies of Catholic boy scouts, young workers and other groups took place throughout the country. As a result of the Weimar relaxation of former strictures against religious assemblies, outdoor services and processions proliferated.

Although the Nazi Party was to make a spectacular gain in the 1930 elections, the Catholic Church in Germany was still an extremely powerful force. However, throughout the late 1920s Hitler had managed to neutralize Catholic fears of National Socialism. Hitler's increasing success was an ominous sign of what John Cornwell rightly calls the beginning of 'a Catholic slide toward National Socialism'.[12] There was still a considerable Catholic feeling of opposition to Nazi thought, however, and it was a tragedy that such opposition did not have greater success in stemming the rise of Nazism. Nevertheless, the National Socialists were nervous of Catholic opposition. Sensing a threat, their area command or *Gauleitung* in Essen contacted the Catholic bishop's office in Mainz. The *Gauleitung* wanted to know whether the bishop shared the views of an outspoken priest in a town called Kirschausen.

This priest had admonished his parishioners with the following guidelines:

No Catholic may be a card-carrying member of the Hitler Party.

No member of the Hitler Party may participate in [parish gatherings] at funerals or other events.

So long as a Catholic is a card-carrying member of the Hitler party, he may not be admitted to the sacraments.[13]

The vicar general of Mainz immediately confirmed that these guidelines were in accordance with official episcopal rulings. Furthermore, it was pointed out that the Hitler Party's policy of 'racial hatred' was 'un-Christian and un-Catholic'. To make himself quite clear, he even went on to say that 'the religious and educational policy of National Socialism is inconsistent with Catholic Christianity'.[14]

Unfortunately not all the other Catholic bishops in Germany agreed with their hierarchical brother at Mainz. The president of the Catholic bishops' conference, Cardinal Bertram of Breslau, contented himself by making a new year's statement with a warning that the Catholic Church in Germany could not tolerate political extremism, or the insanity and wickedness of racism.

Disappointingly, however, this potentially constructive and outspoken position was not followed through. Thereafter, the bishops took a more pluralist approach by directing that parish priests in each area should judge the situation locally on its own merits: 'As guardians of the true teaching of faith and morals, the Bishops must warn against National Socialism, so long and so far as it proclaims cultural opinions that are incompatible with Catholic teaching.'[15] Other bishops were more positive, however, and in the following months the bishops of Cologne, Paderborn and the Upper Rhine stated in unambiguous terms that National Socialism and Catholicism were incompatible, explicitly confirming a key sentence in the letter of the bishops of Bavaria.

In the early 1930s, the Catholic hierarchy in Germany showed a united anti-Hitler front. In the spring of 1931 Karl Trossmann, a Catholic representative in parliament, published a best-selling book entitled *Hitler and Rome*. In it, he described National Socialism as 'a brutal party that would do away with all the rights of the people'. Hitler, he declared, was dragging Germany into a new war that would 'only end more disastrously than the last'.[16] Not long after this another Catholic author, Alfons Wild, was responsible for a widely distributed essay called *Hitler and Catholicism*. He proclaimed that 'Hitler's view of the world is not Christianity but the message of race, a message that does not proclaim peace and justice but, rather, violence and hate.'[17] Other writers followed the same line, and as late as mid-July 1932 the Catholic Church of Germany presented an unshakeable and united front in opposition to Nazism. Ominously, however, this was not the view taken at the time by the Holy See, where the outlook on such matters was increasingly guided and promoted by Eugenio Pacelli, the new Cardinal Secretary of State.

Pacelli's concern with events in Germany was strongly influenced by the threat of international communism. Since the collapse of the Berlin Wall in 1989, followed by that of the USSR itself in the early 1990s, it is perhaps difficult for those born more recently to appreciate the full horror evoked by the former communist goal of world domination. Whatever one's political outlook, and despite Karl Marx's hopes for communism, inhabiting such a soullessly deterministic world would have been well-nigh unendurable for any civilized human being. World communism was possibly the greatest disaster that ever happened to the human race. For over 60 years, its evil shadow fell across the globe. The vigilance of anti-communists, such as Pacelli, was at the time much needed.

The communist perpetrators of that 1917 Russian revolution had declared war on all religions. Although there were less than 1.5 million Catholics in Russia, posing no significant political threat, they were subject to savage repression. In 1921 there were 963 Catholic priests in Russia; by 1930 this figure had plunged to some 300, of whom about 100 were imprisoned. Teaching children under 16 about God was deemed a crime. Untold numbers of clergy, principally Orthodox and Catholic, died in horrible circumstances in the notorious gulags.

An independent Mexican brand of communism had resulted in similar religious persecution since the late 1800s. In 1924, the government of Plutarco Elías Calles formally recognized the Russian communist regime. In the next decade, more than 5,000 Catholics were murdered. It became illegal to be a priest. Clergy thus had to travel the country in disguise. Graham Greene's powerful novel, *The Power and the Glory*, vividly depicts the tribulations of living with such great danger.

In 1933, Spain joined Soviet Russia and Mexico as the third member of the so-called 'Red Triangle', posing a communist threat to the world in general and the Church in particular. Probably only Fascist repression was keeping communism out of Italy and Germany. The great fear for men such as Pacelli was that communist subversion would lead country after country to fall, in a chain reaction, creating a critical mass. Beyond this lay communist world domination, fatal for the Church and for humanity.

Certainly the fear of communism was real enough. But from the days of Pius IX, the Vatican had developed a reactionary stance against social democracy, viewing it as a tendency toward socialism and then outright communism. Pacelli had grown up surrounded by these reactionary views; together with the 'passive anti-Semitism' of the Catholic world of the time, they had become part of his being. Thus the closure of the *Partito Populare* in Italy, following the Lateran Treaty, was viewed as a progressive step. In the early 1930s in Germany, the obvious middle-ground alliance was between the Centre Party and the Social Democrats. But fear of socialism made Pacelli put pressure on the Centre Party to move toward the National Socialists instead.

The Church's reactionary values, no less than its justified fear of communism, thus made it a natural ally of Fascist governments. In Italy, the Lateran Treaty had aligned Church and state. In Germany, the Bavarian and Russian concordats had paved the way for a Reich concordat, which Pacelli was determined to force through.

Meanwhile the Lateran Treaty was exposing the shortcomings of concordats with Fascist states. Under the terms of the concordat, Mussolini had an equal vote with the Vatican in the selection of bishops and archbishops serving in Italian dioceses. Soon he was demanding the appointment of political cronies to positions of importance, while seeking to get rid of clergy of whom he disapproved. 'The Holy Father, and you, too, Eminence, were so concerned about the financial plight of the Holy See, you closed your minds to the eventual consequences', Pasqualina sternly told Pacelli. 'When one bargains with a ruthless dictator, one must be prepared to face a bitter fate.'[18]

Clerical appointments were one bone of contention; religious education was another. The Italian concordat supposedly gave the Church the right to educate children in Catholicism, whereas Mussolini was reverting to the view that the Fascist state must retain authority for such teaching. In addition, Mussolini bitterly blamed the Church for not disciplining clergy and lay Catholics who were protesting against his regime. 'It appears that there may be open warfare between the Fascists and Holy Mother Church', Pacelli told Pasqualina, looking to the plain-speaking nun for a plan of action.[19] Her first response stunned him: 'Return the dirty money and see that the Vatican stands tall against this scheming dictator!'[20]

There was never any chance that Pacelli would take such a blunt message to the Pope. But as it happened, Ratti's views were not much less militant than Pasqualina's. Banging his fist on the table, he railed against the politician he had formerly viewed as a 'man sent by Providence': 'We will not yield to that devil Mussolini! We'll show the world what he is!'[21]

In the following months, over one million Italians of the so-called Catholic Action Group, drawn from a variety of Catholic organizations, protested against the Fascist state. The cries of 'Down with Mussolini!' were drowned by baton-wielding riot police. Church–State relations were in crisis.

Pasqualina's second suggestion to Pacelli was that the Pope write an encyclical denouncing Mussolini's actions. Ratti gave this idea his enthusiastic approval, never knowing that it had come from a humble nun. With Pacelli, he wrote *Non Abbiamo Bisogno* ('We Have No Need'). Pacelli entrusted it to a confidant, one Monsignor Spellman, to secretly convey it to Paris and release it to the world's media. The tone of the document was blunt, accusing Mussolini's Fascist regime of 'acts of oppression' and 'terrorism' against the Church and against members of the Catholic Action Group.[22]

Certainly *Non Abbiamo Bisogno* blackened the image of Mussolini's government in the glare of world opinion. Pasqualina made a third suggestion, also enthusiastically taken up by Ratti and Pacelli. This was to extend an olive branch to Mussolini by inviting him to a private audience with the Pope. On the third anniversary of the signing of the Lateran Treaty, Mussolini duly met with Ratti, and 'Il Duce' bent to kiss the Fisherman's Ring of Pope Pius XI.

For the next decade, until Mussolini's eventual overthrow, Church–State relations were markedly better in Italy. But the Lateran Treaty had nevertheless been achieved at a heavy price. Pasqualina's personal view of political involvement by the clergy is indicative of a strand of conservatism running through the Church: 'The Pope should stop all overt political activity by the clergy.' To her, such action was 'Church interference in matters of the State'.[23] While this view was arguable in Fascist Italy, it would become progressively harder to argue in Fascist Germany, with its atrocious record of persecution. Understandably the populace looked to their clergy for moral guidance.

Several years later, when Mussolini entered the Axis pact with Hitler, another papal denunciation was prepared. Only the death of Achille Ratti, Pope Pius XI, prevented its being issued.

In 1921, when Pacelli had been working on the follow-up to his Bavarian concordat, he acquired an unexpected associate named Monsignor Ludwig Kaas. Kaas was an anomaly, a Catholic priest who was also a professional politician in the Centre Party and, most interestingly, an expert in canon law. Five years younger than Pacelli, Kaas came under the latter's intellectual wing. Seven years later, in 1928, Kaas had become a leader of the Centre Party. By then a close friend of Pacelli, he was beginning to act almost as the latter's private secretary. Kaas thus entered what John Cornwell has aptly termed a political 'double life'.[24] He neglected his political duties in Germany, spending weeks at a time in Pacelli's apartments at the Vatican, working toward a Reich concordat. In short, Kaas became Pacelli's disciple. In one sense, this was a bizarre relationship; in other senses, it was a dangerous one. Germany had ills which it needed more than concordats and canon law to resolve. And while supposedly leading a mainstream political party, despite being a Catholic priest, Kaas was becoming an agent of an organization politically at odds with it.

In 1930 Heinrich Brüning, a Centre Party Catholic and trade unionist, had been made chancellor. His goal was a restructuring of the German economy. Accordingly he introduced a package of austerity proposals, which earned him the unenviable *soubriquet* of 'The Hunger Chancellor'.[25] The proposals were rejected as too harsh, and another general election was triggered. With over 3 million unemployed, political extremism triumphed. The National Socialists increased their share of the vote from 2.6 to 18.3 per cent. At a stroke, their seats in parliament multiplied from 12 to 107. They were now second only to the Social Democrats. The Centre Party lagged behind with 14.8 per cent of the vote, representing 66 seats in the Reichstag.

For the following two years, Brüning was to run a minority government, precariously sandwiched between the Social Democrats and the National Socialists. Despite his economic restructuring, the unemployment figure rose inexorably, from 3 million to nearly 4.5 million in 1930, and then to 5.6 million in 1931. Following on from Scheler and Erzberger, Brüning was an advocate of decentralized management–union relationships. His stance contrasted starkly with that of another prominent Catholic, the leading industrialist Fritz Thyssen, an advocate of centralized control in which unions were as unnecessary as they were unwelcome.

On 13 July 1932 there was a banking crisis in Germany. Panicked customers rushed to withdraw their funds, causing further collapse and the suspension of the banking system. When the banks tentatively opened again on 5 August, the lending rate had soared to 15 per cent. Industry was being decimated; the economy was in freefall. In desperation, Brüning went to Rome to solicit Mussolini's help in pleading with the Allies to get the post-war payments reduced. He also went to the Vatican where, to his astonishment, Pacelli launched into the tactics of a Reich concordat. Brüning tersely told him that this was scarcely the time for it. Pacelli blithely replied that Brüning should form a right-wing government for the express purposes of achieving a Reich concordat.

At this, Brüning bluntly informed Pacelli that he 'misunderstood the political situation in Germany and, above all, the real character of the Nazis'.[26] Yet again, Pacelli was slowing a flagrant disregard for the political climate in Germany. Matters between the two men rapidly worsened. Pacelli attacked Brüning for making separate agreements with the Protestant church. Brüning quite rightly replied that, whether personally Catholic or not, his political role demanded that he should give all churches equal merit.

To Brüning, it was obvious that Pacelli saw concordats as the solutions to life's political problems. In the two years since the Lateran Treaty, Mussolini's Fascists had harassed both the Church and democracy in Italy. For Brüning, this showed that Fascists could sign concordats and then do what they liked, laughing at the Vatican. A German concordat with Fascists would go the same way.

Yet Pacelli remained unmoved by Brüning's passionate yet scrupulous arguments. He repeated that Brüning should make an accommodation with the National Socialists. A weary and exasperated Brüning replied that, whereas the German Social Democrats were not religious but were at least tolerant, the National Socialists were neither religious nor tolerant.

On this unhappy note, Brüning's meeting with Pacelli ran out of time. Immediately, he went into another meeting with the Pope. To his amazement, Ratti praised the German bishops who were speaking out against National Socialism. Evidently Ratti and Pacelli were not of one mind on this matter. At a second meeting with Pacelli, he told him what had transpired with the Pope. He also 'sharply' informed him that after considering their previous discussion, he had decided to abandon a Reich concordat and leave it to his successor.[27]

Brüning bitterly told Pacelli that he supposed 'the Vatican would fare better at the hands of Hitler … than with himself, a devout Catholic'.[28] Pacelli's concordat policy leading to rigid centralization seemed, to Brüning, politically unrealistic given Germany's plight. Certainly it was antithetical to the philosophies of men like Scheler and Erzberger.

However much Pacelli may have been esteemed in Germany, Brüning's observation – that the Secretary of State was loftily ignoring political realities – was one that echoed criticisms of Pacelli made at the time of the Bavarian and Prussian concordats. The partisanship of Pacelli's concordat policy boded ill for German politics.

Quite obviously, after this Brüning was of no further use to Pacelli. Instead he concentrated upon Kass, who attempted to persuade the Centre Party that they should collaborate with the National Socialists 'for a particular purpose over a limited time'.[29] The particular purpose was, of course, a Reich concordat. Meanwhile, Catholics throughout Germany echoed Brüning's dark suspicions of the National Socialists.

Unfortunately for Brüning – and Germany – with 5 million still unemployed in May 1932 he was forced to resign. His successor, Franz von Papen, lifted the ban on Hitler's brownshirt thugs. He also called for new elections on 31 July. They took place in a climate of civil unrest, with hundreds of violent confrontations between the communists and the National Socialists.

The results of the election were decisive. The National Socialists won 37.4 per cent of the vote. The socialists had 21.6 per cent, the Centre Party 16.2 per cent and the communists 14.5 per cent. In a few short years, the National Socialists had come from seemingly nowhere to becoming the greatest power in German politics. With 13.5 million voters they had 230 seats in parliament and, most ominously, what amounted to a private army of 400,000 brownshirts and blackshirts. They were winning at the ballot box, and they were winning on the increasingly bloody streets.

Pacelli's centralist exhortations to do deals with the National Socialists were scarcely echoed by the Catholic clergy in Germany, who banned Catholics from joining the Party. According to them, it contained 'false doctrine', while the utterances of its proponents were 'hostile to the faith'. With prescience, they declared that if it achieved a political monopoly 'the interests of Catholics will prove extremely bleak'.[30]

Meanwhile Kass had written a treatise extolling the Lateran Treaty with Mussolini as the exemplar of State–Church relations. Chillingly, he commented that 'the authoritarian Church should understand the "authoritarian" state better than others'.[31] The Code of Canon Law was being aligned with the principle of totalitarianism. Throughout, the treatise bears the intellectual stamp of Kass's mentor, Pacelli. Using the very same example of the Lateran Treaty, the unfortunate Brüning had warned Pacelli that concordats with Fascists were a doomed venture. The German Catholic clergy were warning all against the Fascist National Socialists. But Brüning had been swept from power, and the German clergy had no power over policy. Vatican concordat policy was being almost entirely decided by Pacelli – the very person who had bankrolled an impoverished Hitler 13 years earlier.

Chapter 7

Shaking Hands with the Devil

On 12 September 1932, at the first meeting of the new parliament, von Papen received a vote of no confidence. He was forced to call yet another election, for 6 November. This would be the fifth election that year in an economically ravaged Germany which was rapidly becoming ungovernable. The communists wanted Germany – at the heart of Europe – to succumb to a Russian-style revolution. The National Socialists wanted a dictatorship. Although they won again, they recorded 2 million less votes this time. Party membership was decreasing. Their star appeared to be waning; but not for long.

In December von Papen resigned, but he came back a month later with a plan for Hitler to become chancellor, while he became vice-chancellor in order to control Hitler from behind the scenes. President Hindenburg rightly viewed Hitler with suspicion; but he nevertheless gave von Papen his support in exchange for protection from financial scandals.

On 30 January 1933, Hitler became chancellor. On February 27, the Reichstag went up in flames. Hitler promptly blamed the communists. The country panicked. Hindenburg played into Hitler's hands by sanctioning the suspension of civil liberties. With Göring controlling the Prussian police, political opponents could be bullied into submission.

On 5 March, Hitler went to the polls to secure an absolute majority. Once again, this proved frustratingly elusive. The National Socialists took 52 per cent of the vote, with 340 out of 647 seats in parliament. The socialists took 18.3 per cent, and the Catholic Centre Party 13.9 per cent.

Hitler may not have feared the Catholic Centre Party; but he certainly feared the Catholic Church in Germany. As mentioned previously, it comprised some 23 million people; moreover, it was extremely well-organized. Catholic associations and Catholic media were steadfastly opposed to National Socialism. The bishops were the moral leaders of Catholicism in Germany. The wily Hitler saw a way to muzzle them. The Lateran Treaty had proscribed Catholic political action in Italy; a Reich concordat would do the same in Germany.

Hitler well knew of Pacelli's obsession with a Reich concordat. Via a dialogue between von Papen and Kass (still in thrall to Pacelli), he was made aware that Kass was prepared to make 'a clear break with the past' and that National Socialism could count on the 'co-operation of his party'.[1] Unconvinced by Vatican policy and string-pulling, the German bishops still remained bitterly opposed to Hitler and everything he stood for. On 10 March, Cardinal

Faulhaber wrote to Hindenburg warning of the 'fear that besets wide circles of the Catholic population'.[2]

Hitler knew that he could use a Reich concordat to silence Catholic protest against National Socialism. But in the murky world of German coalition governments, with votes of confidence one week and elections the next, a Reich concordat was a pipe dream. Hitler realized that his only chance of negotiating a Reich concordat was to do it himself. This required him to have the powers of a dictator – which was what he wanted, in any event. But he could then use a Reich concordat to legitimize his dictatorship, while rendering his political enemies impotent. That was the great prize.

To achieve dictator status required the passing of a so-called Enabling Act. The Centre Party agonized over it. Brüning begged the party to have nothing to do with such an unconstitutional process. Kass, as leader of the party, remained unmoved. Increasingly, he was becoming a go-between for Hitler and Pacelli.

On 22 and 23 March, the Reichstag gathered to vote on the Enabling Act. Kass argued passionately to his colleagues in the Centre Party that supporting the Enabling Act would create a moral hold over Hitler and guarantee his promises to the Catholic Church. Conversely, Brüning denounced the act as 'the most monstrous resolution ever demanded of a parliament'.[3] To Kass, however, the accommodation with Hitler was 'the greatest success that had been achieved in any country for the last ten years [in state relations]'.[4] Owen Chadwick has noted aptly that Kass's 'role in making the party vote for Hitler's Enabling bill of March 1933 is still one of the most controversial acts of German history'.[5]

With Centre Party support and only the Social Democrats opposing, the Enabling Act was passed by 441 votes to 94. Hitler was effectively dictator. He could pass laws without parliamentary approval. He could make treaties with foreign powers. And with his paramilitary brownshirts and blackshirts, together with Göring's Prussian police, he could start turning Germany into a police state.

To morally legitimize his dictatorship, Hitler immediately went on a public relations offensive, hypocritically assuring the populace that Christianity would underpin his rebuilding of Germany. He also did his best to embarrass the German bishops about their anti-National Socialist stance. Back in Rome, Kass and Pacelli were working on a concordat with Hitler. Knowing that the Catholic Church was going to give formal acknowledgement to National Socialism prompted the German Protestant churches to make their own acceptance on 26 March.

On 28 March, the German Catholic bishops issued a statement declaring that 'the designated general prohibitions and warnings [against National Socialism] need no longer be considered necessary'.[6] While the remainder of the statement was ambiguous, the National Socialists immediately seized on it as a moral endorsement from the Catholic Church. The Catholic Centre Party looked ridiculous. The bishops had committed a *volte-face*; to their parishioners, it smacked of hypocrisy and betrayal. In the words of one commentator, 'The souls of well-disposed people are in a turmoil as a result of the tyranny of the National

Socialists ... the authority of the Bishops ... has been shaken by the quasi-approval of the National Socialist movement.'[7]

To Kass however, pondering the 'idea of union' between state and Church, 'an austere and, temporarily no doubt, excessive state discipline' was necessary in Germany. He even went on to say that the Centre Party had been obliged to co-operate in this process since its members were 'sowers of the future'.[8] For Cardinal Faulhaber, however, the situation was much more simple; the bishops had been compromised 'because of the position of Rome'.[9]

On 1 April, the Nazis moved significantly closer to a police state by organizing a boycott of Jewish businesses in Germany and the termination of Jewish employment in professional life, including education, medicine and the law. To Saul Friedländer, it was 'the first major test on a national scale of the attitude of the Christian Churches toward the situation of the Jews under the new government'.[10] No word of protest came from any Catholic quarter at this demonstration of systematic and nationwide persecution of the Jews, either in Germany or in Rome.

Lack of Catholic protest was bad enough, but now something even more potentially dangerous occurred. Cardinal Faulhaber of Munich – generally an enlightened prelate – referring to the attacks by the Nazis on the Jews in a long letter to Pacelli, said that it was pointless to protest against these attacks on the Jews since this could only extend the struggle to Catholics. 'Jews', he told Pacelli, in a sentence which makes the blood run cold, even after all these years, 'can help themselves.'[11]

Faulhaber was willing to extend some help to Jews who had, for ten or twenty years, been practising Catholics after conversion, but this was as far as he would go. The case of Edith Stein was particularly poignant. She was a brilliant German-Jewish philosopher who had been drawn toward Christianity and become a Catholic after reading the autobiography of Saint Teresa of Ávila, the attractive Carmelite mystic of the sixteenth century. In 1922 she became a Catholic. By 1933, she had been accepted for a philosophy post at the German Institute for Scientific Pedagogy in Munich. The decree in April of that year, against the Jews, deprived her of the appointment. In October 1933 she entered a Carmelite convent from which she wrote a passionately worded letter to the Pope, imploring him to 'deplore the hatred, persecution, and displays of anti-Semitism directed against the Jews, at any time and from any source'.[12] Her letter received no reply.

On 7 April, in a supposedly chance meeting, vice-chancellor von Papen told Kass, the Vatican go-between, that a Reich concordat would involve 'the safe-guarding of religious rights for Catholics in exchange for the depoliticising of the clergy and the disbanding of the Centre Party'.[13] On 10 April, the Monday of Easter week, von Papen and Kass began a furious rush to complete a first draft by the following Saturday. The Bavarian concordat had taken three years. The bulk of the Reich concordat was composed in six days. On Easter Sunday and Monday Pacelli and Kass went through the draft, checking the various points. The views of German Catholics and clergy were not solicited; indeed they were not even informed that work was under way. Cardinal Bertram, in response to rumours, wrote to Pacelli on 18 April. He received a bureaucrat's delay of two weeks in reply; and he received a bureaucrat's affected vagueness that 'possible negotiations had been initiated'.[14]

Three weeks later, as the final negotiations were being hammered out, Pacelli coolly informed Faulhaber that although there had been talk of a concordat, there was nothing concrete.

Kass, a supposed leader of the Centre Party, was now working full-time on the concordat and living at Pacelli's Vatican apartments. It was put to him that his behaviour could not be reconciled with his political responsibilities and that he should resign. He refused, on the basis that 'it would upset things in Rome'.[15] An independent commentator tartly noted: 'The future of German Catholicism appears to be decided in Rome. A result of the progressive centralism.'[16]

Hitler and Pacelli had very different reasons for this breakneck rush into a Reich concordat. Hitler knew that a concordat could be presented as a public relations coup, the Vatican seemingly giving its blessing to the Nazis. This was of inestimable value both within Germany and on the international stage. Furthermore, he knew that the depoliticizing of Catholicism in Germany would rid him of powerful internal opposition, ensuring not least the effective demise of the Centre Party. Pacelli was obsessed with a Reich concordat, for the good of the Church and the good of Germany. The canon lawyer in him hoped that a concordat would restrain the excesses of the Nazi Party (although there was scant evidence that the Lateran Treaty had checked the excesses of Fascism in Italy). And as long as the Centre Party existed, with the ever-faithful Kass at the helm, no doubt it could be used as a bargaining chip with Hitler.

Negotiations between Hitler and Pacelli continued throughout April and May. Meanwhile the Centre Party started to disintegrate as hundreds of thousands of disenchanted members defected to the triumphant National Socialists. Kass's resignation, long overdue, was finally demanded. Astonishingly, he gave it by telephone from the Vatican. No greater sign could have been given of where his loyalties lay. Poor Brüning was made leader, once again, on 6 May. In vain, he begged for unity within the Party. But between them, Hitler and Pacelli had taken democratic power out of the hands of this once-proud political organization. An increasingly confident Hitler raised the stakes in the drafting of the concordat by proposing that the Catholic clergy be forbidden from political activity of any kind whatsoever.

At the end of April, Pacelli had told Faulhaber that nothing concrete had been done with respect to a concordat. At the end of May, at a meeting of the German bishops, they were blithely informed that work on the concordat was virtually complete, Pacelli wanted their support, and speed was of the essence. Pacelli was revealing himself as a shamelessly amoral negotiator – using time in his favour by delaying his reply to Bertram in April, then telling Faulhaber an outright lie, and now presenting the concordat as a *fait accompli* and using a 'speed is of the essence' argument to railroad the concordat into being.

Although Pacelli had done his best to stage-manage the meeting of the bishops, there were nevertheless some stormy views expressed. Cardinal Schulte rightly pointed out the Nazis' contempt for law and human rights. To him, 'no concordat could be concluded with such a government'.[17] But it was futile. A majority of the German bishops acquiesced to a resolution to halt their opposition to Nazism on condition that Church rights and liberties were observed, particularly with regard to schools and associations. With the bishops following Pacelli's party line, rebellion in the Church had been staved off.

If there were any lingering doubts as to the good faith of the Nazis, they were violently disabused mere days later. A rally of Catholic apprentices in Munich drew crowds of 25,000 Catholic supporters. Hitler's Nazi bully-boys repeatedly attacked them. Hundreds of young Catholics were beaten up. Peaceful rally members were driven from the streets. To the Nazis, 'political Catholicism' clearly meant anything they wanted it to mean. And their tactics were whatever they wanted them to be – no matter how violent.

Faulhaber wrote to the local bishops, advising them to stop any further Catholic rallies 'since we do not want to risk the lives of our young men and a government ban on youth organisations'.[18] Mindful of dissenters in the Church, he warned that 'clergy who speak imprudently' should be disciplined. How the Nazis must have laughed! They no longer had to attack the Catholic Church, for the Catholic Church was voluntarily rendering itself impotent and subjecting itself to a self-imposed gagging order. Hitler had always (rightly) feared the power of the Church – and he was shrewd enough to continue to do so for much of the next decade. But Pacelli's rigid centralization was turning the Church into a sleeping giant.

In the following month, the Nazis viciously hunted down Centre Party politicians. In Bavaria, 2,000 of their supporters were thrown into prison. The Nazi propaganda machine confidently asserted that 'Catholicism aims in every way to sabotage the orders of the government and to work against it':[19] a far cry from Hitler's earlier avowal that Christianity would underpin his rebuilding of Germany.

Meanwhile the concordat was nearing completion. Hitler's stance was that 'the Catholic Church ... will ensure a ban on all clergy and members of religious congregations from party political activity'.[20] On 1 July, Pacelli went through the final draft with Pope Pius XI. However much Achille Ratti agreed with Pacelli about concordat policy, he was a doughty fighter who had endured his fill of the Nazis' 'alternating abuse and negotiation'. He wanted Hitler to make 'guarantees of restitution for acts of violence'.[21] No such guarantees would mean no concordat.

Brüning was desperately trying to hold together the tatters of the Centre Party, to stand against the police state that was rapidly forming in Germany. With breathtaking cynicism, von Papen told Kass and Pacelli that Brüning's refusal to wind up the Centre Party was preventing the concordat from being concluded. The German bishops told Pacelli not to give credence to von Papen's argument. But to Pacelli, the Centre Party was the final bargaining chip in the negotiations. On 2 July, from the Vatican, Kass telephoned Joseph Joos of the

Centre Party and hurled at him the dreadful words: 'What! Haven't you dissolved yourselves yet?'[22]

Two days later on 4 July, Brüning, bereft of options, made the terrible
decision to voluntarily dissolve the Centre Party. With its passing, democracy
vanished from Germany. Untold millions of people would die terrible, violent
deaths before democracy would return to a country ravaged by war, and a
people once again humiliated by defeat. An irritated Pacelli commented: 'A pity
that it had to come now.'[23] He felt that if he could have hung on to his
bargaining chip just a little longer, his hand would have been strengthened in the
concordat negotiations.

As it happened, Pacelli, the arch-negotiator, was about to receive a masterclass
in negotiation from Hitler. When the Secretary of State believed that the concordat was mere hours away from being a 'done deal', Hitler told Rudolf
Buttmann, a German civil servant and legal expert, to go through the draft
document in painstaking detail. After Buttmann had done this, two issues were
outstanding: the exact distinction between political Catholic associations and
religious ones, and the question of guarantees of restitution for Nazi acts of
violence.

Pacelli and Buttmann argued over these issues throughout 7 July. Failing to
reach agreement over the Catholic association issue, they agreed to leave an
exact definition to a later date. This was a bad decision on Pacelli's part. The
restitution issue was decided by Hitler himself, by telephone.

On 8 July 1933, the Reich concordat was initialled. Pacelli and Kass met with
von Papen and Buttmann. With bitter irony, Pacelli had just received news of a
parish priest having been beaten up by the Nazis. He was so nervous that he
erroneously wrote his full signature on one of the pages. He was achieving his
life's ambition – but at what cost? When it was signed, he raised the question of
the priest. Buttmann smoothly demurred – it was probably a political clergy-
man. And besides, the inhabitants of that particular area were well known for
their volatility...

The bells of St Peter's rang out in joy, even though, had the truth been known,
there was nothing to celebrate in this formalizing of what historians have called
'shaking hands with the devil'. Hitler was beside himself with pleasure. He
authorized the following announcement regarding the concordat:

> The conclusion of the concordat seems to me [wrote Hitler] to give sufficient guar-
> antee that the Reich members of the Roman Catholic confession will, from now on,
> put themselves, without reservation, at the service of the new National Socialist state.[24]
> Therefore I am ordering, as follows:
>
> 1. The disbanding of such organisations as are recognised by the present treaty, and
> whose disbanding occurred without the order of the Reich government, is to be
> rescinded immediately.
>
> 2. All coercive measures against the clergy and other leaders of these Catholic orga-
> nisations are to be revoked. Repetition of such measures in the future is not allowed
> and will be punished on the basis of existing laws.[25]

A few days later, Hitler expressed the spine-chilling opinion that the concordat had created an atmosphere of confidence that would be 'especially significant in the urgent struggle against international Jewry'.[26] This, of course, was in no way the intention of Pacelli or the Church in pressing for the concordat. Nevertheless, Hitler cunningly took the opportunity of stating that in his campaign against the Jews he was merely carrying on, indeed completing, the work that the Church had been doing for nineteen centuries. The Church had stopped short of trying to procure the elimination of the Jews. Hitler would now take the process to its logical conclusion; in other words, he would deliver the 'Final Solution'.

The concordat was officially signed by Papen and Pacelli on 20 July. Typically, Hitler quickly seized the public relations initiative in the legitimization of the Nazi party. On 22 July, he wrote an internal document claiming that the Holy See's treaty with Germany meant the acknowledgement of the National Socialist state by the Catholic Church.

Thus this treaty showed the whole world, clearly and unequivocally, that National Socialism's supposed hostility to religion was a lie.

Pacelli quickly responded in *L'Osservatore Romano* on 26–27 July. He stated firmly that the concordat did not imply any moral endorsement of National Socialism. Conversely, the importance of the concordat lay in the state's acknowledgement of the Church's canon law. Yet the flagrant breaches of human rights by Hitler's thugs gave ample proof of the Nazis' contemptuous disregard of any laws except their own.

The unfortunate Brüning appears to have viewed the Reich concordat with greater honesty than Pacelli.

Behind the agreement with Hitler stood not the Pope, but the Vatican bureaucracy and its leader, Pacelli. He visualized an authoritarian state and an authoritarian Church directed by the Vatican bureaucracy, the two to conclude an eternal league with one another. For that reason Catholic parliamentary parties in Germany, like the Centre Party, were inconvenient to Pacelli and his men, and were dropped without regret in various countries. Pope Pius XI did not share these ideas.[27]

As the days passed, the advantages to Hitler, in the various provisions of the concordat and the ways in which he could exploit it, became more and more apparent. Although it is true that seemingly excellent and far-reaching concessions had been given to Catholics in the field of education, the Nazis now took the opportunity of passing a law against 'overcrowding' in German schools and universities. This was aimed at reducing the number of Jewish pupils allowed into such institutions. A measly quota of 1.5 per cent of school and college enrolments was considered appropriate for non-Aryan or Jewish students.

Most ominously, the papacy and the Holy See, as well as German Catholics as a whole, were being drawn into complicity with racist and anti-Semitic acts of legislation. The once-proud German Catholic Church, glorying in its independence, was now being led into a moral abyss by the consequences of Pacelli's actions.

In August, Sir Ivone Kirkpatrick, British minister at the Vatican, had an in-depth discussion with Pacelli. He noted that Pacelli 'made no effort to conceal his disgust at the proceedings of Herr Hitler's government'.[28] Kirkpatrick reported that Pacelli deplored the Nazi persecution of the Jews. He felt that he must apologetically explain to Kirkpatrick how he had signed a concordat with such people. 'A pistol, he [Pacelli] said, had been pointed at his head and he had had no alternative.'[29] Later he told Francois Charles-Roux, the French diplomat, that he had no regrets about signing because without the concordat, the Church would have had no legal redress against the Nazis.[30]

Pacelli assured Kirkpatrick that 'the Church ... had no political axe to grind. They were outside the political arena.' Furthermore, 'if the German government violated the concordat, and they were certain to do so, the Vatican would have a treaty on which to base a protest'. Pacelli then added, with one of his rare smiles on such serious occasions, 'the Germans will probably not violate all the articles of the concordat, at the same time'.[31]

Herein lies the origin of the argument put forward that the concordat with Nazi Germany was a masterstroke, because now there was an instrument to bind Hitler to the will of the Church, with legal redress against violations. In its *naiveté*, it is little less than a pathetic argument, since it implies that the Pope needs a legal document in order to carry out his mandate as moral arbiter of world affairs. It is the first case ever recorded in papal history of the apparent need of a humanly devised piece of paper, before the Church or the Pope could exercise their moral authority. It is an insult, indeed, to the Church and to the Pope. This is not to say that Pacelli did not, at the time, sincerely believe that such a piece of paper, i.e. the concordat, would immeasurably strengthen the hand of the Church in its relations with Nazi Germany.

The final act of ratification of the concordat left Pacelli in a state of total nervous collapse. By 9 September, before the official ceremonial exchange of signed documents had even occurred, Pacelli had fled once more to his sanctuary at Rorschach. Buttmann asked if he might follow him there to discuss outstanding points of contention. The request was vetoed. The Nazis turned this into political capital, arguing that if Buttmann had been permitted to meet with Pacelli in Switzerland, points of contention in the concordat might have been speedily resolved.[32] The ratification of the concordat was celebrated, shortly afterwards, with a service of thanksgiving held at St Hedwig's Cathedral in Berlin. Nazi flags hung alongside Catholic banners. The *Horst Wessel* was sung inside the church and relayed by loudspeaker to the thousands of celebrants outside. What more powerful symbol could be imagined of the Catholic Church's supposed endorsement of the Nazis?

Before long, the Nazis were busy dismantling the structure of the Catholic Church in Germany. By early October, Cardinal Bertram was cataloguing a plague of protests brought on by 'the totalitarian claims of the State'.[33] These included the dismissal of Catholic civil servants, censorship of the Catholic media, and suppression of Catholic organizations, even 'sewing circles for winter relief'. German bishops complained to Pacelli, urging him to abandon the concordat. The Pope himself was said to be about to protest.

Pacelli, however, twisted the supposed papal denunciation into yet another negotiating ploy. Hitler had forthcoming elections; he needed to continue and, indeed, strengthen his mandate. Papal denunciation could be extremely damaging to his prospects. Pacelli's stance was that the Catholic Church must be protected by the state in Germany, irrespective of human rights abuses or the fate of other Churches. As before, however, Pacelli met his match in the wily Buttmann, who was prepared to buy time by arguing *ad nauseum* as to what precisely constituted a 'political' Catholic organization.[34] The harsh reality was that this was whatever the Nazis wanted it to be. It might change from day to day, according to the whims of expediency – or it might not. By the same amoral token, the Nazis would feel free to promise one thing and do quite another.

Meanwhile, in Germany the spate of human rights abuses continued. Faulhaber, whom the Nazis regarded as 'the spiritual leader of the Catholic resistance to the National Socialist state', gave a number of stirring sermons, but even he admitted that he did not want 'in any way to set out on a course of fundamental opposition'.[35]

During November and December, as vice-chancellor van Papen was getting ready to amalgamate Catholic youth groups into the Hitler Youth, Pacelli and Buttmann continued their verbal sparring. Papal denunciation once more reared its head when Pacelli told Buttmann that the Pope would be addressing the German question at his Christmas address. But '[i]f I could only present something pleasant to His Holiness, I believe the disposition of the Pope would be improved'.[36] 'Something pleasant', a note of intent, arrived the very next day, courtesy of Hitler. The result was no criticism of Nazism in the Christmas speech.

For the first half of 1934, the weary see-saw of post concordat negotiation continued. At one point the Reich prevaricated, pointing out that it had a sworn duty to consult regional states. On 14 May, Pacelli wrote a remarkable missive to Buttmann, upbraiding the Reich for failing to make such regional states toe the party line. Implicit in the rebuke was an accusation that Hitler was being insufficiently dictatorial.

On 30 June 1934 the folly of wordplay was finally exposed, with Hitler's notorious 'Night of the Long Knives'. Erstwhile supporters of Hitler were butchered, along with his Catholic opponents. The Catholic bishops made no protest.

Also in June, Chancellor Dollfuss of Austria signed a concordat with the Vatican. On 25 July he was assassinated. The terror tactics continued, both within and outside Germany. Meanwhile, Hitler had still not published an unequivocal testament of protection for the Catholic Church in Germany. By then, Pacelli had sent ten important communications which had received no reply from the Nazis. Of a total of 54 missives to Berlin, 50 received no reply.

On 2 September, Pacelli informed the German bishops that German concessions were below the degree of religious freedom guaranteed by the text of the concordat. The Secretary of State and distinguished canon lawyer might more accurately have spoken of religious freedom *supposedly* guaranteed. The stark reality is this: in 'shaking hands with the devil', Pacelli had made a catastrophic miscalculation. Hitler had brilliantly utilized the Reich concordat to persuade a potentially deadly enemy to render itself impotent. He had gained the forced obedience of 23 million German Catholics. He had placed the newly legitimized Nazi party centre-stage in the world arena. And he had done all this by conceding, in reality, next to nothing of lasting significance. Pacelli had failed to heed the old saying: *Historia concordatorum, historia dolorum* (The story of concordats is one of sadness). Worse, he had ignored Pasqualina's warning: 'When one bargains with a ruthless dictator, one must be prepared to face a bitter fate.'

Chapter 8

The Flying Cardinal

'I will make him travel, so that he may get to know the world and the world may get to know him. He will be a splendid Pope.'[1] Thus spoke Achille Ratti of Pacelli, in 1936. In failing health, and at nearly 80 years of age, the Pope was defying precedent and anticipating his successor. In addition to being Secretary of State, Ratti had nominated Pacelli as *Camerlengo*, granting him semi-papal power, if the Pope should ever be incapacitated. As Secretary of State and *Camerlengo*, Pacelli was the second most important man in the Catholic Church, far ahead of any rival. One of his inevitable duties would be that of taking charge of the conclave to elect the next pope.

On the face of it, Ratti and Pacelli were unlikely friends. Although Ratti had spent much of his professional life in libraries, there was nothing of the gentle bookman about him. He was blunt, forthright and markedly courageous. He had been an alpinist of repute, climbing the highly rated east face of Monte Rosa. He was 'a man of tremendous personal force and powerful will – a strange equipment, if you will, in a librarian, but one that makes the long obscurity [until the age of 61] more puzzling than his emergence from it'.[2]

In 1921, as Polish nuncio, Ratti had been the sole member of the diplomatic corps to remain in Warsaw when the invading Russian communist army, under Trotsky and Tukhachevsky, reached the Vistula. The then Archbishop Ratti's presence in the capital proved inspirational. Women and children as well as men fought on Our Lady's Day, 15 August 1920, in the Battle of Warsaw. The Red Army was decisively routed; their defeat was one of the definitive battles of the world, and Western civilization was thereby saved. This harrowing experience affected Ratti in much the same way as Pacelli's experience in the Munich nunciature. Both men were scarred by their encounters with communism; both of them would fight it unrelentingly for all of their days.

In many ways Ratti was an old-fashioned despot, making his subordinates (even Pacelli) kneel in front of him for protracted periods. As we have seen, Pacelli was a multi-layered personality with many contrasting facets, from urbane diplomat to tortured neurotic, to silent ascetic. Interestingly, toward the end of his career he would become increasingly like Ratti, a despot, who also would command his subordinates to kneel before him.

Ratti and Pacelli were united in their shared vision of the future of the Church as a 'perfect society, supreme in its own order'.[3] From the dark days of the 1870s, when the doctrine of papal infallibility had been swiftly followed by secular collapse, the Church had struggled to recover its place in the world. Despite its practical difficulties, the Lateran Treaty had saved the Church from bankruptcy and won for Pacelli the red hat of a cardinal. His 1917 Code of Canon Law had given the Church an integrated legal framework for expansion and centralized control. His concordat policy, however problematic, was placing the Vatican once more on the world stage.

From the 1870s, when Pius IX had retreated into the Vatican, a succession of popes and secretaries of state had followed him into self-imprisonment. Pacelli was the first to break this rule. Thus he had become the first such senior Church figure in 60 years to make public appearances outside Rome. In Germany, this had won him (and the Church) crowds of tens of thousands of adoring Catholics. With Pacelli, the cult of public personality began. This would reach its apogee in the early 1960s, with Pope John XXIII. When we see a contemporary pope sweeping in presidential style to a televized audience, in his bullet-proof 'popemobile', we may detect the influence of Pacelli.

Ratti, a man for whom presidential-style public exposure held no attraction, was wise enough to acknowledge that the cult of self-imprisonment in the Vatican had done untold harm to the Church. In any case, the Lateran Treaty had rendered this cult redundant. In grooming Pacelli as his successor, Ratti was moulding a very different pope, one who would exhibit presidential charisma on an international stage. The world of the 1930s was changing rapidly. Telephones, radio and television were ushering in an era of mass communication which we now take for granted. For the Church to make its voice heard it would have to come out, literally and metaphorically, from the hallowed shadows of the Vatican. To Ratti, Pacelli must have seemed the perfect candidate for this new *modus operandi*. Years previously he had criss-crossed Germany, making public appearances; he could do the same in other countries. He would be the modern public face of the Church; he would also be the leader of a formerly obscure canon law conservatism which had taken, in all, 60 years to become the dominant force in Church expansion.

Furthermore, Pacelli's motivation could not have been greater. He was both inspired and obsessed by his 'Great Design'. To Ratti, Pacelli must have seemed the perfect successor; all that he needed was international exposure.

In September 1934, despite the mounting tensions in Europe, the Pope despatched Pacelli to Buenos Aires for the International Eucharistic Congress. By contrast to communist Mexico, Argentina was viewed as the flagship of Catholicism in Latin America. A triumphalist visit would be a public relations coup for the Church, specifically in South America and generally in the world arena.

Back in 1917, Pacelli had travelled throughout war-torn Europe by train, with a special compartment and 60 cases of special food. His voyage from Genoa to Buenos Aires was no less extravagant. His quarters in the ship included an office, a drawing room, two staterooms and a private chapel. His office had a huge desk and part of his personal library. He had a radio-telephone to maintain contact with the secretariat in Rome. At Rorschach, he had managed the nunciature from afar; now he would do likewise with the secretariat. His entourage included four bishops, several secretaries and a bevy of Latin American diplomats, together with his confidant Kass for whom a position had been found in the secretariat.

The press described the ship as a 'floating cathedral'.[4] While on board, Pacelli did not mix with any of the other passengers. Only when the vessel crossed the equator did he make an elaborate appearance to bless the four corners of the earth. Apart from this ostentatious ceremony, Pacelli remained invisible to the other passengers on board ship. His inaccessibility probably added to his majestic status; thus do the famous shield themselves from prying eyes. Pacelli, however, would always need solitude. As Pasqualina had remarked, he had the soul of a mystic. And while fellow passengers might be travelling for pleasure, with Pacelli the bureaucrat it would always be 'business as usual'.

Outwardly however, everything changed at Buenos Aires, where Pacelli met the president and entered the city to tumultuous applause, reminiscent of his leavetaking of Germany. To the greatly impressed Argentines the gaunt, ascetic Pacelli seemed the embodiment of Christ come among them. Hundreds of white-robed priests dragged him through the streets of the capital in a wheeled vehicle. A mere five days in Argentina gave the Vatican the public relations coup it craved. A brief visit to Brazil was no less successful. The world famous *Redemptore* statue of Jesus Christ stands on a hill above Rio de Janeiro with arms outstretched in blessing. Pacelli stood before it and realized its iconic power. In later years this striking image would become his public pose and 'signature', witnessed by millions of adoring Catholics.

On Pacelli's return to Rome he could report faithfully to Ratti: 'I have never before seen an entire nation, rulers and ruled together, bow the head and bend the knee so devoutly before Him who said: "I am a King . . . but My Kingdom is not of this world."'[5] Pacelli's trip to Buenos Aires had marked a watershed for the Church. The dreary years of self-imprisonment at the Vatican were over.

An incident shortly after Pacelli's return further illustrates the seeming paradox of a man who could be a celebrity one moment and a hermit the next. One evening, a secretary bearing an important telegram hastened to Pacelli's quarters. All the lights were turned off. In the dim glow from the windows Pacelli could be seen lying on the floor, his limbs outstretched, at prayer. As the nervous secretary switched on the lights, Pacelli rose to greet him. 'Do not be worried,' he reassured. 'After so much glory and splendour, it is necessary to lie close to the earth to know that we are nothing.'[6]

Pacelli's international visits began to establish an image of him as a religious icon, an ascetic mystic, hands clasped as though engaged in some arcane liturgical ceremony.

He is like someone in an El Greco painting. It is the outward elongation of the emaciated, almost translucent body, as if made only to be a refuge for the soul: it is the fine-drawn face, as in Pascal or the Grand Condé, and most of all the spiritual vitality concentrated in his extraordinary, almost supernatural gaze, unfortunately half-hidden by his spectacles.[7]

A 1935 visit to Lourdes confirmed this sense of ethereal remoteness. It was noted that the Secretary of State always dined alone and his meals never changed; invariably, he would end them with three stewed prunes. He would spend much of the night engaged in prayer or study, and when he lay down to sleep it would be on a chaise-longue rather than a conventional bed. It was as though sleep was but a brief intermission between work and further work. To the end of his life, Pacelli would remain an indefatigable worker.

One afternoon during the Lourdes visit, he requested a visit to the valley of Labigorre near Satin Savin, with its great church. A carriage duly arrived with a priest as a guide. To the surprise of the latter, Pacelli took out his breviary and became immersed in it, wholly ignoring the view. After an hour he murmured: 'And now, Monsignor, let us go back.'[8] The carriage turned around to head back. Pacelli closed his eyes in meditation. When they arrived at his lodgings, he stepped out of the carriage, politely said, 'Excuse me', and disappeared inside.

Pacelli's trip to Buenos Aires was a dress rehearsal for his tour of the United States two years later, in October 1936. This was the first ever visit by a papal Secretary of State. Whereas Argentina had been a generalized public relations initiative, the American trip had a very different agenda – one that Pacelli was keen to downplay. Blandly, he commented to the press: 'I am going to America simply on vacation. I have a great longing to see the United States.' Disingenuously, he responded to further probing with: 'There is no political aspect to my trip whatever.'[9]

In fact, Pacelli had a highly focused political mission. Several years earlier a fiery priest in Detroit, one Father Charles E. Coughlin, had commenced a series of radio broadcasts denouncing President Roosevelt and his New Deal. In so doing, Father Coughlin was acting without the authority of the Church; worse, he was flouting the Church's policy of non-involvement in politics. And worst of all, Coughlin's outbursts were those of a twentieth-century Savonarola. To Coughlin, Roosevelt was nothing better than 'a liar', 'a double-crosser', and 'an upstart dictator in the White House'.[10] The problem of America's Great Depression could be laid at the doors of Roosevelt, 'godless capitalists', Jews and, indeed, communists. It seems that Coughlin was singularly indiscriminate when it came to apportioning blame.

Unfortunately, as with Savonarola, the fiery fifteenth-century friar who caused Pope Alexander VI such grief, Coughlin attracted a legion of followers with whom his views and style clearly resonated. Up to 350,000 letters were sent to him each week, mostly supporting the efforts of 'the radio priest' as he had become known. For a president who needed minority votes, especially the Catholic one, Coughlin posed a grave threat. In 1936 Roosevelt was standing for re-election, and a landslide victory was predicted for his Republican opponent.

The Vatican had a vested interest in Roosevelt's re-election. For some time the President had been working with Joseph P. Kennedy, founder of the Kennedy dynasty, and Bishop Francis Spellman, Pacelli's confidant, who had smuggled the Pope's anti-Mussolini encyclical to Paris. The objective was formal recognition of the Holy See by Washington. Three years earlier, the Soviet Union had been so recognized. The Vatican badly needed similar representation. If Roosevelt were ousted, such representation would be imperiled.

Lastly, Coughlin was costing the Church a great deal of money. Depression or no Depression, America was a vast, wealthy country with a huge Catholic population whose donations to the Church were greatly valued. Now millions of Catholic dollars were going to support the rebel Coughlin instead of the Church.

As with Savonarola, Coughlin was a difficult man to attack directly. When Cardinal O'Connell, Archbishop of Boston, denounced Coughlin from the pulpit as a 'demagogue', the renegade priest received even greater support. To the Vatican, it was obvious that nobody in America was capable of silencing Coughlin. Could Pacelli, the arch-diplomat, succeed where O'Connell had failed?

On the day Pacelli left Europe, Spellman talked to Roosevelt to facilitate a meeting between the President and the Secretary of State. It was imperative that arrangements were kept top secret. Roosevelt was standing for re-election in the following month. The Church could not be seen to be partisan to any particular presidential candidate; neither dare it openly attack 'the radio priest'. To Pacelli, this constituted a 'sword of Damocles' hanging over his trip.[11]

On the domestic front, Pacelli and Pasqualina were concerned to keep her presence on board ship secret from the prying eyes of the world's press, then full of the entanglement of Edward VIII and Mrs Simpson. The public was avid for another 'scandal', no matter how innocent the reality.

As it happened however, the nun's presence went entirely unnoticed by the media. Pasqualina, who had been employed previously in the Vatican's press office, occupied herself by compiling newspaper cuttings so that Pacelli might better understand American culture. She had come a long way from the Stella Maris nursing home at Rorschach; at every step, she had proved invaluable and become increasingly indispensable.

Pacelli arrived in New York to cheering crowds. A prepared statement maintained the party line that he was taking a vacation; any other questions were greeted with a 'distant, inscrutable and determined smile', as one reporter noted with frustration. The same reporter noted that Pacelli:

> smiled cordially but a shade coolly, inviting none of the rough camaraderie which the ultra-democratic ships' reporters and cameramen considered their privilege. There was a continental air of courtesy and dignity, which impressed and somewhat repressed all of us.
>
> Pacelli was withdrawn throughout his interview. Aides said he was not the person the world thought him to be. Some of his most intimate collaborators said that it was bafflingly difficult for even them to penetrate to the depths of his soul.[12]

Pacelli's 'vacation' was a strenuous one. A chartered aeroplane flew him 16,000 miles, from one side of America to another. Invited by Bishop Shehan to the Catholic university in Washington, he revealed the rather surprising fact that he had wished to join its teaching staff; however, the Pope had decreed otherwise. Yet again we find evidence of Pacelli's career equivocation.

The Secretary of State visited 12 of the 16 ecclesiastical provinces and met 79 bishops *en route*. Discussions with these bishops laid the groundwork for conferring with Cardinal O'Connell, Coughlin's failed detractor. As it happened, O'Connell was also a threat to the Vatican, albeit less so than Coughlin. For many years, he had ruled the Boston Irish as though they comprised his personal fiefdom. He had accused Pacelli's friend and mentor, Gasparri, of rigging the conclave in favour of Achille Ratti's election as Pope Pius XI. Ratti had never forgotten this insult and the gap between the papacy and the official leader of America's Catholics had widened, over more than a decade. Finally, O'Connell detested his subordinate, Bishop Spellman, who had worked, prayed and holidayed with Pacelli and was a rising star in the Church for his undoubted abilities as a political and financial 'fixer'. O'Connell was equally colourful. He had been christened 'Gangplank Bill' by his critics, on account of his predilection for boarding pleasure craft bound for the sunny shores of the Bahamas.[13] He was a formidable adversary.

When Pacelli and O'Connell met, they presented an odd couple: Pacelli thin and ascetic, O'Connell every bit the big, tough Irish bruiser. To Pasqualina however, they had an even odder connection. Both of them had a mother fixation. Pasqualina wryly reflected that her destiny seemed to be that of a mother substitute for Pacelli.

Pasqualina and Spellman accompanied Pacelli to his meeting with O'Connell. To Pasqualina's surprise, the archbishop proved a most charming host. However, when dinner had ended and the four of them retired to the library for brandy, it was straight down to business.

Although Pacelli blandly explained that Pasqualina's presence was necessary for taking notes, it seems likely that she was also present as a witness. It was possible that O' Connell might put pressure on Spellman to attest to his version of the meeting. As Pacelli well knew, Pasqualina's loyalty was unimpeachable.

In the event, no such precautions were necessary. Pacelli openly admitted that he had come to the US to silence Coughlin. He had canvassed a wide spread of opinion from his meetings with the 79 bishops. (For this, O'Connell no doubt read that their loyalty to the Vatican and not himself had been assured.) Coughlin would no longer be an irritant, either to O'Connell or the Vatican. He would shortly be abdicating his role and condemning himself to well-deserved obscurity. And the fiction would be preserved that Pacelli would have had merely 'a pleasant and blessed vacation in the United States'.

Just after after Roosevelt's landslide victory, Pacelli had a private meeting with the President. To the press, he calmly announced: 'I enjoyed lunching with a typical American family.'[14] But a highly satisfied Pacelli confided in Pasqualina: 'The President is grateful that the noisy priest will talk no more.'[15] And the *quid pro quo* was that 'White House recognition of the Vatican is assured'.[16]

Shortly afterwards Father Coughlin made his last radio speech, announcing his complete withdrawal from public life and denying that any pressure had been brought to bear by the Church. But 18 years later, in 1954, when Pacelli was nearing the end of his career as Pope Pius XII, Coughlin told a very different story.

Cardinal Pacelli visited America and had conversations with our high government officials, which conversations could be regarded as a type of informal pact ... Small as I was, it was necessary to silence my voice, even though I must be smeared as an anti-Semite, as a pro-Nazi and a bad priest ... Needless to say, the smear was effective, and I was eliminated by devious ways and means – all indirect, yet more effective than were these ways and means direct.[17]

Pacelli's US trip had been a fabulous success. The two objectives of silencing Coughlin and securing an agreement to diplomatic representation had been met. The millions of dollars that had flowed to 'the radio priest' would now flow instead to the wider Church and the Vatican. American Catholics would receive their moral lead from senior clergy, not some renegade priest. The Vatican had become an 'unofficial partner' with Roosevelt and his New Deal. And the prestige of the Church had been notably enhanced. In dealing with enemies such as the Soviet Union, it had greatly strengthened its political force.

Pacelli's US trip also gave a very public demonstration of how far the Vatican had come since the dark days of the 1870s. 'The flying cardinal' was ushering in a new area of high visibility and controlled public relations. Bland public utterances would mask private deals. To Pasqualina, however, the Coughlin affair was further evidence of the Church's double standards. However odious the radio priest, in her eyes, he had been laid low by devious, underhand tactics, probably involving downright lies. Pasqualina had been brought up to serve a Church which rightly occupied the moral high ground. Yet it was becoming increasingly clear to her that the Church could be self-serving and hypocritical when its power was threatened. The luxuriously appointed 11-bedroom mansion occupied by Bishop Spellman showed how the Church's political fixers could reap rich rewards. What, she must have wondered, would Christ have said?

A close-up of Pacelli during his American visit is afforded by observing him during his four visits, between his arduous coast-to-coast journeys, to a certain mansion near Manhasset in Long Island. The house was called Inisfada and belonged to the immensely rich Nicholas Brady, who had been created a papal count for his generous benefactions to the Holy See. Genevieve (or Countess) Brady lived in great state in this luxurious mock-Georgian house where Pacelli, whom she had come to know well, was her guest. Luckily Pasqualina and Countess Brady struck up an immediate *rapport*.

His trips throughout the States were busy and exhausting affairs. At Inisfada he experienced highly welcome periods of recuperation and repose. I have visited the house myself, including the magnificent library-drawing room where Pacelli would relax in the evenings. (After Genevieve Brady's death, Inisfada was sold on generous terms to the Jesuit order as a retreat house and conference and study centre.) Countess Brady subsequently married William Macaulay, who became Irish Ambassador to the Holy See. I often met him, as he was a close friend of my mother's. He told me several revealing anecdotes about the future Pope Pius XII. Bill Macaulay knew a lot about the latter from what he learned from Countess Brady, as well as from his time in Rome.

Inisfada remains to this day something of a shrine to Pacelli. The drawing-room library is as it was during his visit. Despite the presence of many visitors on business, his three stays there proved vital periods of recuperation, under the care of Pasqualina, during his onerous journey.

Chapter 9

With Deep Anxiety

And what would Christ have said about Italy's invasion in 1935 of Ethiopia, then known as Abyssinia? The Ethiopians had pleaded in vain with the League of Nations to thwart Mussolini's expansionist plans. The Vatican had played its usual card of political neutrality, offering merely bland utterances such as the Pope's comment that 'Clouds darken the sky over Italy and Abyssinia.'[1] In Italy, the Church's lack of active opposition to the war was interpreted as a passive endorsement of Mussolini's expansionism. The British foreign minister caustically noted that 'The Pope appears to be so timid as to give the impression that he supports Mussolini.'[2]

In fact, Mussolini was being supported by much more than Vatican impressions. Six years previously, the Church had been bailed out of impending bankruptcy by the Lateran Treaty. The mysterious financier Nogara had multiplied the Italian government's payment of 92.1 million dollars into a fund worth several hundreds of millions of dollars. The Church held significant shareholdings in Italian gas, telecommunications, banking, insurance, chemicals and automotive industries. With consummate irony, a cash-strapped Mussolini, whose donation had saved the Church, now came back to the very same Church to finance his invasion of Ethiopia. And the Church, with its studied political neutrality, was financing the dictator in the antithesis of a just war. To a troubled Pasqualina, no greater hypocrisy could be imagined.

On 3 October, the day of the invasion, guns, tanks, aeroplanes and departing troops were blessed by the Church. The Archbishop of Siena declared: 'Italy, our great Duce, and the soldiers are about to win victory for truth and righteousness!'[3] The Bishop of San Miniato confidently asserted, 'For the victory of Italy, the Italian clergy are ready to melt down the gold of the churches and the bronze of the bells.'[4]

Less than a year later, 50,000 Ethiopian civilians had been killed or injured, many of them by the 250 tons of poison gas which Mussolini's troops sprayed upon defenceless villages. Cardinal Schuster, the Archbishop of Milan and an intimate of the Pope, lauded Mussolini as 'he who has given Italy to God and God to Italy'.[5]

In the Vatican, Pasqualina agonized. Pacelli, the man to whom she had devoted nearly two decades, was now the heir apparent to the papacy and, increasingly, the wielder of power as the ageing Ratti came to the end of his reign. How could he possibly preside over such an amoral regime? Finally she could stand it no longer. 'Christ is the Prince of Peace!' she upbraided him. 'Has the Holy See forgotten Jesus for the profits of war?'[6]

Pacelli was shocked by her outburst. The second most powerful man in the Church was being rebuked, in the strongest possible terms, by a lowly nun. And yet he had no words of defence. The great canon lawyer, the consummate diplomat, could muster no argument. For a saddened Pasqualina, the Vatican was the star in the Church's firmament. But the Vatican also meant the erosion of her ideals, the 'whittling away of conscience', even 'the seduction of me'.[7] What was she to do?

After much painful soul-searching, his face haggard with strain, Pacelli told her: 'I have decided to resign. My conscience troubles me deeply. Your words have caused me to re-examine my conscience, particularly in the matter of Father Coughlin and Holy Mother Church's position in Ethiopia.'[8]

A shocked Pasqualina defensively retorted: 'Eminence, should you not first speak with His Holiness? Perhaps you can convince the Holy Father to correct some injustices and prevent others from happening?'[9]

'I have spoken to His Holiness', Pacelli wearily answered her. 'Pius is not about to change. He forced me to get down on my knees before him and swear never again to defy his authority.'[10]

'But, Eminence, you always seemed to have such influence over His Holiness?'

'That is because I always managed to say what His Holiness wants to hear', Pacelli admitted, his misery complete. Indeed, the British minister to the Vatican had once remarked thus of Ratti: 'His own Secretary of State is said to be often unwilling to make representations which would likely annoy him.'[11] So often in his life, Pacelli the diplomat would deal with conflict by simply avoiding it.

'Pius is an old man', Pasqualina bluntly stated. 'How long has he left to live?'[12] Pasqualina deplored Pacelli's part in what she viewed as the amorality of the Church; nevertheless, if he resigned he was closing the door to the papacy. And what better candidate was there? Pacelli had revealed his principles, albeit tarnished ones; surely she could help him to strengthen them.

For the time being, Pasqualina merely asked Pacelli to take no precipitate action. And as she hoped, as the days went by his resolve weakened. When Ratti had a slight heart attack, Pacelli's duty must have seemed inescapable.

'Eminence, I prayed to Jesus today that He would make you the next Holy Father', Pasqualina told him. 'Dear Sister Pasqualina,' he replied, 'what do you think I should do?'[13]

At that moment, Pasqualina knew she had won. Stifling her exultation, she calmly replied, 'Eminence, I would like you to do what our dear Lord asks, that you remain as Cardinal Secretary of State and serve Him with all your love and integrity.'[14]

The crisis was over.

Meanwhile, in Germany Hitler had created a Ministry of Church Affairs, which supposedly reviewed a host of Catholic organizations suitable for official protection. This created the appurtenance of co-operation with the Church, thus staving off any determined protest. The Nazis made good use of such lack of protest to mount a series of trials against Catholic clergy, citing charges of paedophilia with children in orphanages and schools. Naturally, this weakened the public image of the Church. A second line of attack was against Church organizations moving funds outside the country. The 1930s depression had given rise to complex laws restricting foreign exchange; the Nazis made full use of them.

The Catholic Church in Germany was being simultaneously mollified and weakened by the Nazis; it was also under tight Vatican control. The Spanish Civil War, with a spate of murdered priests and nuns, gave both the Church and the Nazis the realization of how much worse life would be under a communist regime. The Nazis dangled the spectre of communism to give a spurious legitimacy to their actions. Cardinal Faulhaber had a meeting with Hitler in November 1936 and wrote enthusiastically about his encounter:

> The Führer commands the diplomatic and social forms better than a born sovereign ... Without doubt, the chancellor lives in faith in God. He recognises Christianity as the foundation of Western culture ... Not as clear is his conception of the Catholic Church as a God-established institution.[15]

In January, Faulhaber wrote an episcopal letter to be read throughout churches in Bavaria. The themes were Church–State co-operation in the battle against communism, and state respect for the concordat-agreed rights of the Church. Shortly afterwards, the German bishops met at Fulda; they emerged with a list of 17 concordat violations. Led by Faulhaber and two other cardinals, they went to Rome to meet with Pacelli on 16 January. They insisted on papal action.

Pacelli took them to see Ratti, ill in bed with heart disease, diabetes, and ulcers on his legs. The Pope was 'almost unrecognisable, pale, emaciated, his face deeply lined and his eyes swollen and half-closed'.[16] Nevertheless, he gave them his full attention and decided to release an encyclical on the problems facing the Church in Germany.

By 21 January, Faulhaber had written the first draft and passed it across to Pacelli for revision. The encyclical was entitled *Mit brennender Sorge* (With Deep Anxiety). It was smuggled into Germany and printed at 12 different locations. From these it was conveyed by a network of couriers, many of them young boys trudging across fields and rough ground to avoid the roads. The copies were delivered to parish priests, sometimes in the confessional.

Mit brennender Sorge was written in German. It was aimed not only at the German bishops but also the Catholic episcopate, both within the country and outside it. The encyclical sombrely began: 'With deep anxiety and increasing dismay, We have, for some time past, beheld the sufferings of the Church in Germany...'.[17] Moving to the concordat and its aftermath, the Pope noted that the Church's partner had 'sown the tares of suspicion, discord, hatred, calumny, of secret and open fundamental hostility to Christ and His Church, fed from a thousand different sources and making use of every available means'.[18] The worship of God, as allowed by natural law, was being usurped by a creed of race and state.

Doubtless the worship of God, as allowed by natural law, applied equally to the Jews. But there was no explicit reference to the terrible treatment of German Jews. And the attack on Nazism was diluted by another encyclical, *Divini redemptoris*, published just five days later, making an even greater attack on communism. The Nazis quickly struck back, confiscating every copy of the encyclical they could lay their hands upon. The printing presses were tracked down and put out of business, their staff imprisoned. From the Ministry of Church Affairs came a letter to the bishops asserting that the encyclical was 'in flat contradiction to the spirit of the concordat ... [There are] serious attacks against the welfare and the interest of the German nation.'[19] Hitler ranted: 'When they [the Churches] attempt by any other means – writings, encyclicals, etc. – to assume rights which belong only to the State, we will push them back into their proper spiritual activity.'[20]

A Church protest of a very different kind was made on 18 May 1937, by Cardinal Mundelein of Chicago to 500 diocesan priests. In language which could not have been more blunt, Cardinal Mundelein demanded: 'Perhaps you will ask how it is that a nation of 60 million intelligent people will submit in fear and servitude to an alien, an Austrian paper-hanger, and a poor one at that, and a few associates like Goebbels and Göring, who dictate every move of the people's lives?' The cardinal acidly suggested that 60 million German brains had been removed without their previous owners having noticed anything untoward.[21]

In retaliation, Göring resumed the trials against Catholic clergy, which had been temporarily suspended. Yet the Nazis scarcely had to police the Church for, under Pacelli's stewardship, the Church was policing itself. A mere two months after Cardinal Mundelein's denunciation of Nazism, Pacelli greeted some pilgrims from Chicago with soothing words about their cardinal 'who is so solicitous and zealous in defence of the rights of God and of the Church and in the salvation of souls'.[22]

Shortly afterwards, following a meeting with Pacelli, Diego von Bergen, the Reich ambassador, reported to Berlin:

> In striking contradiction to the behaviour of the Pope, however, are the statements of the Cardinal Secretary of State during the call that I made on him on the 16th, the day before the Pope's discourse ... The conversation was of a private nature. Pacelli received me with decided friendliness and emphatically assured me during the conversation that normal and friendly relations with us would be restored as soon as possible; this applied particularly to him, who had spent 13 years in Germany and had always shown the greatest sympathy for the German people. He would also be prepared at any time for a discussion with outstanding personages such as the foreign minister and Minister President Göring.[23]

Pacelli's policy of conciliation posed little threat to the Nazis. *Mit brennender Sorge*, summarizing the Pope's position, could be taken in two ways: a cry for mass protest on the part of Germany's 23 million Catholics, or merely another attempt to get the Nazis to respect the concordat. Churchmen were split into the rebels, wanting protest, and the dominant appeasers, led by Cardinal Bertram.

Pacelli managed to keep a foot in both camps, despite being an arch-appeaser. His many years of diplomacy aided him. As Scholder caustically noted: 'It says much for the skill of Pacelli that both parties felt that he was on their side.'[24]

In general, a point until now rarely and inadequately made, *Mit brennender Sorge* carefully avoided making any outright condemnation of Nazism's moral evil, and left the way open for future reconciliation. The encyclical's original publication infuriated the Nazis; but when Hitler came to study its actual terms, he could hardly believe his luck.

In May 1938, Pacelli went to Budapest to open the International Eucharistic Congress. His announcement made no reference to the Anschluss, the recent annexation of Austria by the Nazis. Nor did he make any reference to the virulently anti-Semitic regime in Hungary. Instead, he spoke with sociological blandness of each country's 'promoting its unwritten laws and contingencies'.[25] *Unwritten* laws? An interesting viewpoint from a man who had spent decades promoting canon law as a rigid structure for the government of the Church.

On the theme of 'love in action', Pacelli sharply delineated the differences between Christians and Jews:[26] 'As opposed to the foes of Jesus, who cried out to His face, 'Crucify Him!', we sing Him hymns of our loyalty and our love. We act in this fashion, not out of bitterness, not out of a sense of superiority, not out of arrogance towards those whose lips curse Him and whose hearts reject Him even today.'[27] Moshe Herczl notes sadly, 'Pacelli was sure that his audience understood him well.'[28]

From 1933 to 1938, the Nazis had been systematically weakening the Catholic Church in Germany. Soon after coming to power, Hitler had remarked to Hermann Rausching that the best method of ridding Germany of effective Christianity would be to 'leave it to rot like a gangrenous limb'. However, he added contemptuously: 'But we can hasten matters. The parsons will be made to dig their own graves. They will betray their God to us. They will betray anything for the sake of their miserable little jobs and incomes.'[29]

In the previous century, Bismarck's cruel but crude *Kulturkampf* had swiftly dissipated its power against a Catholic population paradoxically united by adversity. But the Nazis were far more clever and subtle. The concordat guaranteed near-total political impotence from the Church. Breaking the concordat's terms at local levels ensured that the Nazi leadership could always cite 'plausible deniability', i.e. disassociate themselves from the actions of their subordinates. With a police state and unofficial paramilitary thugs, detractors could easily be intimidated. In 1930s Germany, it took a brave man – or woman – to stand up to the Nazi Party.

Thus Catholic opponents of the regime could be dismissed from their posts; missionaries could be prosecuted for infringements of currency laws; members of Catholic organizations could be 'persuaded' to join the Nazi Party. Meanwhile the churches stayed open, and Mass would be celebrated as normal. The implicit message was clear: the Church might carry on if its members remained compliant.

But beneath the façade lurked an ever-grimmer reality – especially where

German Jews were concerned. In November 1938, some 800 Jews were brutally murdered. A further 26,000 Jews were sent to concentration camps. A 'degradation ritual' systematically deprived Jews of successive vestiges of citizenship and humanity.[30] Jewish children might not attend state schools. Jews were not allowed to attend cinemas, theatres, concerts and other cultural events. Increasingly, Jews were treated not as people but as hated objects. The larger German population, both Catholic and otherwise, was itself dehumanized by both active participation in and passive acceptance of Jewish degradation.

At Budapest, Pacelli had declaimed:

> We love our times, despite their danger and their anguish ... precisely because of that danger, and because of the difficult tasks that the age imposes on us; we are ready to dedicate ourselves wholly and unconditionally, regardless of ourselves; otherwise nothing great and decisive can result.[31]

Years earlier, Cardinal Faulhaber had chillingly stated: 'The Jews can look after themselves.' For the Church, little if anything had changed. For the Nazi Party, the Final Solution was coming ever closer.

Recently a draft has come to light of an encyclical which Ratti commissioned in 1938 on Nazi anti-Semitism. It is entitled *Humani generis unitas* (The Unity of the Human Race) and is available in a French translation. In words as chilling as Faulhaber's, it notes that 'the Church is only interested in upholding her legacy of Truth ... The purely worldly problems in which the Jewish people may see themselves involved, are of no interest to her.'[32] This contrasts markedly with Ratti's famous declaration of 6 September 1938. Tearfully, the Pope had reflected upon the parlous situation of European Jews. 'It is impossible for Christians to participate in anti-Semitism', he declared. 'We recognize that everyone has the right to self-defence and may take the necessary means for protecting legitimate interests. But anti-Semitism is inadmissible; spiritually we are all Semites.'[33]

Two dominant themes are implicit in Ratti's encyclical. There is the familiar one that by rejecting and killing Christ, the Jews damned themselves and are, in some mysterious way, cursed throughout eternity. Thus their problems, while regrettable, are seen to be of their own making. The second theme, also familiar, is for the Church always to hold the moral high ground ('upholding her legacy of Truth') and never risk 'being compromised in defence of Christian principles and humanity by being drawn into purely man-made politics'.[34] Yet, as Pasqualina had seen, the Church was quite prepared to compromise its ideals when expediency demanded – as long as such compromise was kept secret.

It is not known whether Pacelli was involved in the production of this draft encyclical. His position in the Church and his close relationship with Ratti would suggest that he was involved; but this is supposition, no more. Certainly the warning against 'being compromised' aligns with Pacelli's positioning of the Church during World War Two. And a defence of the Church against anti-Semitism also aligns itself with Pacelli's post-World War Two position. The theme of the accursed sons of Abraham could have come from Pacelli's old schoolmaster, Signor Marchi, with his diatribes against the 'hard-heartedness' of the Jews.

So this curious draft encyclical, forgotten for so many years, seems to censure the Nazis, defend the Church, and acknowledge a special fate meted out by history to the Jews. Three Jesuit scholars, notably the American Father, John Le Farge, presented the draft to Wladimir Ledochowski, the head of the Society of Jesus. He passed it to the editor of *Civiltà Cattolica*. Was it delayed deliberately? By the time it reached the Pope, on 9 February 1939, he had only one day left to live.

Senior figures in the Church were undoubtedly stalling the release of this encyclical, presumably for fear of provoking the Nazis. Given his long-term predilection for appeasement, it is hard to believe that Pacelli was not involved in these stalling tactics. When he became Pope he buried the encyclical, thus surely indicating his true feelings about it. Even given its sad prejudice, a papal condemnation of anti-Semitism might have made a difference – but, as with so much speculation in history, we shall simply never know.

In September 1938, Mussolini's government had passed a law giving foreign Jews six months to leave the country. Anti-Semitism was creeping ever closer to the Vatican. Pius X had died, they said, of a broken heart as the Great War erupted. To Pius XI, slowly succumbing to heart disease and diabetes, it must have been agonizing to know that, once again, Europe was collapsing into ruin. Many years before, as a fervent mountaineer, he had risked life and limb on the high Alpine peaks. Soon, he knew, death would come to millions who had not chosen any such risk, who merely wanted to live a normal existence. Their normality would become a charnel house.

In January 1939 the British prime minister, Neville Chamberlain, and his foreign secretary, Lord Halifax, had a meeting with Mussolini and then the Pope. The doughty Ratti wasted no time asking their views; instead, he harangued them on the dangers of appeasement. Above all else, they must stand up to Hitler. But to the exhausted pontiff, they clearly lacked resolve. To him they were like a pair of 'slugs',[35] strikingly ill-prepared for dealing with conflict.

Ratti fixed a meeting with his bishops for 11 February 1939. It was both the anniversary of his coronation and the tenth anniversary of the Lateran Treaty – although there was no sense of rejoicing. Rumour in the Vatican had it that the Pope was going to make a much more uncompromising statement on anti-Semitism. But at the beginning of February he had a heart attack, then another. Finally, on 10 February, his body finally gave in. He had come so tantalizingly close to making an announcement which, as with the missing encyclical, just might have made a crucial difference.

The last words of Achille Ratti, Pope Pius XI, are heart-rendingly poignant: 'Instead of talking about peace and goodwill to men who are not disposed to listen, I prefer now to talk about them to God alone.'[36]

Chapter 10

Pastor Angelicus

'At last the obstinate old man is dead!'[1] Thus was Mussolini's heartless comment on the death of Ratti. From his successor came a very different reaction. 'Those who saw Cardinal Pacelli bend over the body of the dead Pope, to kiss the forehead and hands, understood how much he had loved him. For once, he betrayed emotion.'[2]

Ratti's death, on the eve of his denunciation of Fascist anti-Semitism, had come at a most convenient time for Mussolini. Indeed it was rumoured that the death of the pontiff had come at a *too* convenient time and that Ratti had been injected with poison by his doctor, Francesco Petacci, the father of Mussolini's mistress, Claretta Petacci.[3] To the end of his life, Cardinal Tisserant remained of the opinion that Ratti had been murdered. Certainly it seems Mussolini was desperate for the text of Ratti's speech to be suppressed. To this end Count Pignatti, Italian ambassador to the Vatican, visited Pacelli, who told him: 'It will remain a dead letter. It will be put in the secret archives.'[4] As with the lost encyclical, *Humani generis unitas*, another challenge to Fascism was buried.

The death of Ratti left the Church at a political crossroads. Pacelli's diplomatic triumphs, the Reich concordat and the Lateran Treaty, remained in little more than name. *Mit brennender Sorge* stated the Church's grave dissatisfaction with matters in Germany. The Pope's aborted speech and *Humani generis unitas* would have expressed equally grave dissatisfaction with matters in Italy. For Hitler and Mussolini, preparing for war, there were three main papal options. The new Pope might be sympathetic to Fascism and thus lend moral legitimacy to the dictatorships of Germany and Italy. Conversely the Pope might be opposed to Fascism, which would be a potential disaster since Catholic-influenced America might move politically closer to Britain and France. The third option was that the Pope would be a simple 'holy man', devoted to prayer and matters spiritual, thereby denying the Church any significant political role.

In the three weeks between the death of Pius XI and the conclave to elect his successor, Rome buzzed with speculation. The spectre of war magnified the usual papal jockeying, so much so that Cardinal Baudrillart met the French ambassador to the Vatican with the sarcastic, if not entirely undeserved, greeting: 'I have come to learn how my government wants me to vote.'[5]

The victor of the conclave would require the votes of two-thirds of the 62 cardinals. He would have to be acceptable to almost all of the 35 Italian

93

cardinals; he would also have to be acceptable to at least a quarter of the 27 non-Italian cardinals. Pacelli, as Secretary of State and *Camerlengo*, was by far the most powerful figure in the Church, as well as being the best-known senior churchman in the world. Yet there was an argument that secretaries of state tended to lose conclaves because cardinals wanted popes markedly similar – or markedly dissimilar – to the previous incumbent. And there is always an argument that the qualities of an excellent second-in-command are not necessarily those of an ultimate leader. (Giulio de' Medici, in the sixteenth century, had been a superb second-in-command to Pope Leo X, but proved a consummate disaster as Pope Clement VII, whose papacy culminated in the sack of Rome.)

On a personal note, Pacelli might have been weakened in spirit after serving under the autocratic Ratti, who had sternly made his close colleague and longtime friend kneel before him for up to an hour at a time. As we have seen earlier, the British minister to the Vatican had noted of Ratti: 'His own Secretary of State is said to be often unwilling to make representations which would likely annoy him.' Pacelli himself had agreed with this view by admitting privately to Pasqualina: 'I always managed to say what His Holiness wants to hear.' Would such a man make an able pope in a world sliding towards world war? Certainly the fierce, bearded Cardinal Tisserant, who had seen military service as an intelligence officer in the First World War, did not think so. His view of Pacelli was scathing: the Secretary of State and *Camerlengo* was 'indecisive, hesitant, a man more designed to obey orders than to give them'.[6]

And what of Pacelli himself? Pasqualina found the likely leader to nearly half a billion Catholics distraught with anguish: '*Miserere mei!* Have pity on me!' he implored.[7] In the 40 years since his ordination, his career in the Church had been spectacular: the 1917 Code of Canon Law, the concordats, the trips to South and North America. Now he was poised for the greatest prize of all – and he was in despair.

For half of her life, Pasqualina had cared for this brilliant, difficult man. She knew his dark depressions all too well. Sympathy was a waste of time; his despair would run its course and eventually burn itself out. Steeling herself to matter-of-factness, she brusquely admonished him: 'You do all the brooding you like, Eminence. There is no time to waste. I go to prepare the papal quarters for your presence.'[8]

For Pasqualina, Pacelli was by far the best possible leader of the Church, despite his glaring faults. She served Jesus and she served Pacelli. Years before, she had come to the Vatican without any authority beyond a sense that what she did was for the best. Now, with Ratti dead and Pacelli lost in indecision, she bustled about making administrative decisions, again with no authority but her aura of leadership. Her simple words of comfort to Pacelli had the power of a blood oath: 'Jesus is always with you and I will never desert you.'[9]

In all of history, there was no known instance of a woman being present in a conclave. Only cardinals were allowed to vote; only male servants were allowed to enter with them. But Pasqualina knew how perilously frail was Pacelli's state of mind; and she made her decision. 'I go with you to the conclave and remain at your side throughout the election', she told him.[10]

'No!' The *Camerlengo* and Secretary of State was outraged at the temerity of the nun. 'Yes! I go there', she told him with utter conviction. 'Tell me if Jesus Christ ever excluded any woman from His household ... Eminence, I have prayed to Jesus for the inspiration to help make you a good, strong Pope.'[11]

At this, Pacelli's reserve broke. After their nearly 25 years together, his emotional defences finally collapsed. He clung to her, like the mother she had become to him. Pasqualina looked at him and whispered, 'Dear God, please help us!'[12]

By an ingenious internal arrangement, Pacelli's private apartment (notionally called 'Cell 13') was linked with the conclave area, without disturbing the sealing of the whole from the outside world. Pasqualina, without moving, could thus be 'present at the conclave'.

On 1 March 1939, 19 days after the death of Pope Pius XI, 62 cardinals gathered to elect his successor. Pacelli, as leader, greeted his fellow prelates, while Pasqualina's entrance was greeted with shock. She marched past the august fathers of the Church, her head held high in defiance. 'Nuns have a way of discreetly avoiding eye contact', she recalled years later.[13] She knew that her action was one of high risk.

Her presence, if interpreted as scandalous or simply too unbecoming, could wreck Pacelli's chances of the papacy. But if she had not entered the immediate conclave area, there was an even greater risk of Pacelli cracking up under the strain. A discreet arrival could be viewed as 'sneaking in' and might thereby foment scandal. No, her only recourse was to be dignified and open, daring all. Pacelli's predilection for special foods and medicines was well known; preparing these gave her an excuse for being among the cardinals.

Looking back on the conclave many years later, Pasqualina reflected, 'Eminence was an ailing man and too distraught at the moment to act decisively. I felt it was my responsibility to protect him, and, in so doing, serve the Holy See. At the time, Eminence was 63 and I was 45. Both of us too old to be ridiculous ... In my heart, there was only one paramount consideration. As long as Jesus knew everything was right, that was all that counted.'[14]

Just before the conclave was sealed, a startled pressman noticed Pasqualina coming out of a side door, indicating a woman's presence where no woman had ever been seen before. Sensing a scoop, he went straight to the Vatican press office. Despite issuing a firm 'No comment', the press relations people were privately just as surprised as the reporter. Several days later, the following explanation emerged:

> Special authorisation of the Congregation of Cardinals permitted Mother Pasqualina to remain there so that Pacelli should lack nothing of his customary diet, or of the medicines necessary to his well-being. It was generally felt that Pacelli would suffer were he deprived of his own particular way of living, which was the more necessary to him since he had just relinquished his duties as Secretary of State to assume the onerous task of *Camerlengo*.[15]

Although Pasqualina's presence had been hidden for so many years, if Pacelli became Pope the glare of the media spotlight would be far greater, thus necessitating extreme caution. But for Pacelli to function, he required special treatment. He needed particular food; he needed his special medicines. Above all, he needed Pasqualina. Even before he entered the Church, he had avoided the rigours of the seminary in favour of living at home. When he was ordained it was at a special private seminary, remote from his classmates. For many years, as a young priest, he had contrived to remain at home, close to his possessive mother. Now, at the conclave, which he was strongly tipped to win, he availed himself of special treatment yet again, living in his papal apartments rather than the dreary stalls, alongside his fellow cardinals. Instead of his mother he had Pasqualina close by him, anticipating and fulfilling his every need.

Conclaves are sealed gatherings. The proceedings of a conclave are regarded as matters of the utmost secrecy. Nevertheless, human nature being what it is, we know a great deal about most conclaves. Each ballot paper says, in Latin: 'I choose as Sovereign Pontiff The Most Reverend Lord Cardinal _____.' And each cardinal makes his choice.

According to the writer Giancarlo Zizola, Pacelli received 28 votes on the first ballot and 35 on the second.[16] Pasqualina recalled that Pacelli received 35 votes on the first ballot. Whether it happened on the first or second ballot, with 35 votes Pacelli was only seven votes away from a two-thirds majority.

As Pacelli was going into the second ballot, he slipped badly on the steps. At this, it is said that Cardinal Verdier exclaimed: 'The Vicar of Christ, on earth!'[17] Pacelli struggled to his feet and made his way into the conclave clutching his left arm, clearly in pain.

Zizola declares that at this ballot, at 5.25 p.m. on 2 March, the very first day of voting, Pacelli was elected Pope with 48 votes, giving him a majority. Another commentator, Charles-Roux, has the notable French cardinal, Tisserant, still voting against Pacelli in the belief that he was the wrong choice.[18] Yet another writer notes that according to one participant, as the final vote was called out 'the holy Cardinal [Pacelli], pale and deeply moved, closed his eyes, and, as though afraid, lost himself in prayer. Some minutes passed in that solemn silence'.[19]

Pasqualina had a different account. She claims that on being elected Pope, Pacelli simply turned it down. It is believed that in the entire history of the papacy, this had occurred only once before – in the previous conclave in 1922, when Cardinal Laurenti turned down his nomination and Achille Ratti became Pope Pius XI instead.

Pasqualina claims that Pacelli cried out: 'I ask that another ballot be cast. I ask that each Eminence search his heart and vote for someone other than me!'[20] She says that with this Pacelli walked out of the hall, leaving his fellow cardinals in a state of shocked disbelief.

Pasqualina recalls that she ran out after him and found him in the Square of Saint Damaso, lost in thought and riven by doubt and insecurity, now that the hour of reckoning had finally arrived. With the onset of war, the papacy would be buffeted between the superpowers. Whoever became Pope would have to make terrible decisions. According to Pasqualina, it was then that Pacelli slipped and fell heavily on the marble steps. As the Swiss guards rushed to his aid she cried, 'Dear Jesus, help him!'[21]

'*Miserere mei!*' Once more from the stricken Pacelli came an outpouring of emotional pain. 'I am not worthy!' he told her. 'Something within me cries out in despair. I do not hear the voice of Our Dear Lord – as I had expected at this most important moment – saying to me, "Eugenio, you have the moral strength, the physical stamina to be Christ's Vicar on Earth." '[22] Pacelli limped away, half-supported by the nun.

'Dear Eminence, it is not for you to decide', she fervently whispered. 'Jesus has spoken and has chosen you, Eugenio Pacelli, to be the Holy Father.'[23] They went into the papal chapel and began to recite the Lord's Prayer. At the fateful words 'Thy will be done. . .' Pacelli paused, pondering deeply.

With Pasqualina at his arm, Pacelli went back into the hall of astonished cardinals and took his place on the throne for the next ballot. Pasqualina's terrible fear was that in view of Pacelli's odd behaviour, another candidate would be chosen. But, she says, her fears were unfounded. She claims that the next vote was unanimous. Eugenio Pacelli had, for the second time, been elected Pope.

Pacelli's 63rd birthday was on 2 March 1939. Elisabetta had once told Pasqualina that at Pacelli's christening, two days after his birth, a Monsignor Jacobacci had held the baby aloft and prophesied: '63 years from today, the people of St Peter's and all Rome will loudly praise this child.'[24] Pasqualina's thoughts flashed back to this odd prophecy. But would it be realized – would Pacelli accept?

'*Accipisne electionem?*' Cardinal Caccia-Dominioni, Dean of the conclave, sternly demanded of Pacelli. For an anguished Pasqualina, it must have seemed as though 40 years of Pacelli's life and 20 years of hers had led inexorably to this moment. Faced with the supreme prize, all that it took was one simple word of acceptance.

And yet, amazingly, Pacelli did not utter that word. He stood transfixed, as though in turmoil. As the seconds ticked away, the suspense became agonizing. The expressions on the cardinals' faces slowly began to change, from joy to bewilderment, to a kind of baffled anger, and finally to something approaching despair.

At last, his voice broken by extreme tension, Pacelli croaked, in a hoarse whisper, '*Accepio.*'

It was enough. The cardinals broke into a huge cheer. The one-day conclave had been the shortest for 300 years. It was the first time since 1667 that a secretary of state had been made Pope. It was the first time in well over 200 years that a Roman had been made Pope. Pacelli, who had faithfully served four popes, became the supreme leader of the Catholic Church. In honour of Achille Ratti, he took the name of Pope Pius XII. He was the first Pope since 1846 to begin his reign as ruler of a sovereign state.

At the age of 63, it seemed likely that Pacelli's reign would be a long one. His grandfather Marcantonio had lived to 102. His great-uncle Felice had lived to 103. All the signs were auspicious: from his entry into the Secretariat of State in 1901, Pacelli's career in the Church had been one of continuous distinction. Over the centuries, conclaves had thrown up many strange results; but if ever a cardinal was elected Pope on merit, surely it was Pacelli.

Soon his election would impact on the lives of millions of people, of many religions and many nationalities.

On 12 March 1939, Cardinal Eugenio Pacelli was crowned Pope Pius XII. Pope Leo XIII and Pope Benedict XV had been crowned in the privacy of the Sistine Chapel. Pope Pius XI's coronation, although more public, was a relatively modest affair. But Pacelli decided on an event of unparalleled splendour, at extravagant cost. It would be the first coronation to be filmed from beginning to end, and the first to be broadcast internationally by radio. It would also be the first papal coronation in more than 90 years to take place outdoors, before the crowds in St Peter's Square.

By 3.00 a.m., the first of the 40,000 ticket-holders were waiting patiently at the steps of St Peter's Basilica. Their numbers would later be swollen to some 70,000 spectators in St Peter's Square. Elsewhere in Rome multitudes thronged the streets, bringing the total estimated number to more than a million. Hilaire Belloc wrote: 'It was an astonishingly fine sight, the finest I have ever seen in my life....'.[25] Tom Driberg noted that the coronation was 'one of the most magnificent ceremonies I have ever attended'.[26] Dignitaries included former kings as well as princes, princesses, dukes and counts. Nazi Germany was the only significant country to fail to send a national figure; Diego von Bergen, the Vatican ambassador, sufficed instead. When Hitler had visited Rome Pope Pius XI refused to meet him, proffering the transparent excuse that he was absent at Castel Gandolfo. Evidently Hitler had not forgotten the snub.

Pacelli cut a remote, ethereal figure, lost somewhere between man and deity. Members of the white-gloved Black Nobility carried him on the *sedia gestatoria*, the papal sedan of august tradition. He was fanned by *flabelli*, long poles topped by ceremonial feathers. His pallid face was gaunt as ever, his dark eyes gazing imponderably upon the supreme triumph of his life, his darkest dread come true. The choir of the Sistine Chapel sang, 'Thou art Peter, and upon this rock I will build my Church.'[27] The master of ceremonies solemnly intoned, 'Remember, O Holy Father, that thus passes the glory of the world.'[28]

Even as he spoke, 40 Nazi divisions were mustering. *Wehrmacht* troops were poised on the Czech border, awaiting the order to invade.

The Cardinal Deacon Caccia-Dominioni placed the papal tiara on Pacelli's head. 'Receive this Tiara, adorned with three crowns, that thou mayest know thou art the father of princes and of kings, the ruler of the world, the Vicar on earth of our Saviour Jesus Christ, to Whom is honour and glory for ever and ever, Amen.'[29]

Prophecy had it that the 262nd Pope since St Peter would be known as '*Pastor Angelicus*', the Angelic Shepherd. It was said that Pacelli endorsed this tradition and wished to be known thereafter as 'Pastor Angelicus'. By the end of the day, the cry was everywhere: 'Pastor Angelicus! Pastor Angelicus!'[30]

'Holiness, forgive my bewilderment, but I fail to understand your extreme changes of heart', Pasqualina cautiously began.[31] To her, the splendour of the coronation was 'a shocking display of pomposity', bewildering to reconcile with Pacelli's self-abasement during the conclave.[32]

'At the conclave', Pacelli replied patiently, 'I was confronted with the realization that I – merely an ordinary man – was to be placed in an extraordinary position as Christ's Vicar on Earth. This thought humbled me greatly and gave me good reason to search one final time into my mind and soul to determine if I was worthy. But the coronation was quite another matter. The pomp and adulation were not for me, but for the honour and glory of Almighty God. I am only a symbol to remind the faithful to adore Him.'[33]

In Pacelli's accomplished rationale, there is more than an echo of his reflection following the visit to Buenos Aires: 'After so much glory and splendour, it is necessary to lie close to the earth to know that we are nothing.' Always there are paradoxes in Pacelli – the suave diplomat and the silent ascetic; the bureaucrat and the mystic; the glittering receptions and the austere private furnishings; the shameless cosseting and the relentless toil. It is tempting to speculate that Pacelli secretly loved the limelight, adored adulation, yet went in constant denial of these typically human desires. And perhaps it is as simple as this. Or maybe Pacelli abased himself as a man, yet simultaneously glorified himself as a vessel of God. Certainly his mood swings, from black depression to wild euphoria, seem to have accentuated the qualities of these sharply differing personae.

'What do you plan to do about Hitler?' Pasqualina asked bluntly. 'As Holy Father, you have the influence to speak out effectively against him.'[34]

'The world, unmindful of broader values, all too often seeks simplistic solutions to many complex problems', he told her. 'When a mere man becomes the Holy Father, he cannot allow emotion or impulse to sway his decisions. The Holy Father must constantly ask of himself many questions. His Holiness cannot afford to act rashly, but must seek solution on the side of what is best in the long run for the greater good of humanity as a whole.'[35] At this, the nun remained staunchly unconvinced.

'Certainly you, Holiness, are not implying that a despot like Hitler, in the long run, serves the greater good of mankind?' she ventured.[36]

'By no means, Sister Pasqualina', he answered. 'In the case of Hitler, it would be all too easy for the Holy Father to follow what might seem rational or obvious or inevitable to the world. If the Holy Father were to think only in a temporal manner, that would be the political and popular move to make. But there are many millions of the Catholic faithful whose minds have been captured by Hitler – and these blinded souls would be lost to Holy Mother Church, were our actions to be overt or extreme. If these souls are to be saved, the Holy Father must act with discretion. Of course Hitlerism must be destroyed, but our method must be subtle. We must be deliberate, yet we must remain temperate. Pray for me, Sister. It is not easy being Holy Father.'[37]

Perhaps sensing Pasqualina's continued unease, Pacelli added, 'It is inevitable, for all the reasons I have expressed, that the Holy Father shall invite, at any and all times, a ceaseless crossfire of criticism and attack, even hate. From this sad and hopeless position, Church and papacy can never expect to escape. We must forever endure the onerous weight of criticism.'[38]

Pasqualina now knew the sad truth: Pacelli would moderate; he would mediate. But he would not fight. What, she wondered helplessly, had happened to the man who had once stood beside her in the nunciature at Munich, and outfaced the communist thugs with a courage that had become legendary?

As if sensing how greatly he had failed her, Pacelli slowly rose to his feet. His face was devoid of expression. Shrouded in loneliness, he stepped into an adjacent room and closed the door firmly behind him.

As Pope Pius XII, Pacelli was now the undisputed leader of the Catholic Church, numbering half a billion people. Half the population of Hitler's Greater Reich was Catholic; a quarter of the Nazi military elite, the SS, was Catholic. As supreme arbiter of moral values on earth, he was in a unique position to say what was right – and what was wrong.

Understandably, the most powerful politicians of the day asked themselves what manner of man was the new Pope. More pertinently, they pondered what side (if any) he would take in the increasingly likely event of a Second World War. The more they studied him, the more they must have realized that they were dealing with an enigma, a creature of mystery and paradox.

Pacelli had broken the outdated tradition of self-imprisonment in the Vatican. His unprecedented public exposure had made him more widely known than any other pope in history. Such exposure, culminating in the extravaganza of the coronation, was generally viewed as an initiative to decentralize and demystify the Church. The ironic reality was that, for decades, Pacelli had been relentlessly centralizing the Church as a core element of his Great Design. And the urbane bureaucrat hid the soul of a mystic, who would one day make the unprecedented papal claim that Our Lord, Jesus Christ had appeared before him.

Four years previously Pacelli's brother, Francesco, co-architect of the Lateran Treaty, had died. Since then Pacelli had been distant from his siblings, even Elisabetta. He was no less distant from many of his colleagues in the Church. His secretary, the Reverend Robert Leiber, was discretion personified. Pasqualina and two assistants from her order in Germany attended to his domestic needs with near-fanatical devotion.

In Italy, Pacelli's elevation to the papacy was greeted with delight; after all he was a Roman, ruling in Rome. Abroad, reaction was mostly favourable. D'Arcy Osborne, British minister at the Holy See, reported to his political masters at the Foreign Office that Pacelli had 'great personal charm', a 'saintly character', and 'great political experience'. He was 'the sort of paragon that the *Pastor Angelicus* should be'. Just one note of reservation sneaked into an otherwise blameless encomium. D'Arcy Osborne was 'not quite sure how strong a character he [Pacelli] is, working as he did under an autocrat like Pius XI'.[39] As previously noted, Cardinal Tisserant had made a similar, albeit characteristically blunter, comment. For him, Pacelli would always be 'indecisive, hesitant, a man more designed to obey orders than to give them'.

Pacelli's visits to North and South America had won him enduring popularity. But his special relationship with Germany was scarcely acknowledged in sneering Nazi newspaper comments: 'The election of Pacelli is not favourably accepted in Germany, since he has always been hostile to National Socialism' (*Berliner Morgenpost*); 'Many of his [Pacelli's] speeches have made it clear that he does not fully grasp the political and ideological motives which have begun their victorious march in Germany' (*Frankfurter Zeitung*); 'Pius XII is not a *Pastor Angelicus* . . . Pacelli has never been a pastor of souls, a priest in the pulpit. For nearly 40 years, he has been a diplomat, a proponent of the Vatican's worldly politics' (*Danziger Vorposten*). In Austria the Nazi newspaper, *Graz*, denounced Pacelli as 'a servile perpetuator of Pius XI's doomed policy . . . but, for the German people, it is of no importance whether a Pius XI or a Pius XII sits in the Vatican'.[40]

Perhaps gimlet eyes at the British Foreign Office had noted D'Arcy Osborne's reservation in being 'not quite sure how strong a character he [Pacelli] is'. On 2 March Sir Robert Vansittart took the wise insurance policy of inviting to lunch someone with highly pertinent experience of Pacelli – the former statesman, turned political *émigré*, Heinrich Brüning.

Afterwards Vansittart informed the Foreign Secretary, Lord Halifax, 'Brüning does not share the general optimism in regard to [the then] Cardinal Pacelli.'[41] Brüning had confided in Vansittart his opinion that 'Pacelli may still have in his mind the possibility of proceeding by way of treating with the present regime in Germany and Italy.'[42] Even worse, in Brüning's view, Pacelli had already effectively delivered 23 million German Catholics into the evil power of the Nazi Party. Pacelli's predecessor, the doughty Ratti, may have snubbed the Führer – but his wily German opponent would exact a gloating revenge upon the Church.

The implications of Hitler's revenge were to bear terrible consequences, which have rippled throughout history to our own time and, tragically, seem set to continue far beyond it.

Chapter 11

Darkness over the Earth

While always talking about love and humanity, they [clerics] are, in fact, interested in only one thing, power – power over men's souls, and hence over their lives. The Catholic Church is like a scheming woman who at first contrives to give her husband the impression that she is helpless and guileless, only to take over power, finally holding it so securely that the man has to dance to any tune she plays.[1]

Thus did Hitler declare his true feelings about the Church. Close to his death, Pope Pius XI had been equally forthright:

Let us call things by their true name. I tell you, in Germany today, a full religious persecution is in progress. A persecution which does not shrink from using every weapon: lies, threats, false information, and, in the last resort, physical force ... A lying campaign is being carried on in Germany against the Catholic hierarchy, the Catholic religion, and God's Holy Church ... The protest we make before the whole civilised world cannot be clearer or more unequivocal.[2]

As we have seen, the 'missing encyclical', *Humani generis unitas*, did not reach Pius until 9 February. On 11 February he was due to hold a meeting with his bishops, where he was expected to denounce anti-Semitism in the strongest possible terms. His death, on 10 February, could not have come at a more convenient time for Hitler and Mussolini. Even on his own deathbed many years later, Cardinal Tisserant still fervently believed that Pius had been poisoned by Doctor Petacci. It is one of those tantalizing riddles of history, to which we will probably never know the answer.

In 1919, at the nunciature in Munich, Pacelli had bankrolled an impoverished 'anti-communist' named Adolf Hitler. Now, 20 years later, Hitler was undisputed master of Germany, while Pacelli was undisputed master of the Catholic Church. At their first meeting Pacelli had wielded immeasurably more power than Hitler, who had walked in off the street without an appointment, little more than a vagrant. A letter from General Ludenforff had been his only *bona fides*. And yet somehow he had secured an astounding victory.

Did Hitler set the tenor of their relationship at that very first meeting? Did he create some kind of arcane psychological dominion over Pacelli? True, by 1939 Hitler ruled Germany and would shortly rule most of Europe. But Pacelli possessed not only the moral loyalty of half the population of Germany but that of half a billion people, world-wide. Again and again in the years to come,

Hitler, wisely, would be very careful indeed not to engage the Catholic Church in direct confrontation. But again and again, throughout those same years, Pacelli would behave as though Hitler held all the power and he held none. From such a seasoned diplomat and world-class negotiator, this stance is both staggering and perplexing.

'In 1878, Leo XIII, at the beginning of his Pontificate, sent a message of peace to Germany. In my modest person, I should like to do something of the same sort.' Pacelli looked up from his proposed letter to Hitler and asked of his German cardinals, 'Is that all right? Does it need altering? Or amplifying? I should be most grateful for your Eminences' advice.'[3]

Cardinal Bertram hastened to reassure: 'I don't see there's anything to add.' Likewise, Cardinal Schulte gave his seal of approval: 'As far as its contents are concerned, excellent.' Pacelli summed up the objective: 'If it's treated as a purely protocolar affair, the implication about the bad state of affairs for the Church may be missed. And we are concerned, above all, with what is best for the Church in Germany. For me, that is the most important question.'[4]

'Do we address him [Hitler] as "Illustrious" or "Most Illustrious"?' Pacelli queried. ' "Most Illustrious!" ' Cardinal Schulte scoffed. 'That's really going too far. He hasn't earned that.'[5] Pacelli and his German cardinals were concerned to arrive at the most suitable salutation for the man who was bent on destroying the Catholic Church in Germany. Eventually a bland letter began: 'To the Illustrious Herr Adolf Hitler. . .'.[6]

For Pasqualina, taking notes at the meeting, it was 'frightfully condescending conversation being carried to pathetic extremes'.[7] Many years later she sadly concluded: 'It was like watching a Shakespearean tragedy. There was the Pope and his council of Cardinals on their knees to Hitler.'[8] To her, 'a Pontiff of Christ [must] not only preach the word of God but practise his teachings and be a moral force, irrespective of all costs and sacrifice'.[9] Spiritual values must predominate over temporal ones.

'The Holy See today stands alone as a viable instrument of peace', she reminded Pacelli after the meeting. 'Hitler is making a mockery of the Catholic Church. The Holy See can prevail against Nazism only if the Holy Father speaks with strength and without fear of consequences.'

Knowing that she was failing to breach Pacelli's defences, she pushed harder. 'Holiness, you will recall that Pius XI, on the eve of his death, condemned Hitler and the Nazis. As you know, my good and loving friend Pius XI's encyclical of denunciation was in complete contradiction to everything that was decided today.'[10]

At this Pacelli's reserve finally broke; yet, typically, he still refused to acknowledge her argument. 'Keep to your place as a woman and a nun! And let the dead rest in peace!'[11]

For 20 years, Pasqualina had devoted her life to Pacelli. How dare he treat her thus! She stalked out, her heart bitter, knowing that he would repent and return to the one person whom he would always need.

That night, as she was about to go to bed, there was a timid knock at the door of her room. She hesitated. As she was about to unfasten the latch, she heard him meekly say, 'Sister Pasqualina, I have remembered you in my prayers this evening. Now have a good night's sleep.'[12] It was Pacelli's characteristically oblique way of apologizing and reaffirming how much she meant to him.

On 15 March 1939, just three days after Pacelli's coronation, the *Wehrmacht* invaded Prague and took control of Czechoslovakia, under Hitler's pretext that 'the Jews in Czechoslovakia were still poisoning the nation'.[13] The next objective was Danzig, gateway to the Baltic. Poland was looking increasingly ripe for Nazi acquisition.

Five days later, on 20 March 1939, the Archbishop of Canterbury spoke to the House of Lords. He proposed an alliance against war. This alliance would be outside the normal political parameters. In effect, it would be Christians – of all nationalities – opposing war. Generously he proposed that the newly elected Pope Pius XII might accept the presidency of a Christian conference to avert catastrophe.

Pacelli refused. For him, any such joining of Catholics, Protestants and the Orthodox Church would carry implications of parity – and this he could never accept. For him, the Catholic Church was the one true Church. However laudable the cause for a common Christian front, it was more important that the status of the one true Church in 'splendid isolation' should be upheld at all times.

With Europe slipping ever closer to war, Pacelli looked to his own peace conference. He had chosen, as a papal coat of arms, a dove carrying an olive branch. His policy would be one of strict neutrality, with the rule of law a moderating influence over violent passions. Meanwhile, on Good Friday, Mussolini invaded Albania. Pacelli did not speak out. At about the same time, however, he sent a telegram to General Franco, congratulating him on Spain's 'Catholic victory'. In Iberia, he appeared willing to ignore his policy of strict neutrality – and some 500,000 deaths.

After securing Mussolini's support for his peace conference, Pacelli looked to the rulers of Germany, Poland, France and Britain. The British were suspicious of Mussolini's involvement. Hitler listened 'with deference' to the proposed plan for a peace conference and blithely assured Archbishop Cesare Orsenigo, Pacelli's nuncio in Berlin, that he saw no need for war. He would not attack Poland, 'unless forced by ill-advised Polish provocations'. Orsenigo wrote to Pacelli: 'I think ... that, if Poland would calm down and be silent, without, for the time being, giving in on any point, the motive for a war, at least for the moment, would be set aside.'[14]

The notion of a peace conference was debated among the guest nations. Then, on 10 May, Pacelli abruptly withdrew. The papal nuncios were told by the Secretariat of State that there was no longer any danger of war. Elsewhere though, it has been suggested that Mussolini derailed the proposed conference, fearing to face France, with whom he was in conflict over disputed Northern African territories, in front of Poland, Germany and Britain. Publicly, Mussolini and Ribbentrop stated that political tensions had decreased; privately they drew up their 'Pact of Steel', by which Italy and Germany would fight together. On 22 May it was signed, in Berlin.

On 4 June, Pacelli made overtures to the British that he was prepared to mediate personally between Poland and Germany. Pacelli hinted that the British guarantee to defend Poland was making mediation difficult. He seemed eager for Poland to appease Germany.

British diplomats were astounded. At the Foreign Office, Sir Andrew Noble declared that Pacelli was aiming to 'exorcize the devil with soft words', and hoped that 'the Pope would see his way to make clear to the world the incompatibility between the worship of God and the worship of the State'.[15] There was a strong opinion that Pacelli should confine his attentions to matters spiritual, and leave professional politicians to get on with their business. President Roosevelt was informed by his ambassador in Warsaw that the Poles believed Pacelli was pro-German and had no understanding of Poland at a grassroots level. To Pacelli, European countries were above all pieces on the chessboard of his Great Design. He distrusted the French, was fearful of the British, and kept the Spanish at a distance due to their dogmatism and pride. Even the Americans were regarded in a poor light, as a culture already in decline without ever having had an apogee. Pacelli regarded Europe as the centre of the world, and Germany as the political and economic centre of Europe. Ironically, his lofty indifference to domestic political considerations had first been noted in Germany, many years before.

By August, war seemed unavoidable. In a last-ditch attempt, Lord Halifax prevailed upon Pacelli to make a radio broadcast in favour of peace. Four different drafts were prepared, condemning the communists and Fascists in increasingly vehement terms; typically, Pacelli chose the most moderate. His radio appeal contains his only well-remembered dictum: 'Nothing is lost with peace. Everything may be lost with war...'.[16]

In his superordinate role of one 'standing above all public disputes and passions',[17] Pacelli assured the world of his willingness to be a broker for peace. Mussolini, who feared that a world war could mean the 'end of civilisation', also worked behind the scenes. But events were sliding toward inevitable conflict. On 31 August 1939 Pacelli made a 'last appeal in favour of peace'.[18] A day later, on 1 September, Hitler invaded Poland. On 3 September, Britain and France declared war on Germany. World War Two had begun.

Pacelli and Pasqualina were praying together when they learned the news of the invasion of Poland and the inevitability of war. Pacelli went rigid with shock, before rushing into his private chapel and breaking down in tears. 'How unwise you must think I am, at times', he miserably apologized to Pasqualina.[19] She looked at him with sorrow. Nearly 40 years later, she recalled that 'His Holiness looked so old and pitifully tragic at that moment.'[20]

As ruler of a sovereign state, Pacelli declared neutrality. Stalin is alleged to have rhetorically demanded: 'How many divisions has the Pope?' This demonstrated not only the communist premier's dismissive contempt of the Church, but also a certain *naiveté*. It was a mistake that the wily Hitler never made. The Pope may have had no divisions, but he had well-nigh half a billion subjects. The early Christians had no divisions either; but they grew to wield more power than even Hannibal and a host of other military aggressors.

On 17 September, the Russians also invaded Poland. In the first month, an estimated 70,000 fatalities occurred. By the end of World War Two, six million Poles had been killed or injured; half of these were Jews. Most of the 35-million population of Poland was Catholic. Of the 2,000 priests and bishops, some 700 were killed and another 700 imprisoned. The Poles looked to Pacelli to protest on their behalf.

Certainly, on 18 September Pacelli had spoken of 'new and incalculable dangers' deriving from the 'sinister shadow, daily closer and more threatening, of the ideology and actions of the enemies of God'.[21] The Jews were Hitler's *bête noire*; the Bolsheviks were Pacelli's *bête noire*.

But while the Bolsheviks were indeed the enemies of God, Nazi behaviour in Poland was no less godless. Pacelli's elliptical comments seemed to mask a greater and more fundamental silence. To the Polish, the British and the French, this silence was baffling. Was Pacelli 'keeping his powder dry' for a role as an international peacemaker? Surely it was far too late in the day for that. Was he remaining silent for fear of worsening the situation for the Poles? Simultaneously invaded by two hated armies, it was difficult to see how their situation could be much worse. Édouard Daladier, the French premier, expressed his surprise that Pacelli had failed to condemn the invasions. A British report noted the Polish anger at Pacelli's silence, and declared that 'papal pronouncements since the outbreak of war have pusillanimously evaded the moral issues involved'.[22] But it was left to Daladier to state more bluntly that Pacelli's continuing silence was tantamount to assent.

On 20 October Pacelli finally broke his silence, with the encyclical *Summi pontificatus* (Of the Supreme Pontificate.) This has become known in the English-speaking world as *Darkness over the Earth*. It asked all nations to recognize the kingdom of Christ. It noted that 'The blood of so many who have been cruelly slaughtered, though they bore no military rank, cries to heaven, especially from the well-loved country of Poland ...'.[23]

The encyclical was greeted with approval by Britain and France. The *Daily Telegraph* headline of 28 October read POPE CONDEMNS NAZI THEORY, while *The Times* noted NEW IDOLATRY CONDEMNED.[24] The French air force dropped many thousands of copies of the encyclical over Germany. Conversely, Germany regarded it as a breach of Pacelli's neutrality – even though there had been no direct reference to Nazism. In Poland the German invaders reprinted the encyclical, substituting 'Germany' for 'Poland'.

The Great Design envisaged a pyramid of power, with most of the half-billion Catholics in the world at the base, and one man – the Pope – at the apex, ultimately making decisions on behalf of all. Now, Pacelli was that man. Although nobody knew the Curia better, his managerial style paid scant heed to consensus or delegation. In his own way, Pacelli was as autocratic as Ratti had ever been. He had his tiny circle of confidants, his 'kitchen sink' cabinet. And he also had a mercurial temperament, ranging from Churchill's 'black dog' of depression to moods of wild euphoria.

Today we would probably regard Pacelli as suffering from manic-depression. It is most important to note that such a view of him does not necessarily invalidate his competence. Churchill himself suffered not only from depression but from alcoholism; neither precluded his extraordinary leadership during World War Two. Similarly, President Kennedy's handling of the Cuban missile crisis of 1961 remains a most impressive achievement, considering his suffering from agonizing back pain and developing an increasing reliance on medication, including amphetamines. But when power over half a billion lives is concentrated in the hands of an autocrat who suffers from savage mood swings, it is extremely worrying to say the least.

In November 1939 Pacelli, the advocate of scrupulous political neutrality, amazingly became implicated in a conspiracy to overthrow Hitler. General Beck, former chief of staff of the army, was the main conspirator. Beck's plan, post-coup, was to withdraw from Poland and Czechoslovakia, and restore democracy to Germany and Austria. Such actions would expose Germany both to military annihilation and civil war. To nullify the first risk, the conspirators needed assurances that neither Britain nor France would use such a coup for their own military benefit.

Hans Oster, an intelligence officer and co-conspirator of Beck's, suggested using Pacelli as an intermediary between the plotters and the Allies. Oster had known Pacelli when he was nuncio in Germany. He sent a colleague, Josef Müller, to Rome to meet Ludwig Kass, the former German politician turned administrator of St Peter's Basilica. Kass put Müller in contact with Robert Leiber, Pacelli's private secretary. The idea was for Pacelli to communicate with Neville Chamberlain, via D'Arcy Osborne, the British minister at the Vatican, and Lord Halifax of the Foreign Office. Suitable guarantees could be conveyed back to the Germans, via Müller.

Pacelli spent just one day weighing up the pros and cons of the conspiracy. Then, on 6 November 1939, Müller was assured that the Pope would do 'all he can'.[25] Pacelli made his crucial decision without any consultation with Cardinal Maglione, his newly elected Secretary of State. He was prepared to risk the fate of the Catholic Church on a conspiracy of dubious provenance – which could have easily been a 'sting' operation by the Germans.

Conspiracies benefit, above all, from two factors. As few people as possible should know the overall plan; thus do terrorist organizations advocate cell structures, where members of each cell are ignorant of the activities – or even the existence – of others. By contrast, this conspiracy had Beck-Oster-Müller-Kass-Leiber-Pacelli-Osborne-Halifax-Chamberlain as a nine-person communication loop. Compromise or penetration by German or Italian Intelligence would have spelled disaster. It must be remembered that the Vatican had been under surveillance for decades. For instance, it is estimated that nearly 40 per cent of the Vatican's encrypted radio messages in World War Two were successfully deciphered by Italian decoders. There is also evidence that Vatican staff members (including members of the cipher section of the Secretary of State) had been compromised by members of Italian Intelligence. Keeping secrets in Rome was a perilous business.

Notwithstanding the need for expert planning, conspiracies also require brisk timing, for each day increases the risk of exposure. But despite Pacelli stating on 6 November that he was prepared to do 'all I can', D'Arcy Osborne was not approached until almost a month later, when he lunched with Kass, on 1 December. The first meeting was swathed in generalities; a second meeting did not take place until 8 January, 1940. It was not until 12 January that Osborne finally met with Pacelli, who told him that a west European offensive was planned by the Germans in February. If Hitler were deposed in a coup, the offensive might be aborted. But the conspirators needed suitable British assurances. D'Arcy Osborne sent a secret message to Halifax, as follows:

> He [Pacelli] wished to pass the communication on to me purely for information. He did not wish, in the slightest degree, to endorse or recommend it. After he had listened to my comments on the communication he had received and passed on to me, he said that perhaps, after all, it was not worth proceeding with the matter and he would therefore ask me to regard his communication to me as not having been made. This, however, I promptly declined, as I said I refused to have the responsibilities of his Holiness' conscience unloaded onto my own.[26]

Pacelli once again makes selective use of his studied neutrality, with his emphasis first on 'information only' and then on discussions being 'off the record'. Hitler would have greeted both caveats with derision, and punished Pacelli and the Church with equal savagery. When Osborne told Pacelli that, quite reasonably, the French allies would have to be told of the proposed coup, Pacelli felt that 'having thus salved his conscience, he would not even expect any answer'.[27]

Above all else, perhaps, conspiracies require steeliness – to proceed or to abort. Pacelli, having embraced this conspiracy in a fit of rash enthusiasm, was now showing his characteristic indecisiveness. By not even expecting an answer, he was also voluntarily choosing political impotence – *and putting the very existence of the Catholic Church at risk, for no benefit whatsoever.*

Understandably, Osborne found the whole affair 'hopelessly vague' and wondered whether it was indeed a German counter-intelligence sting. He noted that Pacelli's 'spontaneous offer, after my expressions of scepticism, to cancel his communication to me shows that he does not relish being used as a channel and that he has little expectation of any result. But he certainly cannot be reproached for acting as he has.'[28] Although Pacelli could not, perhaps, be reproached by the British government, he could certainly have been reproached by his College of Cardinals – had they known of his actions.

On 17 January, Halifax read Osborne's letter to the British war cabinet, who agreed that the French government should be informed; a month later, however, it seemed that this had not yet happened. The German offensive had not happened either, due supposedly to bad weather. The conspirators still had no assurances from the British, never mind the French. No sources had been disclosed by Pacelli, so the British could not evaluate the intelligence. Halifax noted curtly in a letter to Osborne that 'If any progress is to be made, a definite programme must be submitted and authoritatively vouched for.'[29] Patience was running out and tempers were, perhaps, fraying. When Pacelli confided in Osborne that the conspirators had confirmed their desire for a change in government, that worthy testily replied that 'if they wanted a change of government, why didn't they get on with it. I added that, even if the government was changed, I didn't see how we could make peace so long as the German military machine remained intact.'[30] Events then entered a period of stalemate. The British wanted to know the identities of the conspirators, to evaluate their *bona fides*; the conspirators wanted a British guarantee. Both sides seemed to lack the will to break the deadlock.

Early in March the German foreign minister, Ribbentrop, met with Mussolini to entice Italy into the war. He also requested an audience with Pacelli. Given that Ratti had absented himself to Castel Gandolfo, to evade Hitler, Ribbentrop wanted the Nazi propaganda coup of a meeting with the Pope. He also wanted to stop Pacelli's criticism of the Nazis, however mild and oblique. When the two men met Ribbentrop arrogantly used the rationale that Germany would win the war, to preclude any consideration of peace initiatives. Pacelli's protestations about Nazi attacks on Catholics and Church property were summarily rebuffed; Ribbentrop pointed out that Hitler had the full support of the German people. Scornfully he declared that 'Even today, the clergy has not yet understood that it is not their business to meddle in politics.'[31]

Pacelli's request for a Vatican envoy to be appointed to war-torn Poland was similarly sidestepped by Ribbentrop. By now, Pacelli must have realized that he was getting nowhere. His near-40 years' experience of diplomacy was wasted on Nazi supposed omnipotence. He bluntly asked Ribbentrop whether he believed in God. The German minister scathingly replied in German: 'I believe in God but I am not addicted to any church.'[32] Pacelli sarcastically repeated the phrase a couple of times and then told Ribbentrop that he could not help wondering if it was true.

Pacelli's uncharacteristic behaviour at this meeting is illuminating. As a well-mannered man, being rude or sarcastic was alien to his nature. Or was he on a 'high' at the time? It seems that the pressures of conspiracy were, in one way or another, taking their toll upon him. And it also seems that he was exhausted by Nazi hypocrisy. It was now transparently obvious that Ribbentrop had met him solely for unilateral purposes of propaganda and control. The German minister had no intention of any political give and take.

On 30 March, Pacelli wrote again to D'Arcy Osborne. The Beck conspiracy was stillborn, and by then he had discovered that other peace overtures had been made to Britain. He was miffed. The British regarded him as 'more open to influences than his predecessor', and Osborne added 'he is more ready to listen and to weigh opinions, and less rigid and uncompromising in his own views and actions. But it does not at all follow that he is unstable and easily swayed.'[33]

And yet Pacelli *had* been both unstable and easily swayed. On the spur of the moment, he had insinuated the papacy into a potentially deadly plot. He had compromised it with unknown partners (who turned out to be utterly feeble). He had laid it open to a sting operation. He had waved a spurious white flag of neutrality, which British fair play may have been prepared to respect, but which Hitler would undoubtedly have scorned. He had allowed time to drift by, when every day increased the risk of exposure. Above all, he had been hopelessly, endlessly, indecisive.

To Leiber, Pacelli's shocked secretary, Pacelli 'went much too far'.[34] To historian Harold Deutsch, the whole affair was 'among the most astounding events in the modern history of the papacy',[35] while in the opinion of another historian, Owen Chadwick:

> The Pope risked the fate of the Church in Germany and Austria and Poland and perhaps he risked more. He probably risked the destruction of the German Jesuits ... He took this big risk solely because his political experience saw that, however unsuccessful this plan was likely to turn out, it was probably the one remaining chance of halting the coming invasion of Holland and Belgium, of saving untold bloodshed, and bringing peace back to Europe.[36]

Throughout his entire career, Pacelli's normal political *modus operandi* was one of risk avoidance. It cannot be stressed too much that this was in no way whatsoever due to physical cowardice. At the nunciature in Munich, in 1917, he had stood up to the communist thugs with a rare courage; as the Vatican came under physical threat later on in World War Two, the Pope acted always with complete unconcern for his own safety. Of Eugenio Pacelli, it can be said with certainty that he was no coward.

But he was 'a man afraid'. He was always abnormally sensitive, and the dreadful experience of Munich had somehow blighted his being. All through his life he seemed to be pursued by a nameless dread, which cast a shadow over his days and filled his few sleeping hours with horrible nightmares. For decades Pasqualina, the woman who loved him, had to endure his agonized screams, ringing out in the dead of night.

Pacelli was raised by canon lawyers and became a canon lawyer himself. Logic and due process were his favoured political instruments. But these are part of the armoury of a diplomat rather than a politician. Above all, a politician must be a risk-taker.

For most of his career Pacelli failed to take risks when, perhaps, he should have taken them. His continued silence about Nazi atrocities in Germany and the invasion of Poland was, as we shall shortly see, part of a much greater silence about many terrible events throughout World War Two. Yet, with the Beck conspiracy, Pacelli went from risk avoidance to taking the wildest risk imaginable. Was he in an uncontrollable mood swing from black depression to manic high, when Muller's proposition arrived? Certainly, spending just one day evaluating it and coming to a unilateral decision, with no significant managerial consultation, seems unbelievably remiss. Perhaps Pacelli felt that his subordinates would simply recommend 'No'. Maybe he did not trust them to keep their silence.

Every day of the weary months while the plot dragged on increased the chances of a leak. If the plot had leaked – or if it had been a German sting operation – Hitler would have been served an unimaginably powerful propaganda coup. At one stroke, the Pope's credibility would have been ruined in the eyes of the world. All Hitler had to do was ask his partner, Mussolini, to cut off the water and electricity supplies in order to compel the Vatican to cease operations. And what then? A deposed pope and a Nazi stooge in his place? A forced unholy marriage between Catholicism and National Socialism?

Certainly, with the Beck affair, Pacelli's true attitude to Hitler is revealed. But he gambled the independence of the Church for no gain whatsoever. His willingness to do 'all I can' makes a mockery of his claims to political neutrality. And it sits uneasily with his relative silence as Europe dissolved into the fearful chaos of war.

Chapter 12

'Ecclesiastical Lust'

Wars are fought with money, no less than with soldiers and weapons. It was obvious to Pacelli that the Church was also fighting a war, not just for the hearts and minds of Catholics of all countries but for its continued independence and, perhaps, its very existence. Throughout the 1930s, he had viewed Hitler and Mussolini as Fascist rat-catchers who were keeping the communist vermin at bay. However, with the outbreak of hostilities the political landscape had become very much more complex and frightening. France, one of the most long-standing Catholic countries in Europe, was at war with the Vatican's 'allies', as defined by the Reich concordat and the Lateran Treaty. A shifting political landscape demanded that the Vatican 'punch above its weight' on the world stage.

Soon after Pacelli took over from Ratti, he discovered a shocking secret hidden away in his predecessor's confidential files. The New York archdiocese, the most powerful in the Church apart from the Vatican, was more than 28 million dollars in debt. Furthermore it was a debt that was increasing rapidly, by the day. As we have seen, the 2,000-year-old Catholic Church had been saved from bankruptcy by the Lateran Treaty in the 1930s. Now it was facing another financial crisis – ironically, in the richest country in the world.

For 18 years, New York's archbishop had been a certain Cardinal Hayes. He had earned the *soubriquet* 'The Cardinal of Charity', by his willingness to help the needy from Church funds. On one occasion Bishop Spellman, Pacelli's confidant, had mentioned to him that throughout the 1930s, he had seen queues of supplicants standing outside Cardinal Hayes' house. The old man hadn't the heart to turn anyone away.

Now he had died, leaving behind a financial crisis of staggering proportions. (Twenty-eight million dollars then would be a vast sum today.)

New York Catholics, accustomed to Hayes' *largesse*, wanted another 'Cardinal of Charity'. Bishop Stephen Donahue, Hayes' *protégé*, seemed the obvious candidate. But to Pius XI the indiscriminate handout policy had been a disaster, to be terminated forthwith and never allowed to recur. And he had his own nominee, Archbishop John McNicholas of Cincinnati, a generous benefactor to the Vatican. The papers for the McNicholas appointment were actually on the Pope's desk awaiting signature when he died.

'Bishop Spellman has told me that President Roosevelt does not like Excellency McNicholas', Pacelli confided in Pasqualina. 'He [McNicholas] has been preaching against Roosevelt's "peace propaganda", which he feels could lead America into war, and he has even urged Catholics to form "a mighty league of conscientious non-combatants".[1]

Pacelli's visit to America had been the crowning triumph of his career as Secretary of State. Coughlin, 'the radio priest', had been silenced. The prestige of the Church had soared. Important diplomatic links had been made with Roosevelt. All of these achievements had been enhanced by Spellman's behind-the-scenes facilitation, not least with the American President.

'Bishop Spellman is President Roosevelt's favourite holy personage', Pasqualina declared. 'That is simply because His Excellency has the mind and tact to appreciate the delicacies required in conversing with a man like the President. Bishop Spellman quite wisely never forgets that Holy Mother Church always requires good friends in high places.'[2]

Then, with characteristic bluntness, the German nun went straight for the obvious solution. 'Holiness, since you have already set your mind against Excellency McNicholas, why not appoint Bishop Spellman? But appoint him on his merit, not merely to appease Roosevelt! Holiness, he is loyal to you. He is shrewd, and knows how to persuade people to donate large sums of money and valuable gifts. Bishop Spellman was the best money-raiser the Vatican ever had.'[3]

Characteristically, Pacelli procrastinated. As day followed day, and Archbishop McNicolas's appointment remained unsigned, rumours spread that Pacelli was trying to wriggle out of Ratti's commitment and find an excuse to give the position to his 'pet', Spellman. Both Spellman and McNicholas were left in quandaries of doubt. Finally, one evening when Pacelli and Pasqualina were kneeling together in the papal chapel, the Pope whispered to her: 'My decision is made. You have convinced me, Sister Pasqualina. Your friend is in!'[4] Shortly afterwards, Spellman's appointment was officially confirmed. McNicholas, who had been assured by Ratti that the post was his, was given no explanation whatsoever. Doubtless he pondered the vicissitudes of regime change. He had come so very close to attaining the most important position in the Catholic Church in America.

Spellman's appointment was greeted with dismay by the Curia. When he had first come to Rome in 1925, he had been the recipient of blatant racism on the part of the Italians. Contemptuously assigned the job of playground director, he had shamelessly wheeled and dealed with an enviable dexterity. In time, the 'hotshot from Boston' had curried favour with both Ratti and Pacelli. Back in America, he thrived. During Pacelli's American visit, the austere Pasqualina had been shocked by the luxury of Spellman's residence. The former playground director had become a confidant not only of the Pope, but also of the American President. Now he would become the premier Catholic in America. His erstwhile tormentors in Rome must have been beside themselves with envy. The hotshot from Boston had given them a resounding lesson in career management.

If Spellman's appointment was deemed disastrous, the manner of its making was regarded as scandalous. Rightly, the senior members of the Curia suspected Pasqualina's influence over Pacelli. To these powerful, often pompous, elderly men, nuns were little more than chattels. That a simple nun should wield such influence over the Pope was an affront to their entrenched values.

Much later in Spellman's career, a certain Archbishop Sheen would emerge as a rival for the affection of the American public. Rev. D. P. Noonan, writing in his biography of Sheen, notes of the Catholic Church that:

> The thirst for power among priests, Monsignors, Bishops and Cardinals [goes] totally unchecked, simply because there [is] no one to check it ... Ambition is the ecclesiastical lust![5]

For many years Spellman's former superior, Archbishop O'Connell, had done his best to make life miserable for the 'Boston hotshot'. On hearing of Spellman's appointment, O' Connell sneeringly observed: 'That's what happens to a bookkeeper when you teach him how to read.'[6]

Many years before, when Pasqualina had first met Spellman, she had taken an instant dislike to him. But, over time, he had endeared himself to her, as well as to Ratti and Pacelli. He had also noticeably grown in stature during the same years that Pacelli, sadly, had become more careworn and inward-looking.

Spellman was an unashamed opportunist; but, as Pasqualina had observed, he was also a man of considerable talent. Roosevelt was another opportunist – so the President and the newly created Archbishop made good company. Spellman boasted that he was an intimate of the ruler of America *and* the ruler of the Catholic Church. Certainly he was the key intermediary between these two men. And whenever he became too grandiose, there was always Pasqualina to prick 'Spelly's' bombast and bring him back down to earth.

To his credit, though, Spellman went straight to work. His mission was firstly to clear up the financial mess in New York, and secondly to put the Church on a secure economic footing in the US. He inherited a near-catastrophic situation. Besides the 28-million-dollar debt in New York, another 200 million dollars was owed throughout America. A lesser man would have buckled under the strain of such an enormous task.

Remembering the success that the Vatican had experienced when they enlisted the services of the mysterious financier Nogara, Spellman formed a partnership with a Wall Street financier called John Coleman. The pair of them organized a series of fund-raising events, remorselessly targeting 'men who mattered'. Trading on perennial human vanity, they sold memberships of the prestigious Knights of Malta for sums ranging from 50,000 to 200,000 dollars. With an enviable neatness, Spellman rewarded Coleman by making him head of the Knights. Coleman subsequently became known as 'The Pope of Wall Street'.

Membership fees from the Knights and other organizations were promptly invested. The New York archdiocese created its own bank, and began to borrow and lend money. In Italy the Church had invested heavily in the industrial infrastructure; Spellman and Coleman did the same in America, operating through shell corporations to keep ownership secret. In Italy the Church had eschewed 'ethical investment', for instance, in buying stock in pharmaceutical companies which made birth control products. (This, of course, did not stop it from denouncing birth control.) A similar line in ethical pluralism was adopted in America. Spellman denounced the 'loose morals' of films such as *Forever Amber* and *Baby Doll*, both made by Paramount, where blocks of shares were owned by the Church.

Pasqualina had sagely noted that 'Bishop Spellman was the best money-raiser the Vatican ever had.' Within a few years, Spellman and Coleman had turned a 28-million-dollar deficit in New York into a 182-million-dollar surplus. They had a particular interest in construction; dozens of Catholic schools and churches were erected. Spellman began a tradition of donating a million dollars a year to the Vatican, sometimes nonchalantly presenting it personally, in cash and cheques, in a black satchel. Spellman's extraordinary financial success made him even more detested in the Curia. Cardinal Tisserant contemptuously referred to him as 'Cardinal Moneybags', conveniently forgetting Spellman's loyalty, his ability, and the Church's desperate need of the funds which he supplied in such abundance.

Spellman's ability as a political fixer brought unexpected benefits when America entered the war, after the Japanese attack on Pearl Harbour. At that time Nazi submarines controlled the North Atlantic, off the American coast. In January 1942, 21 ships were torpedoed. In February, another 27 vessels went to watery graves. In March, a staggering 50 ships were sent to the bottom of the ocean. It was a crisis of epidemic proportions.

Spellman had been made chaplain-general of the US Catholic armed forces, with 2,700 chaplains reporting to him and an overall pastoral responsibility for 2,000,000 people. President Roosevelt called him to the White House and tersely informed him of the situation. Counter-espionage intelligence suggested that the Germans were being notified of naval targets by spies and saboteurs at key ports. It was an open secret that the Mafia controlled the docks on the east coast. The Mafia were Italian – and Catholic. Roosevelt wanted nothing less than a senior Catholic churchman to intercede with the leaders of organized crime on behalf of the war effort. He had decided that Spellman was the man for the job.

Spellman was flabbergasted. He realized that Roosevelt must know that Frank Costello, a Mafia elder statesman, was a regular churchgoer, sometimes seen at prayer in Spellman's own church, St Patrick's Cathedral. Frantically hedging his bets, Spellman told Roosevelt that naturally he would first have to ask the Pope for permission.

Roosevelt read Spellman well. 'There is no substitute for victory, my dear bishop. Tell the Holy Father for me what my good friend, Winston [Churchill], so wisely said in defining wartime morality. "If, by some strange stroke of fate, the devil came out in opposition to Adolf Hitler, I should feel constrained, at least, to make a favourable reference to the devil in the House of Commons." '[7] With this admonition ringing in his ears, Spellman made his uneasy way to Rome.

'The President wants me to seek a deal with the underworld for the United States government', a distraught Spellman told Pasqualina. 'How am I to present such a horrible idea to the Holy Father? And how can I afford to turn down Roosevelt?'[8]

'Nothing that any politician says or seeks surprises me any longer', the nun dryly replied.[9] Her time in the political snake-pit of the Vatican had made her worldly-wise. The Teaching Sisters of the Holy Cross at Altötting, all those years before, must have seemed to belong to another world.

'Would you please broach the subject with the Holy Father before I speak with him?' Spellman begged. 'I will then be guided by your advice.'[10] Spellman had no desire to offend either of his patrons, Roosevelt or Pacelli. Equally, Pacelli had no desire to offend Roosevelt. In common parlance, Spellman wanted to 'pass the buck' to Pacelli, who was just as determined not to accept it. And both Spellman and Pacelli were world-class negotiators.

'Mother Pasqualina, you are such a splendid diplomat in such matters', Pacelli murmured. 'Whisper in our American friend's ear that he has no need to bring up such talk with me. It would be far more pleasant if His Excellency and I confined our private audience tomorrow to a brief prayer.' But then Pacelli added the key words: 'I have full confidence in Archbishop Spellman's discretion. The decision is his.'[11] Pacelli was elevating deniability to an art form. Meanwhile, hundreds of lives were being lost in the icy waters of the North Atlantic. Spellman knew what he had to do.

Operation Underworld began soon afterwards. Costello met Spellman in an anonymous Manhattan tenement. 'We all have a patriotic duty to perform for our country in time of war', the Archbishop reminded the mobster. For his part, Costello assured Spellman of his good faith. 'I am both honoured and overjoyed to be of service to my Church and my country.'[12]

Costello was as good as his word. He conferred with an associate, Charles 'Lucky' Luciano. Luciano, the 'boss of bosses', in effect the CEO of organized crime in the United States, was serving a 30- to 50-year sentence in the New York Prison, for crimes such as running large-scale prostitution rackets. But Luciano, even behind bars, wielded more power on the docks than all the US law enforcement agencies put together. The boss of bosses put the word out that sabotage was to stop. Within a few weeks, it had stopped. Nazi saboteurs were mercilessly punished. The U-boat menace was deflected, and the Germans started to lose control of the North Atlantic. The subsequent introduction of radar meant that U-boats themselves could be detected silently, without their knowledge. In months, their status changed from hunters to prey. It is estimated that more than 80 per cent of Nazi submariners perished at sea.

Spellman's access to Luciano, via Costello, led to even greater consequences later on in the war, when the Allies invaded Europe via the Sicily landings. Luciano once again proved his worth to the US government. As with the docks of New England, the mountains of Sicily were controlled by Mafia 'men of honour'. Luciano interceded with these 'men of honour' to sabotage the occupying forces of Sicily and assist the Allied invasion. Sicily became the Allies' bridgehead to Southern Europe. Without Luciano's intervention, the Allies would have encountered immensely greater opposition. Luciano and his 'men of honour' had saved Allied lives, military resources, and – vital for an invasion – time.

Luciano had proved his worth to the US wartime effort with a patriotism undoubtedly tinged with self-interest. Fear of adverse public opinion prevented his domestic release with a government pardon. If Luciano was to be freed from jail, he must be spirited out of the country. Italy was his homeland. Mussolini, however, remained a bitter enemy of the Mafia. Luciano would be a marked man.

Only after Mussolini's overthrow and assassination, in 1945, was it possible to absolve Luciano of 40 years of his 50-year prison sentence, and set him free. Returning to Italy, he discovered that premature retirement ill suited his avocation as criminal mastermind. Soon he was back to his old ways – an embarrassment to the Italian and American governments, and to the Church. When he died in Naples in 1962, aged 65, it was claimed that he was facing imminent arrest for smuggling 150 million dollars' worth of heroin into the US, during the previous 10 years.

Ironically, Luciano had gone to meet a producer eager to make a film of his life story. Like so many other gangsters, he yearned to be immortalized in print or celluloid with, no doubt, selectively edited, highly favourable accounts of his exploits.

'It was a blessing when he [Luciano] passed away', Pasqualina admitted. 'I remember saying a prayer to Jesus for the repose of his soul.'[13] This seems an honest epitaph from the nun to the gangster. When she was asked whether the Vatican had aided the US authorities in facilitating Luciano's move to Italy, Pasqualina refused to comment. Her silence speaks volumes.

However embarrassing Operation Underworld might have been to the Church, it was a desperate time which called for desperate measures. Costello and Luciano were gangsters, yet they delivered their side of the bargain. However queasy and under duress Spellman may have been, he acted with courage – a courage which ultimately saved thousands of lives and helped to win a war which threatened all of civilization. Costello's relationship with the Church is commemorated with the gift of the magnificent bronze doors of St Patrick's Cathedral in New York. Doubtless they were a constant reminder to Spellman of what he had done.

In their own ways, Costello and Luciano served the Church well. So too did Spellman. When he died nearly 30 years later, the Church in the US had gone from a $280 million deficit to a net worth of more than 80 billion dollars, with annual revenues of over 150 million dollars in the New York archdiocese alone. The Catholic Church became 'the biggest corporation in the United States'. Lay membership more than doubled, from 21 million to over 45 million. It was a golden age of Catholicism. Archbishop O'Connell's sneering jibe at Spellman, 'That's what happens to a bookkeeper when you teach him how to read', merely demonstrated O'Connell's paucity of spirit. Spellman transformed himself into a business *maestro* and brought huge financial benefits to the Church. However unpopular at the time, Pasqualina's recommendation of Spellman was an inspired choice, for which her many detractors never gave her any credit.

On a personal level Spellman proved a loyal friend to Pasqualina, many years later, when Pacelli was dead and her life was desolate.

Chapter 13

The Croatian Genocide

Pacelli's Serbian concordat of 1914 – his first diplomatic coup and the initial part of his Great Design – had been an attempt to surmount the centuries-old schism between Western and Latin Christianity (i.e. Roman Catholicism) and the Orthodox Church. Serbia was a religious bridgehead to the East. However, the Russian Revolution of 1917 dramatically changed the political landscape. Subsequently, for Pacelli, the East came to represent not only erstwhile Christian territory to be retaken; it also marked the birthplace of his *bête noire*, the communist scourge which threatened the future of mankind and the survival of the Church.

For Europe, Pacelli's Serbian concordat was a blunder of the first order. Selfishly pursuing religious aims regardless of the Austro-Hungarian Empire contributed, however unwittingly, to the outbreak of the First World War. Not content with this disaster, Pacelli's 1919 donation to the destitute Hitler in Munich bankrolled the emergent Nazi Party.

Astonishingly, in 1940, a third diplomatic blunder by Pacelli made it 'inevitable that Mussolini would enter the war'.[1]

On 3 May, Pacelli learned of the forthcoming invasions of Holland and Belgium. His informant was none other than Josef Müller, the courier in the abortive Beck plot to topple Hitler. The relevant nuncios were alerted, as were the foreign offices of France and Britain. However, Italian Intelligence intercepted the warnings to the nuncios; and when Pacelli confided the news to Crown Prince Umberto of Italy, Mussolini was promptly informed.

Pacelli had breached Vatican neutrality in the most spectacular fashion imaginable. Any international peacekeeping role was now forfeit. In Berlin, his actions were understandably viewed as espionage. In Rome, a reluctant Mussolini was left with no viable option but to enter the war. As the historian Owen Chadwick wrote: 'Mussolini could do no other than prove to the Germans that he totally rejected the Pope.'[2]

On 10 May the Nazis invaded Luxemburg, Belgium and Holland. Pacelli sent telegrams of condolence to the respective sovereigns. To the Italian and German governments, these communications were unwonted interference. Conversely, the French and British governments were angry at Pacelli's refusal to issue a condemnation of acts of territorial aggression and the flouting of international law.

Pacelli had struggled to keep the Fascist regimes of Spain and Italy out of the war.[3] Spanish neutrality continued, but on June 10 Italy declared war. Although a sovereign state, the Vatican was nevertheless in a dangerous position. Two weeks previously, 7.6 million dollars in gold bars had secretly been transferred to the US as a precautionary measure.[4]

Before long, Fascist thugs roamed the streets of Rome, beating up the innocent and vulnerable. A cry went out: 'Death to the Pope!' Pacelli declared himself unafraid of being put in a concentration camp. He joined a long line of popes who were fully prepared to die.

Italy's entrance into the war made Rome an enemy city to Britain and France. Throughout World War Two, Pacelli repeatedly implored the Allies not to bomb the city. For this, he has been vilified. Pacelli's pleading for special status was not tainted by cowardice; rather, for him, Rome was the sacred cradle not only of Christianity but, indeed, of civilization itself. Preserving Rome meant preserving a potent symbol of all that was good about the human race. Sadly, for Pacelli and Rome, such arguments carried little credence with ruthless men determined to win, no matter what the cost.

Yugoslavia, with its historical division between Serbs and Croats, was a powder keg set to explode. For hundreds of years, Catholic Croats had been oppressed by Orthodox Serbs. In many ways, the religious/ethnic conflict paralleled that of Northern Ireland. Catholic Croats were denied opportunities for education and professional advancement. Their resentment had festered into outright hate.

In 1940, Mussolini had ordered a campaign in the Balkans. Ironically, this was welcomed by certain high-ranking members of the Vatican. Yugoslavia was viewed as the defending line between Italy and communism. But when Mussolini proved incapable of achieving victory over the Greeks, Hitler came to his aid. Yugoslavia blocked land access to Greece. Therefore Yugoslavia had to be enticed into the Axis web. On 25 March 1941 in Vienna, a pact was signed between Germany, Italy and Yugoslavia. In response, two days later, a Serbian coup toppled the regency. The rebels declared that Yugoslavia was joining the Allies and not the Axis powers.

On 6 April 1941, the Nazis retaliated by invading Yugoslavia. Belgrade was bombed and 5,000 civilians were killed. On 10 April, Zagreb was captured. The Fascist state of Hungary joined Italy and Germany in determining the future of Yugoslavia. The country was partitioned. The dominant segment was an independent state of Croatia, ruled by Ante Pavelic and his *Ustashe* ('Those who rise up'). Pavelic and the *Ustashe* had many years of terrorist experience behind them. Mussolini's government had sponsored their training and propaganda.

Catholic Croats numbered some 3,300,000 people. Conversely, Serb Orthodox Christians amounted to over 2,000,000. In addition, there was a mix of ethnic, religious or political groups such as Muslims (750,000), Protestants (70,000), Jews (45,000), Gypsies and communists. The Croats were not bothered by the Protestants, of largely German descent; nor, surprisingly, were they concerned with the Muslims. But the Orthodox Serbs and the Jews were marked down for extinction.

On 25 April 1941 Pavelic banned the Cyrillic script, thereby effectively dispossessing the Serbs from their cultural version of the written word. In May, anti-Semitic laws were brought into being. Jews could not marry 'Aryans'. Jewish capital, Jewish professions and Jewish businesses would be subject to compulsory 'Aryanization'. In June, Serb Orthodox primary schools were closed down. The familiar – and horrible – tactics of Nazi Germany were being employed. Political, social, professional and personal identities of hated ethnic minorities were removed by a totalitarian state. Shortly afterwards, the first batches of Jews were deported from Zagreb to the concentration camp of Danica.

Clearly, to remain Orthodox Christian was to mark oneself as a hated Serb. Understandably, for their survival Serbs flocked to join the Catholic Church. On 14 July, the Croatian Ministry of Justice told the Yugoslav bishops that 'the Croatian government does not intend to accept within the Catholic Church either priests or schoolmasters or, in a word, any of the intelligentsia – including rich Orthodox tradesmen and artisans – because specific ordinances in their regard will be promulgated later, and also so that they shall not impair the prestige of Catholicism'.[5] In other words, the door of forced conversions was being slammed shut.

From the outset, it appears that there was significant communication between the Holy See and the newly formed Croatian government. For instance, the Curia helped to draw up rules of conduct for Orthodox churches taken over by Catholic Croats. Diplomatic links were forged; in Rome, Pavelic was received by Pacelli. *De facto* recognition of the new regime was given by the Vatican. An apostolic legate was appointed to Zagreb.

Undoubtedly Croatia was a bulwark against communism. But it was 'not the result of a heroic rising by the people of God but of outside intervention'.[6] Pacelli was endorsing military intervention by Hitler and Mussolini. Worse, he was tacitly approving the formation of a totalitarian state whose genocide would shortly rival that of Nazi Germany.

The cold, brutal facts are these. Between 1941 and 1945, the *Ustashe* murdered over 500,000 Serbs, Jews, gypsies and communists. Of the 45,000 Jews, 30,000 were killed. The *Wehrmacht*, no strangers to violence themselves, were revolted by the horrible scenes of carnage. By early June 1941, only two months after the invasion, a German general reported that 'the *Ustashe* have gone raging mad'.[7] In July, the same general reported German unease and helplessness. 'Six battalions of foot soldiers' had to stand by while 'the blind, bloody fury of the *Ustashe*' was unleashed upon defenceless populations. This was 'ethnic cleansing' with a vengeance – before the vile term had even been invented.

The Italian army was heavily involved in Croatia. German repugnance was superseded by Italian humanity. One estimate has it that by mid-1943 the Italians had protected over 30,000 Yugoslav civilians, including over 2,000 Jews. This happened despite the Italians' position as Axis allies.

Was such Italian humanity Vatican-influenced? We do not know. Jonathan Steinberg's research suggests that it was not. He concludes:

A long process, which began with the spontaneous reaction of individual young officers in the spring of 1941, who could not stand by and watch Croatian butchers hack down Serbian and Jewish men, women and children, ended in July 1943, with a kind of national conspiracy to frustrate the much greater and more systematic brutality of the Nazi state. *It rested on certain assumptions about what being Italian meant.* [Italics added][8]

On 6 March 1942, Cardinal Tisserant told a Croatian diplomat that Franciscan priests were actively involved in the carnage: 'I know for sure that the Franciscans in Bosnia and Herzegovina have acted abominably, and this pains me. Such acts should not be committed by educated, cultured, civilized people, let alone by priests.'[9] On 27 May he quoted German figures that '350,000 Serbs had disappeared', and that in 'one single concentration camp there are 20,000 Serbs'.[10]

Tisserant's intelligence was quite correct. Shockingly, armed Franciscan priests had taken part in the atrocities with gusto. After the war, Pasqualina would unearth evidence of Franciscan banditry in Sicily. But, as Tisserant rightly said, Franciscan behaviour was not only an insult to the priesthood; it was also an insult to humanity.

In addition to racial hatred, religious war had broken out in the Balkans. The Bishop of Mostar made the bizarre claim that there 'was never such a good occasion as now for us to help Croatia to save the countless souls'.[11] The old dream of using the Balkans as a bridge to re-establish Christianity in the domains of the Orthodox Church was coming true. But as Franciscans killed, looted and set fire to homes, religious 'fervour' was not a dream; it was a nightmare. The Sub-Prefect of Mostar admitted that in Ljubina alone, 700 schismatics had been hurled into a pit.[12]

Did the Holy See know about these atrocities? Undoubtedly it did. Ramiro Marcone, Pacelli's apostolic delegate, had military aeroplanes put at his disposal to travel across Croatia; and he was free to come and go at will between Rome and Zagreb. The Croatian bishops, who had intimate local knowledge, had regular access to the Pope on their *ad limina* visits. Courtesy of D'Arcy Osborne, the UK minister in the Vatican, Pacelli could receive translations of BBC broadcasts. On 16 February 1942, one of these broadcasts bluntly described the situation in Croatia:

> The worst atrocities are being committed in the environs of the Archbishop of Zagreb. The blood of brothers is flowing in streams. The Orthodox are being forcibly converted to Catholicism and we do not hear the Archbishop's voice preaching revolt. Instead, it is reported that he is taking part in Nazi and Fascist parades.[13]

Directives to the Croatian Bishops indicate that the Vatican knew about the enforced conversions from July 1941 onwards. The Vatican was insistent that those wishing to convert to Catholicism should be turned away when it was apparent that their conversions were for the wrong reasons. The 'wrong reasons' were, of course, avoidance of murder.

On 14 August, a letter was written to Maglione, the Secretary of State, by the

Sister Pasqualina's favourite photograph of Pope Pius XII (Private Collection)

Sister Pasqualina Lehnert, a German Roman Catholic nun who served as Pope
Pius XII's housekeeper (circa 1935) (Private Collection)

Germany, III.Reich: Concordat between the Reich and the Vatican. Signing ceremony Rome, Vatican: Sitting from left: Prelate Ludwig Kaas, Vice-chancellor Franz von Papen, cardinal secretary of state Eugenio Pacelli, head of department Rudolf Buttmann (German charge d'affaires at the Vatican), Eugen Klee (embasssy counsellor). 20.07.1933 (Ullstein Bild)

Pope Pius XII gives the "Urbi et orbi" blessing to a crowd filling St. Peter's Square on Easter Day, 1952. (© /ANSA/Corbis)

Sister Pasqualina Lehnert arrives at The Pontifical North American College in Rome, Jul. 20, 1970. (AP Photo)

SA meeting in Dortmund on 9 July 1933. Hitler, at the speaker's pulpit, giving a speech in front of SA division. (Photo: akg-images)

president of the Union for the Israelite Community of Alatri. It mentioned 'residents of Zagreb and other centres of Croatia who have been arrested without reason, deprived of their possessions and deported'. It told of 6,000 Jews abandoned on a desolate island with no food, water or protection from the elements. Attempted help was 'forbidden by the Croat authorities'.[14] The letter pleaded for the Holy See to intervene with the Italian and Croatian governments. There is no record of any such intervention. Indeed, there is no record of a response to the letter.

Marcone, the papal representative, a Benedictine monk and philosophy lecturer, was a diplomatic *ingénue*, good for public appearances such as being photographed with the odious Pavelic, but for little else. Clearly Pacelli had selected a man who could be guaranteed 'not to rock the boat'. If further proof of Pacelli's position were needed, in March 1942 he spoke thus to Nicola Rusinovic, the Croatian diplomat who was Marcone's opposite number: 'Recommend gentleness to your government and government circles, and our relations will work themselves out. As long as you behave correctly, the form of the relations will come of their own accord.'[15] Correct behaviour? Gentleness? Hundreds of thousands of innocent people were being butchered.

By early 1942 the true situation in Croatia was known to anyone in the world who cared to listen to a BBC broadcast. At the Secretariat of State in the Vatican the relevant officials, Maglione, Montini and Tardini, made it clear that they were aware of cries for help from the beleaguered country. Yet their negotiations with the Croatian diplomats followed an unwavering pattern of 'simulated attack, patient listening, generous surrender'.[16]

Meanwhile Pacelli maintained cordial relations with the genocidal regime. In July 1941, he greeted the Zagreb chief of police and 100 members of the Croatian police force. In February 1942, he received a *Ustashe* youth group visiting Rome. In December 1942, he received another such group. In 1943, in conversation with one of the Croatian diplomats, the Pope 'expressed his pleasure at the personal letter he had received from our Poglavnik [Pavelic]'.[17]

In fact, as late as 1943, Pacelli, in the course of speaking about Croatia, could remark quixotically that he was 'disappointed that, in spite of everything, no one wants to acknowledge the one, real and principal enemy of Europe; no true, communal military crusade against Bolshevism has been initiated'.[18] Clearly his Bolshevik *bête noire* was as strong as ever.

Despite Tisserant's blunt concern, there was no condemnation from the Vatican. Confronted with the Croatian genocide, Pacelli simply remained silent – even when Hitler's true intentions about the Church were becoming abundantly clear. Diplomatic representation was maintained with the disgusting Croatian government, and the Holy See was kept well informed as to the true situation in a country which had become a charnel house. The dreadful 'ethnic cleansing' of Croatia was a precursor to Hitler's Final Solution of the extermination of central European Jews. And Pacelli's silence on Croatia was the precursor to a still greater silence.

On 22 June 1941, Germany invaded the USSR. For Pacelli, the prospect of political alignment of the communists with the Allies must have seemed a nightmare scenario. Conversely, the invasion signalled an opportunity for the reunification of the Orthodox Church with Rome. While Nazi propaganda showed freedom of religion apparently being restored, Pacelli resisted Axis pressure to endorse the invasion as a religious crusade. Nevertheless priests were trained in readiness to follow the Nazi invaders, and re-establish Catholicism in the conquered territories.

Any notions of reunification were sharply dismissed, though, by Hitler's belated declarations of hatred toward Christianity. For years, Pacelli had preserved increasingly tenuous relations between the Vatican and the Fascists, believing the communists to be worse enemies. For instance in 1941, on Pacelli's orders, Vatican Radio broadcasts on anti-Catholic activities in Poland and Germany had been suspended. Allied opinion was contrary; for them, the broadcasts were good propaganda. The *Manchester Guardian* had termed Vatican Radio 'tortured Poland's most powerful advocate'.[19] But it was not widely known that in Germany there had been 'martyrs of the air-waves' – Catholics who had been exposed to Nazi retribution for listening to these broadcasts.[20]

In July 1941, Hitler declared: 'Christianity is the hardest blow that ever hit humanity. Bolshevism is the bastard son of Christianity; both are the monstrous issue of the Jews.'[21] In December 1941, he made his intentions unmistakably clear:

> The war will come to an end and I shall see my last task as clearing up the Church problem. Only then will the German nation be completely safe ... In my youth, I had the view: dynamite! Today I see that one cannot break it over one's knee. It has to be cut off like a gangrenous limb.[22]

So by 1942, despite all his measures to preserve working relationships with the odious Fascists, Pacelli had been forced to acknowledge the unpalatable truth:

> Yes, the communist danger does exist *but, at this time, the Nazi danger is more serious.* They want to destroy the Church and crush it like a toad. There will be no place for the Pope in the new Europe. They say that he is going to America. I have no fear and I shall remain here. [Italics added][23]

Chapter 14

The Final Solution

One afternoon in May 1940 Cardinal Tisserant, Pasqualina's arch-enemy, strode past her into the Pope's vacant office, sat down in the papal chair and began to puff away at a huge cigar. The little nun rushed in, furiously berating him: 'Eminence! Remove yourself at once from the Holy Father's place. And put out that cigar this instant!'[1]

Cowed by her fury, Tisserant rose to his feet and stamped out his cigar.

'The papal conclave made a mistake!' he shouted at her. 'What the Holy See needs is a wartime Pope, not a diplomat!'[2]

'Quite the contrary!' Pasqualina snapped. 'What His Holiness needs is loyalty among his hierarchy. Pius certainly does not need cardinals who take the side of their nation before the welfare of the Holy See! You know very well, Eminence, the Holy See must maintain neutrality in war!'[3]

'Neutrality ... perhaps. But how can the Holy Father remain silent when we keep hearing reports day after day of the persecutions of our own clergy and the killings of the Jews? ... You, woman, have a great deal of influence with His Holiness. Tell Pius to stand up as Jesus Christ would stand up! Otherwise, you too are as much at fault as the Pope himself!'[4]

With this parting shot, Tisserant stormed out. Pasqualina stood dazed, staring after him. However disagreeable Tisserant could be, nobody doubted his ability. He knew 13 languages and was fully prepared to speak his mind in all of them. On this occasion, Pasqualina sadly reflected, she could hardly dispute the justice of his argument.

On 13 May 1940, referring to Mussolini's annoyance at the telegrams regarding the invasions of Holland and Belgium, Pacelli stated (according to Cardinal Montini, the Under-Secretary of State):

In certain circumstances, the Pope cannot keep silence. Governments put political and military considerations first ... for the Pope, on the other hand, that consideration [i.e. to speak out] is the first, and it is one that he absolutely cannot ignore. His Holiness said, in this connection, that he had recently had occasion to read the letters of St Catherine of Siena who, writing to the Pope [Gregory XI], warned him that God would subject him to the most severe judgement if he did not react against evil, or fulfil what he believed to be his duty. How could the Pope in the present instance make himself guilty of so serious an omission as to stand by, indifferent, to events of such importance, when the whole world awaits a word from him?[5]

On 11 June 1940, one day after Italy entered the war, Tisserant wrote thus to Archbishop Suhard of Paris:

> Germany and Italy will set about destroying the inhabitants in the occupied areas, as has been done in Poland ... The Fascist and Hitlerite ideology has transformed the consciences of the young ... all those under 35 are ready to commit any crime, granted they can attain the goal set by their leaders ... I'm afraid that history may be obliged in time to come to blame the Holy See for a policy accommodated to its own advantage and little more. And that is extremely sad ... above all, when one has lived under Pius XI.[6]

Similarly, Archbishop Spellman – no friend of Tisserant – wrote to Cardinal Maglione, Secretary of State, sharply criticizing his patron:

> The prestige of the Pope has declined sharply in America, owing to the Pope's unclear pronouncements. On account of pro-Axis statements by the Italian bishops, American Catholics no longer have the same confidence in the Pope's impartiality, because he is behaving first and foremost as an Italian, who probably sympathizes with Mussolini's imperial ambitions.[7]

How ironic that Pacelli would be accused of being both pro-German and pro-Italian. Maglione deemed the letter too offensive to be shown to the pontiff. Months later, Pasqualina discovered it and was shocked. Knowing Spellman as she did, his letter deserved to be taken seriously.

On 10 June 1940, the day of Italy's entrance into the war, Pasqualina went into Pacelli's office, where he was still working, late at night. The pontiff looked weary. He informed her of Mussolini's decision. They spoke of their fears that Rome would be bombed. And Pacelli told her of the mounting criticisms from lay Catholics and Churchmen that the Pope was not speaking out about the Nazi atrocities against the Jews.

'The Holy Father may go down in history as being anti-Semitic', he confessed. 'The Holy See must aid the Jewish people, to the best of our ability. But everything we do must be done with much caution. Otherwise the Church and the Jews themselves will suffer great retaliation.'

Pacelli's eyes moistened. 'Better that the world think of Pius XII as being anti-Semitic than for the Holy See to wear its valour and virtue on its sleeve so that the Nazis can claim more victims.'[8]

> The Jew is the ferment of decomposition in peoples ... The heaviest blow to humanity was the coming of Christianity. Bolshevism is Christianity's illegitimate child. Both are inventions of Jews... Saul became Paul and Mordechai became Marx.[9]

In 1919, Hitler had assured Pacelli that he fought communism '[f]or the love of Almighty God!' Now he venomously asserted: 'The time will come when I'll settle my account with them [the Church].'[10] Communism and Christianity were bundled indiscriminately together, and laid at the door of the Führer's perennial scapegoat.

In Hitler's eyes, virtually everything that was bad was ultimately the fault of the Jews. For instance, Germany's defeat in World War One and its subsequent humiliation were caused 'by lack of insight into the racial problem, especially the failure to recognise the Jewish danger'. In 1939, in a miracle of hypocrisy, Hitler had even managed to blame the Jews for the coming conflict:

> If international finance Jewry, in and outside Europe, should succeed in plunging the peoples of Europe into another world war, then the result will not be the bolshevisation of the world and a victory for world Jewry but the annihilation (*Vernichtun*) of the Jewish race in Europe.[11]

Two years later, Hitler was in a position to carry out his foul promise. His dreadful target was the extermination of the 11 million Jews in Europe.

'I go the way that Providence dictates with the assurance of a sleep-walker.'[12] In July 1941, Hitler told Reinhard Heydrich to make ready for 'a complete solution'. By September 1941, all German Jews had to wear the dehumanizing Yellow Star. The German Catholic bishops asked that the onus to wear the Yellow Star be removed *for Catholic Jews only*. Their request was refused.

In October 1941 the Final Solution began, with the first transportations of Jews to eastern concentration camps, from which they would never return. The same month, it was decreed by the Nazi hierarchy that poison gas was to be the preferred method of extermination. The German bishops wondered whether they should protest, again in favour of *Catholic Jews only*. They decided to remain silent, in order to avoid antagonizing the Nazis.

Pacelli, with his Great Design, had striven for a monolithic Church, with the Pope at the apex of a vast hierarchy of half a billion people. Were the German bishops making a grassroots protest – or were they following the dictate of Pacelli? The answer to this question would have been of scant comfort to the tens of thousands of Jews herded together into cattle wagons.

In November 1941 Goebbels stated, in words of chilling inhumanity: 'No compassion and certainly no sorrow is called for, over the fate of the Jews … Every Jew is our enemy.'[13] Himmler, the head of the SS, told Hoess, the camp commandant of Auschwitz, that 'if it [Hitler's order for a "final solution"] is not carried out, then the Jews will, later on, destroy the German people'.[14]

With Teutonic thoroughness, mass transportation was carried out, until 1944. The dread names of Auschwitz, Dachau, Sobibor and Treblinka have entered history. Six million Jews died. As long as the human race endures, their terrible deaths must never be forgotten.

On 9 February 1942, Hitler declared publicly that 'the Jews will be liquidated for at least a thousand years!'[15] On 18 March, the Vatican was notified of violent Jewish repression in France and Eastern Europe – countries where the Pope had influence. Partisan attacks on the Nazis were punished with savage reprisals. Shortly afterwards, when Reinhard Heydrich, architect of the Final Solution, was assassinated, 1,300 suspects were liquidated, together with all the male inhabitants of Lidice, which was charged with sheltering the assassins.

On 11 June, D'Arcy Osborne wrote:

> It has been made clear to me that H.H. [His Holiness] is in rather bad odour with the F.O. [British Foreign Office], and, I daresay, the British public too. It's a good deal his

own fault, but, on the other hand it isn't, *he being as he is*. I'm sorry about it, but I think there is much to be said on his side. [Italics added][16]

By now the US had entered the war, following the Japanese attack on Pearl Harbour. Harold Tittman, the US representative at the Vatican, begged Cardinal Maglione, Secretary of State, to denounce the slaughter at Lidice. Maglione refused, commenting that Vatican denunciation would merely make matters worse. On 16 June 1942, Tittmann reported that, in his view, the Pope was spending his time on religious concerns, rather than attending to the harsh political realities. Even Osborne acidly remarked that Adolf Hitler 'needed more than the benevolence of the *Pastor Angelicus....*'.[17]

On 25 June 1942 the *Daily Telegraph* carried an article stating: '...more than 700,000 Polish Jews have been slaughtered by the Germans, in one of the greatest massacres in the world's history'.[18] Shmuel Zygilebojm, the originator of the report, was to kill himself afterwards, despairing at what he considered to be the indifference of the Western powers.

On 30 June a second article came out, with the headline: MORE THAN 1,000,000 JEWS KILLED IN EUROPE.[19] On 30 June and 2 July, the *New York Times* reported the carnage. On 21 July a protest rally was held in Madison Square Garden. The Western world was now fully aware of the Nazis' horrible machinations.

On 31 July D'Arcy Osborne, despairing of Pacelli's continuing silence, wrote thus:

> The fact is that the moral authority of the Holy See, which Pius XI and his predecessors had built up into a world power, is now sadly reduced. I suspect that H.H. [His Holiness] hopes to play a great role as peace-maker and that it is partly, at least, for this reason that he tries to preserve a position of neutrality as between the belligerents. But, as you say, the German crimes have nothing to do with neutrality ... and the fact is that the Pope's silence is defeating its own purpose because it is destroying his pro-spects of contributing to peace. Meanwhile he canalises his frustration by being the *Pastor Angelicus*, thereby exhausting himself and sapping his own morale. It is most unfortunate that that Irish monk, Malachi, wasn't it, selected '*Pastor Angelicus*' for the 262nd pope. If he had said '*Leo Furibunds*' [Ferocious Lion] things might have been very different. A film is being made here, for world distribution, to be called '*Pastor Angelicus*'. I cannot say how I deplore this. It is like Hollywood publicity.[20]

In the summer of 1942, the hour-long film *Pastor Angelicus* was made. It began and ended with a statue of the good shepherd, Pacelli/Christ, holding a lamb on his shoulders. The narrative told the story of Pacelli's life, from earliest days to his elevation to the papacy. It showed his daily routine. A sequence of guns firing, and a sequence of a ship sinking, symbolize the war. But for the most part, the film dwells on the timelessness of the papacy and the tranquillity of holiness. The Pope is emblematic of all that is good in the world. And he is ever-vigilant. Late at night he toils in his office, ceaselessly serving the needs of sleeping humanity.

If *Pastor Angelicus* did not dwell on the carnage of war, neither did it dwell on the true situation of the Pope. Certainly, Pacelli rarely stopped working for the greater good of humanity. But his lifestyle had gone from ascetic to unnaturally frugal. The former gourmet, who had once chartered a special train to transport his food, now ate the bare minimum to survive. By the end of the war, the six-foot Pope weighed less than nine stone. Always gaunt, he became skeletal. He refused to have his apartment heated, even in the bitter cold of Rome winters. It was as though he was punishing himself, as though he was a man condemned to eternal torment.

'Holiness, the world believes little of the truth of the Nazi atrocities', Pasqualina told Pacelli in August 1942. 'It remains for you, as Holy Father, to speak out. The people will then be convinced, and they will rise up in righteous indignation.'

'Roosevelt and the British have already spoken out against these alleged war crimes', Pacelli responded. 'Their words have done practically no good.'

'That is because people do not accept such stories, coming from the Allied leaders with vested interests.'

'But even our own clergy in Germany have no real evidence, just hearsay, that these alleged exterminations are taking place', Pacelli persisted.

'Could it be that the clergy, like most people, refuse to believe that such a holocaust could be perpetrated by civilized men?'

'You feel that Roosevelt is telling the truth; that the American president can be trusted?' Pacelli's scepticism was obvious.

'I feel that no politician can be fully trusted', Pasqualina acknowledged 'Holiness, may I suggest that you speak with the president, perhaps through Archbishop Spellman. Demand the truth! If full assurance is given by President Roosevelt that these atrocities are taking place, perhaps Your Holiness should then prepare an encyclical denouncing these horrible war crimes. *If you, as Holy Father, were to reveal the mass extermination of Jews, people all over the world would believe you. Every decent human being on earth would rise up. The sheer force of right over terrible evil would prevail, and the Nazi philosophy would be crumbled in its own disgrace.*' [Italics added][21]

'I told His Excellency [Spellman] that the Holy See would not become a propaganda machine for either side, the Allies or the Axis', Pacelli told Pasqualina.[22] Nevertheless he telephoned Spellman in New York, and asked him to speak with Roosevelt.

'Your Holiness, President Roosevelt has given me every assurance that the vicious Nazi war crimes are entirely true', Spellman informed Pacelli in a return phone call. 'Thousands of Jews are being gassed to death in concentration camps and other thousands are being burned alive in ovens.'[23]

A distraught Pacelli summoned Diego von Bergen, the German ambassador to the Vatican, and denounced the Nazis with a cold fury. Von Bergen heard him out. Then, with silky menace, he replied: 'I shall report your feelings, my dear Holy Father, to the Führer. Do not be too surprised if relations between the Third Reich and the Papacy are broken off.'[24]

'In such an event, there could be but one outcome – the downfall of the state', Pacelli told him with cold finality.[25]

But despite his standoff with von Bergen, Pacelli maintained a public silence. Guenter Lewy comments thus:

> A public denunciation of the mass murders by Pius XII, broadcast widely over the Vatican radio and read from the pulpits by the bishops, would have revealed to Jews and Christians, alike, what deportation to the East entailed. The Pope would have been believed, whereas the broadcasts of the Allies were often shrugged off as war propaganda.[26]

In the event, Pacelli waited until 2 June 1945, when the war was over, before making an unequivocal condemnation of Nazism.

From World War Two until the present day, a war of opinion has raged over whether public denunciation by Pacelli of Nazi atrocities would have been productive or counterproductive. Three instances of grassroots Catholic protest, one in 1936 and two in 1941, indicate that the supposedly omnipotent Nazi Party – and even Hitler himself – were forced to take heed of the feelings of ordinary Germans.

In 1936 a Nazi decree was passed, ordering the removal of crucifixes from schools in Oldenburg, northern Germany. Catholics in the town of Cloppenburg were indignant. The resulting groundswell of protest spread, even among the Nazi Party itself; indeed, members of the Hitler Youth actively supported the protestors. Within a few weeks, the decree was countermanded. Subsequently, when crucifixes, together with Christian prayers and hymns, were banned in Bavaria in 1941, a 'mothers' revolt' threatened to remove children from the schools. Again, the Nazi hierarchy backed down.

In 1940, a euthanasia programme was introduced. Over the following year and a half, some 70,000 Germans were liquidated on the grounds that they were mentally infirm. Many of them were sent to the very gas chambers which were later used to kill the Jews. In February 1941, in Bavaria, the inhabitants of the village of Asberg staged a mass protest against the deportation of these unfortunate people, who were being sent to their deaths. As before, protestors included Nazi Party members. To the horror of the establishment, specific protest broadened into more general anti-Nazi fervour. Police reports noted that 'numerous political jokes and rumours of a character particularly detrimental and hateful to the state, for example vindictive jokes about the Führer, leading personalities, the party, the army, and so forth, were being spread'.[27]

Later in 1941 Bishop Clemens von Galen, who had been involved in the previous protests, delivered three sermons denouncing the euthanasia programme. He pointed out that the spurious notion of 'mercy killing' could be applied, willy nilly, to disabled people, the elderly, the sick, even wounded soldiers, in fact any segment of the population which found disfavour with the Nazis for any reason. Galen's sermons were printed and distributed; at Münster Cathedral, there were silent demonstrations by thousands of protestors.

The Nazi leadership was sharply divided about what action should be taken. Bormann and others argued that Galen should be executed. Goebbels gave the counter-argument that disposing of Galen would result in the inhabitants of

Westphalia ceasing to support the Nazi Party. The final decision on Galen's fate was not for Bormann or Goebbels to make; it was for Hitler, alone. And Hitler decided to let Galen remain unscathed. Although elements of the euthanasia programme continued, great care was taken to keep them out of the public eye.

As far as is known, Bishop Galen's resistance to the Nazis received no backing, either overt or covert, from the Vatican. Indeed, as it flew in the face of prevailing Vatican policy, he may well have encountered resistance from his own side. Certainly his courageous stance showed that the German people could be mobilized to active protest.

After examining these instances of public protest, Guenter Lewy concluded thus:

> That German public opinion and the Church were a force to be reckoned with in principle and could have played a role in the Jewish disaster as well – that is the lesson to be derived from the fate of Hitler's euthanasia programme.[28]

The tragedy is threefold. Pacelli failed to protest directly at Nazi atrocities during the War. Centralized Vatican control – a key part of his Great Design – acted to stifle protest at lower levels. And the elimination of Catholic politics in Germany – another aspect of his Great Design – removed the very mechanisms by which protest might have been amplified.

The actions of Bishop Galen, a brave man, and a lonely voice in the prevailing political wilderness, perhaps indicate what might have been. Nazism may have severely dented the humanity of the German people; but it failed to destroy it.

In the words of another historian, J. P. Stern:

> It seems beyond any doubt, that, if the churches had opposed the killing and the persecution of the Jews, as they opposed the killing of the congenitally insane and the sick, there would have been no Final Solution.[29]

Chapter 15

The War in Rome

The Allies landed in Sicily in July 1943. 'Lucky' Luciano, the imprisoned mobster, commanded the Mafia to give assistance. The tide of the war was turning and a net was starting to close around the Axis powers. On 19 July, despite Roosevelt's blithe assurances to Pacelli, air raid sirens sounded in Rome. The sky was filled with over 500 American bombers targeting the railway terminal. Inevitably some of the bombs went astray; hundreds of innocent civilians died.

At the Vatican, Pacelli and Pasqualina watched the bombers swooping low over St Peter's. Anger flickered in the Pope's eyes at Roosevelt's betrayal. Then, casting such emotions aside, he reached for the telephone and spoke tersely with Monsignor Montini, acting Secretary of State.

'How much cash is there in the Vatican bank?'

'About two million lire, Holiness', Montini told him.

'Draw it out immediately and take the first car you find in Saint Damasco Courtyard. We will join you.'[1]

Pacelli and Pasqualina dashed down the stairs to meet Montini in the courtyard. A huge black bag was stuffed with money. Pacelli pointed at a small car nearby. All three of them jumped into it. 'Go as fast as you can!' Pacelli told Montini.

The little car sped through the streets of Rome. Bombs exploded all around them. Great buildings collapsed into heaps of rubble. 'Faster!' Pacelli shouted, heedless of the danger. 'Faster! Faster!' he yelled, pounding the dashboard impotently with his fist. 'Faster! Faster!'[2]

They screeched to a halt in front of the railway station. The police and military had set up a barricade to prevent further loss of life. The building was engulfed in clouds of smoke. Dozens of trains were on fire. Bombs continued to rain down and explode on all sides. People screamed in agony as they burned to death. Bodies and lumps of flesh were strewn all over the rubble.

'*Il Papa! Il Papa!*' At the sight of Pacelli, a great cry went out. Hundreds of Romans clustered around him, clutching at his cassock in grief-stricken desperation. Pacelli and Montini gave the last rites to dozens of the dying.

All three of them struggled to save everyone they could. When nothing more could be done for the dead and the injured, Pacelli told Montini and Pasqualina to give all the money to those in need. As they began, a distraught mother came up to the Pope and shoved the body of her dead child into his arms. Pacelli stood, holding it tenderly, speaking what words of consolation he could to people who had lost well-nigh everything.

Throughout the night, they toiled. Finally, at dawn, they headed back to the Vatican, exhausted, their robes spattered with blood. Pacelli dictated to Pasqualina a letter for Roosevelt. 'As bishop of this sacred city,' he wrote, 'We have constantly tried to save Our Beloved Rome from devastation. But this reasonable hope has, alas, been frustrated.'[3]

For Pasqualina, such diplomatic blandness was irreconcilable with the atrocities they had just witnessed. But, she sadly reflected, it was Pacelli's way. Did he think he was saving Rome from further harm? If so he was mistaken, for three weeks later, on 13 August, the Allies bombed Rome again.

Returning from the destruction of the second attack, Pacelli summoned Pasqualina and Tisserant. It was as though his anger at the Allies had turned inward, as though his closest colleagues had somehow become the real enemy. 'As long as I remain the Holy Father, the Holy See will never again violate its rule of neutrality', he warned them. 'The scoundrels on both sides in the present war have shown their dishonour. In the future, the Holy Father shall continue to listen to you both, as I have in the past, but I will remain firm, within my own better judgement.'[4]

At the first bombing, it had been Pacelli, not Mussolini, who ministered to the people of Rome. *Il Duce* remained only in name. In truth, Mussolini was tired and prematurely aged. Five days later, on 24 July, he was voted out of office. The Fascist Party was disbanded and a provisional government formed. Marshall Badoglio, the temporary ruler, publicly stated that war would continue, while privately suing for peace.

On the night of 25 July 1943, Pacelli and Pasqualina were at prayer together, when an exuberant Tisserant rushed in. 'Great news, Holiness! The guineas [Italians] have come to their senses at last! The king has put that bastard Mussolini in chains!'[5] Horrified by such language in the presence of the pontiff, Pasqualina furiously slapped him across the face.

Tisserant stumbled back in rage. 'This is what happens when you bring a woman into a man's world!' he roared at Pacelli. 'Well, let me tell you more, Holiness.' He stabbed the air with his finger, first at Pacelli, then Pasqualina. 'Word has been received by the Sacred College that the other son of a bitch, Hitler, is about to retaliate for the taking of that Fascist, Mussolini!' Tisserant drew himself up to his full height and shoved his bearded face up close, against Pacelli. 'Hitler has ordered your capture, my dear Pope. Indeed, if you resist, the Nazis, those stinking slime, have been ordered by *der Führer* to shoot you dead!'[6]

Pacelli and Pasqualina stood horrified. Nobody said anything. Anger and frustration poured out of Tisserant. Suddenly he turned and stormed out, slamming the door behind him.

Typically, Pacelli made no move to increase his personal protection, although a terrified Pasqualina instructed the Swiss Guards to exercise ceaseless vigilance. Word had got back to Hitler that she was forging identity cards to smuggle

Jewish refugees into the Vatican. She always suspected – but could never prove – the existence of a pro-Nazi traitor within the hierarchy.

The Germans invaded Italy on 9 September. Hitler made his intentions abundantly clear: 'I'll go into the Vatican! We'll grab it! Yes, the whole bunch in there! I couldn't care less ... We'll drag them out, the whole swinish pack of them ... We'll have no more attempts by the Church interfering in matters of State ... The time is coming when I'll settle my account with the Pope!'[7]

Shortly afterwards Karl Wolff, commander of the SS and the German police in occupied Italy, flew to Hitler's 'Wolf's Lair' in Prussia. He met with the Führer to discuss the 'occupation of the Vatican and the transfer of Pope Pius XII to Liechtenstein'.[8] Hitler gave Wolff a secret mission to occupy the Vatican and kidnap the Pope, together with the members of the Curia. The Pope would be brought either to Germany or to neutral Liechtenstein. Either way he would be whisked away from the advancing Allies, to deny any political advantage.

Three months later, Wolff had completed a feasibility study for the kidnapping. He met again with Hitler and presented his conclusions. 'Give up the Vatican project', Wolff bluntly advised.[9] The Catholic Church was a huge stabilizing influence in Italy. Invading the Vatican and removing the Pope would most likely inspire a potent backlash. Any Nazi gains would quickly be nullified.

Hitler accepted Wolff's conclusions. The kidnap plan was abandoned. Interestingly, Pacelli's plan to remove Hitler and Hitler's plan to remove Pacelli both came to nothing. Yet again, Hitler dared not attack the Catholic Church directly. *It was as though he could sense a power which Pacelli could not.*

On 12 September, on Hitler's orders, Mussolini was rescued by a crack German commando unit and installed as puppet dictator of Saló, in northern Italy. Imprisonment had made the former *Il Duce* mad for revenge. Hitler encouraged his former accomplice to vent his aggression on the Vatican. Neo-Fascist thugs streamed into Rome, intent on killing the Jews and attacking the papacy. Pasqualina begged Pacelli to take defensive action. Sometimes it was as though the Pope had been dazed by the unrelenting stress of the war and the preceding years of struggle. In Pasqualina's shrewd estimation, Pacelli was also too keen to 'leave everything in the hands of God'.[10]

As the Nazis too advanced upon Rome, Pasqualina implored Pacelli to act. 'We must barricade the Jews in St Peter's.'

'Go and tell the Swiss Guards of my orders to seal the basilica!' Pacelli affirmed. 'But first, see that all Jews within the Vatican take sanctuary there.'

'And you, Holiness? Where will you remain?' Pasqualina asked, her voice breaking with fear that he would be killed.

'The Holy Father shall stay here, in the palace!' Pacelli replied. 'Let us see if any man, Hitler and Mussolini included, dares to attack the Pope, the symbol of Jesus Christ on Earth!'[11]

Despite her dread, Pasqualina felt a spurt of pride. Pacelli's outward physical courage had never been in doubt.

'We were not intimidated then by pistols pointed at us and we will be even less frightened this time', the Pope gently chided her, as both of them inevitably remembered the Bolshevik outrage at Munich, back in 1919.

'Holiness, with your permission, I will remain here with you!'

'You do not have my permission!' the Pope ordered her. 'Go! Take sanctuary in the palace's cellars.'

'No, Holiness!' Pasqualina refused. 'After the Jews are safely sealed in the basilica, I will return here. With or without your permission! My place always is at your side!'

Pacelli shook his head in surrender. 'Hurry back, Mother Pasqualina!' he gently whispered, sinking to his knees in prayer.[12]

When he rose from meditation, Pacelli stationed the Swiss Guard along the 'border' – a broad white line painted across the pavement, separating the Vatican from Rome. The Fascists steadily drew nearer. Just in time the German field marshal, Albert Koshering, realizing that a public relations disaster was imminent, ordered his troops to hold fire and respect Vatican neutrality.

Although disaster had been narrowly averted, the situation remained serious. Koshering proclaimed a state of martial law; serious infringement was punishable by death. Telephone calls were monitored. Private correspondence was prohibited. The Italian Fascist police were augmented by the yet more sinister German secret police. Rome was put under surveillance. Special heed was given to Vatican City.

At his election four years previously, Pacelli had known that the new Pope would have to face immense ordeals. Now he found himself personally responsible for the fate of both the Vatican City and Rome, together with the entire Catholic Church. The barbarians were at this gate. As with so many of his predecessors, his greatest weapon was moral authority.

In 1943 there were about 7,000 Jews in Rome. The Italian capital had held a Jewish population for more than 2,000 years. Apart from brief periods of relative humanity, these two millennia had been times of savage repression. The Nazis' Yellow Star had its horrible antecedents in the compulsory yellow badges formerly meted out to the inhabitants of the ghetto. In all of this time, the Jews of Rome had kept their faith and observed their religious practices.

With the arrival of the German troops, Ugo Foa, president of the Jewish community, advised calmness and normality. Conversely, Israel Zolli, the chief rabbi, feared genocide and urged Jews to flee Rome. He was over-ruled by Foa. With terrible irony, Zolli's opinion was shared by Baron von Weizsäcker, German ambassador to the Holy See. Von Weizsäcker had been second-in-command to Ribbentrop in the German Foreign Ministry. His presence in Rome indicated the importance that Hitler gave to dealing with the Vatican.

Keen to avoid conflict, von Weizsäcker told Pacelli that the Nazis would honour the Vatican as an independent state. The *quid pro quo* was that the Vatican would co-operate. To date, Pacelli had, by and large, remained silent about Nazi atrocities in occupied countries. Now Rome itself was part of an occupied country.

Von Weizsäcker's greatest fear was reserved not for Pacelli but for the SS, who would soon be bent on their dread task of rounding up Jews. Should this happen beneath the windows of the Vatican, the seasoned career officer knew that he would be facing a diplomatic crisis.

On most evenings, Pacelli and Pasqualina strolled through the rose-scented papal gardens. It was virtually the only respite the pontiff had from a life of toil that often lasted from early morning until well past midnight.

'Holiness, if you cannot bring yourself to denounce Hitler, then the least the papacy can do is lend its full support to the Jewish people whom the Nazis are persecuting ... Holiness, we can provide sanctuary within the Vatican for thousands of Jews escaping Nazi Germany', Pasqualina insisted.[13]

Pacelli ruminated over her words, before finally saying what she yearned to hear.

'Dear Sister Pasqualina, Our Holy Saviour speaks through your mind and heart. You have moved the Holy Father at last!' Pacelli raised his hand and blessed her.[14]

Thus was formed the bland-sounding Pontifical Relief Committee, in reality the greatest aid programme in the history of the Church. A meeting was convened with the German army commander, Kesselring, Pacelli, Pasqualina and Tisserant. In return for Pacelli's issuing a statement in L'Osservatore Romano that Vatican territory was being respected, Kesselring agreed to Pasqualina's idea of having identity cards issued for visitors to the Vatican.

Kesselring had been surprisingly amenable. By contrast, the College of Cardinals was aghast when Pacelli put Pasqualina in charge of the Pontifical Relief Committee. Although the initiative had been her inspiration and she had had extensive experience in Munich following World War One, such considerations mattered little. A nun chairing a committee of prelates? 'No!' shouted the fiery Tisserant. 'Has His Holiness gone mad?'[15]

Faced with rebellion from within, Pacelli procrastinated. Typically, Pasqualina took matters into her own hands, as she had done on so many occasions before. In a cellar of the Vatican, she started to process pleas for help from the beleaguered Jews of Nazi-occupied territory. When an angry Tisserant found her hard at work late one night, the tiny nun was so worn out that she pointed to a dead rat in a corner of the cellar. 'If you don't leave me alone, I'll throw it at you!' she shouted.[16] Wisely, Tisserant retreated.

Soon Pasqualina had issued hundreds of forged identity cards. Often she would stand with Pacelli at the Vatican windows, anxiously watching Jewish refugees present these cards to Nazi border police in order to gain refuge in the Vatican. During the remainder of the war, thousands of Jews crossed that painted line between Nazi-occupied Rome and the sanctity of the Vatican. At least 15,000 refugees were accommodated at Castel Gandolfo, which Kesselring had also agreed to protect.

Pasqualina's Pontifical Relief Committee distributed food, clothing, medicine and money to the needy. Some 7,000 dollars a day was spent on food alone. Catholics from all over the world were asked to donate cash, which was smuggled in. Those attending papal audiences brought food. Pasqualina ran a highly complex logistical operation, which would have taxed the abilities of a corporate chief executive. And she ran it knowing that the Nazis suspected her, and that their spies were everywhere. A charm offensive toward the sympathetic von Weizsäcker kept the Vatican railway bringing in much-needed food and supplies. Refugees were spirited out of Rome in trucks allegedly used for food delivery. The fortunate ones reached neutral countries such as Switzerland and Spain. Meanwhile, back in the Vatican, Pasqualina hid hundreds of Jews in the cellars. In secret tunnels, by dead of night, she moved fugitives whom the Nazis would dearly have loved to lay their hands upon.

And yet Pasqualina's desperate efforts were not enough to save the Jews of Rome.

In the second week of the German occupation, SS Major Herbert Kappler, a subordinate of Himmler, was told to deport the Jews. He went to Foa and told him: 'It is your gold we want in order to provide new arms for our country. Within 36 hours you will have to pay 50 kilograms of gold.'[17]

At 11 a.m. on 27 September 1943, the gold collection began in the synagogue. For the first few hours, donations were sporadic. It was suggested that the Pope might be approached for help. Meanwhile, a stream of Roman citizens started to come forward, bringing family heirlooms such as jewellery and medals to be sold for gold. Their donations were not loans: they were gifts.

At 4 p.m. word came back from the Vatican. A loan had been authorized. The priest bringing the news stated quite categorically that the money was a loan, not a gift. 'It is obvious we want it back.'[18] There was no interest payable; and there was no repayment period.

In the end, the Jewish leaders reached their target without the need of Vatican help. The gold ransom was delivered in full and on time. With mortal insult the Nazis weighed it twice, accusing the Jews of cheating.

No receipt for the extorted fortune was tendered. Kappler's chilling message to the Jews read thus: 'To the enemy, who is being relieved of his arms, one does not give receipts.'[19] The gold went to Berlin and sat uselessly in cardboard boxes on a ministry office floor for the duration of the war. The Jews of Rome had paid their gold ransom – to a deadly enemy who had no earthly intention of keeping their promise.

At 5.30 a.m. on Saturday 16 October, the SS entered the ghetto of Rome. Using a previously prepared list they went from house to house, ripping out wires so that the alarm could not be passed by telephone. A document was handed to the head of the house, stating what each family could bring. Apart from personal effects such as jewellery and money, items such as clothing, bedding and 'food for eight days' were allowed.[20]

A brave lady, Principessa Anza Pignatelli-Aragona, was alerted by a telephone call from a friend, who had seen the Nazi trucks in the streets. She went straight to the Vatican and was brought to Pacelli, at prayer in his private chapel. Pacelli instantly telephoned Maglione and told him to contact von Weizsäcker.[21] Even as they spoke, the first trucks filled with terrified Jews were passing through Rome. In the words of one onlooker, 'The eyes of the children were dilated and unseeing. It seemed as if they were asking for an explanation for such terror and suffering.'[22] Another onlooker remembered 'the maddening fear that had overtaken them'.[23]

For over two decades, Hitler had studiously avoided direct confrontation with the Catholic Church. Quite obviously, he felt that the Church was too powerful to attack outright. Now the war had come to Rome. The Jews were being taken, within sight of the Vatican. The Pope was absolute ruler of the enemy which Hitler so feared.

Pacelli told Maglione, his secretary of state, to send for von Weizsäcker. The German diplomat was shaken to the core. In his shame, he said to Maglione: 'I am waiting for you to ask me why I remain where I am.'[24] In von Weizsäcker's words, 'pressure from all sides was building, calling for a demonstrative [papal] censure of the deportation of the Jews of Rome'.[25] With supreme irony, a great deal of the pressure was coming from the Germans themselves. Albrecht von Kessel, the German consul in Rome, urged the Pope to make 'an official pro-test'.[26] The German military and diplomatic elite feared that deportation of the Jews would spark riots and insurrection from the Romans.

Maglione asked von Weizsäcker to intervene. Conversely, von Weizsäcker asked for the only possible intervention with any chance of success – a papal protest. Maglione was noncommittal. Von Weizsäcker asked, 'What will the Holy See do if these things continue?'[27]

Maglione replied, 'The Holy See would not wish to be put in a situation where it was necessary to utter a word of disapproval.' Further on in the conversation, Maglione said:

> I wanted to remind him that the Holy See had shown, as he himself had acknowledged, the greatest prudence in not giving the German people the least impression of having done or wished to do, the least thing against the interest of Germany during this terrible war.[28]

To the amazement of the Germans, no papal protest was made. In the end, the Germans themselves composed two letters for Berlin, one supposedly from the German bishop, Alois Hudal, the other from von Weizsäcker himself, warning that 'the friendly relations between the Curia and ourselves [the Germans]' were being put in jeopardy.[29]

At Nuremberg, von Weizsäcker had this to say:

> Hitler's persecution of the Jews was considered by me from its very inception to be a violation of all the rules and laws of Christianity ... It is a matter of course that I would have chosen any way to help the Jews.[30]

On Sunday 17 October, news of the outrage broke in the world press. The following day more than 1,000 Jews were taken to the railway station, put in cattle trucks and deported. As the train journeyed through Italy, the Vatican was informed of its progress. Lack of sanitation, together with hunger, thirst and cold, soon reduced the occupants to a pitiful condition. The Bishop of Padua pleaded for papal action; none was taken.

139

Back in Rome, both Pacelli and the Germans were more concerned with a communist-inspired uprising. Pacelli wanted increased policing on the streets. When Osborne visited Pacelli, he was told that there was no complaint to be made against the German military and police presence. Vatican neutrality had been observed. In his despatches to England, Osborne noted dryly that it was the opinion of 'a number of people that *[Pacelli] underestimated his own moral authority and the reluctant respect in which he was held by the Nazis*, because of the Catholic population of Germany'. [Italics added][31]

Within a week of the deportation, more than 1,000 Jews had been murdered at Auschwitz and Birkenau. Nearly 200 Jews – 149 men and 47 women – were kept alive as slave labour. Only 14 men and one woman survived. Settimia Spizzichino, the single woman, a former guinea pig of the evil Doctor Mengele, was found lying under a pile of corpses when the Allies liberated Bergen-Belsen.

In 1995, 50 years later, Settimia Spizzichino had this to say in a BBC interview:

> I came back from Auschwitz on my own. I lost my mother, two sisters, a niece, and one brother. Pius XII could have warned us about what was going to happen. We might have escaped from Rome and joined the partisans. He played right into the Germans' hands. It all happened right under his nose. But he was an anti-Semite Pope, a pro-German Pope. He didn't take a single risk. And, when they say the Pope is like Jesus Christ, it is not true. He did not save a single child. Nothing.[32]

Pacelli, Pasqualina and their helpers sheltered legions of refugees in the Vatican and at Castel Gandolfo. But when the Jews of Rome had a great and terrible need of the Pope, the *Pastor Angelicus* did not help them.

Von Weizsäcker's Nuremberg assertion that, for him, Jewish persecution was 'a violation of all the rules and laws of Christianity' sits oddly with a traumatic meeting which he had with Pacelli in 1943. By courtesy of an intermediary named Kurt Gerstein, Pacelli had received an unequivocal report of death marches, mass shootings and gassings. Jewish bodies had been made into soap. Lampshades had been made from Jewish skin and inscribed with Gothic characters and the dreaded swastika. Pacelli confronted von Weizsäcker: 'We must state that We wish the German people and their Leader all God's blessings, *but if such is true and if it continues, We will be forced to speak*' [Italics added]. Von Weizsäcker replied, 'The German people, led by their Führer, are fighting for their historic destiny and the Christian heritage of Europe against the twin enemies of Bolshevism and international Jewry. Nothing must be done to affect our unity, because nothing can break it. One People. One Leader. One Fatherland. *Ein Volk. Ein Führer. Ein Vaterland.*'

'*Ein Volk, Ein Führer, Ein Vaterland...*' Von Weizsäcker's conversation to Pacelli was interspersed with this sinister rant, repeated as spurious justification. For weeks afterwards Pacelli's sleep was tormented by a recurring nightmare, where lines of Gothic script entwined themselves around him like evil serpents. Caught in their suffocating embrace, he could neither breathe nor think lucidly. '*Ein Volk, Ein Führer, Ein Vaterland ... Ein Volk, Ein Führer, Ein Vaterland ...*'

It was as though he had written this farrago of nonsense himself, and yet ... It was running all over his body, up his side, across his shoulder. In the cold grey of dawn he would start awake, muttering: 'It's all over my body, it's at my throat.'

It is difficult to know whether this recurring nightmare was worse than his other periodic nocturnal agony, relating to his traumatic encounter in the Munich nunciature. Both were horrendous, occurring regularly and becoming, if possible, even more vivid and terrible in the last years of his life. Pacelli's non-response at the time to the revelation of Nazi atrocities plagued him with guilt ever afterwards.

Throughout the autumn of 1943 the Vatican, formerly remote, seemed caught in the vortex of war. On 14 August, the day after the second bombing, Rome was declared an open city. Yet several weeks later it was bombed again; this time, Vatican City was specifically targeted. 'We never found out which side it was, the Allies or the Axis, that sent the bombers', Pasqualina reflected many years later. 'But we had our suspicions. Twice deceived in the past, how could we have further confidence in anybody?'[33]

Mussolini's rescue had revived the spectre of Italian Fascism. Bands of thugs were descending on Rome. There was a constant threat of communist insurrection. The German occupiers were understandably nervous. In short, there was extreme pressure for Pacelli to flee Rome for a neutral country.

On 9 February 1944, the Pope summoned the Roman cardinals to a meeting in the Sistine chapel. Five years previously the prelates had sworn oaths of fealty in the same place. Pacelli absolved them from those oaths: 'We release you from any obligation to follow our fate. Each one of you is free to do what you think best.' Pacelli made it quite clear that he would remain as bishop of Rome. 'If anything should happen to the Holy Father, if the Holy Father is imprisoned or killed, you must gather together wherever you can and elect a new Pope.'[34]

Pasqualina watched from the back of the chapel. Overcome by emotion the cardinals, one by one, refused to leave their master. Instead they pledged their faith anew. Tisserant was among the first to come forward. For once, all the cynicism was gone from his face. Pacelli's words had moved him in a way that Pasqualina could never have imagined.

Despite Allied assurances, Rome was attacked repeatedly in the following weeks. American bombs rained upon the Vatican and Castel Gandolfo, where 15,000 refugees were sheltering. More than 500 people were killed; many of them were Jews. The buildings of Castel Gandolfo itself were almost destroyed. American explosives amounting to 576 tons were dropped on the famous abbey of Monte Casino, reducing it to rubble. Again, many refugees were senselessly killed.

March 12 was the fifth anniversary of the Pope's coronation. For the first time since the German occupation, Pacelli made a public appearance. A crowd of 300,000 listened to him attack both the Allies and the Axis powers for their breached promises and their attacks on the city: 'How can we believe that anyone would dare to turn Rome, *this noble city, which belongs to all times and all places*, into a field of battle and thus perpetrate an act as inglorious militarily as it is abominable in the eyes of God?' Pacelli demanded [Italics added].[35]

On 4 June 1944, Rome was finally liberated. Pasqualina 'felt enormous relief. I had sympathised with His Holiness throughout, in maintaining the Holy See's historic position of neutrality in warfare. But, in my daily prayers to Jesus, I begged Our Lord that Hitler and Mussolini be defeated. I told His Holiness of my prayers and hope early in the war. *Every day thereafter, the Holy Father prayed along with me for the same intentions*' [Italics added].[36]

One night in July Pasqualina received a secret visitor, Claretta Petacci, the daughter of Achille Ratti's doctor and the mistress of Mussolini. She wanted the Pope to act as an intermediary with the Allies. Mussolini was prepared to repudiate the Nazis.

Pacelli was furious when Pasqualina told him of her meeting with Claretta. 'You spoke alone with that woman, without my knowledge and permission!' he shouted.

'Holiness, how do you know the truth of such scandal?'

'Ask anyone in the Vatican. Ask those among the hierarchy!'

'And what do you suppose they whisper about us, Holiness? I have been living under your roof since I was a young girl. We know that, in God's eyes, our lives are pure. Yet who, even among the Sacred College of Cardinals, believes the truth about us? Why, then, Holiness, are you so quick to judge others?'

Pacelli was dumbfounded. Pasqualina took his hand and kissed it.

'Holiness, let us hope and pray that we are not the only decent people alive. Even though you are Pope and I a nun, we are not the best of humans, nor the worst, either.'[37]

As she had done so many times before, Pasqualina managed to calm Pacelli down. At first he wanted nothing to do with Mussolini. Finally he relented. Mussolini was to tender his peace plan to the Archbishop of Milan. From there, it went to Pasqualina.

'Holiness, I suggest you forward the proposal to Allied headquarters. It will help greatly to shorten the war and save many lives.'[38]

Accordingly Pacelli sent the plan to Eisenhower with a covering letter, written personally, urging its acceptance. But the US president curtly turned it down. By then, as in World War One, the Allies wanted peace on their terms. If that meant further loss of life – particularly in the concentration camps – so be it.

Pasqualina had the sad task of telephoning Claretta to tell her of Eisenhower's refusal. On 25 April a stricken Claretta wrote to the Bavarian nun: 'I am following my destiny. I don't know what will become of me, but I cannot question my fate.'[39]

By the time Pasqualina received the letter, she knew that Claretta and Mussolini had been killed by anti-Fascists. Barbarically, their bodies were hung up by their heels, in the Piazza Loreto in Milan. 'A lesson for all who would persecute the human race to see and learn by,' Tisserant gloated.[40]

Shortly afterwards, Hitler killed himself in his bunker in Berlin. On 7 May 1945, the war in Europe was over. On 2 September 1945, with the Japanese surrender, World War Two finally ended. After six years, the seemingly invincible Nazis and Japanese had been defeated. Millions upon millions of people had died to preserve the greatest prize of all – civilization itself.

Chapter 16

An Uneasy Peace

For Pacelli, the end of World War Two meant exchanging one set of problems for another. Rome was a divided city – erstwhile collaborator versus resister, communist versus Fascist. Rabbi Zolli was denounced by his own people. The fugitives leaving the Vatican were replaced by fugitives from the Allies. Europe was in turmoil. The demands on Pacelli and Pasqualina's relief programme intensified. The Vatican Information Service had expanded into a bewildering variety of sub-sections: missing persons, prisoners, refugees, deportees, orphans, sick people. . . As many as 1,800 letters a day poured into the Vatican, imploring help. Vatican Radio sent up to 27,000 messages a month, to dozens of countries. The logistics of getting food, clothing and medicine to where they were desperately needed seemed never-ending. Preventing further loss of life became a key priority. Another priority was giving protection to the former victors of Europe, now the vanquished. The endings of wars are always a time where grudges are repaid viciously, and the Vatican found itself in the unenviable position of defending erstwhile persecutors against bloody revenge. All these efforts amounted to an enormously impressive feat of Christian charity.

Although Pacelli was widely acclaimed as a moral symbol of victory, and the various Allied leaders flocked to have their photographs taken with him, he was not consulted on the planning of the new Europe and his attempts as a peacekeeper were brusquely ignored. The relationship between Pacelli and Roosevelt had deteriorated sharply when the latter's perfidy had been exposed by the bombings of Rome. *L'Osservatore Romano* criticized the Grand Alliance of Yalta on the grounds that:

> It would mean a return to the distinction between great and small, strong and weak, rich and poor, victors and vanquished, thus classified in perpetuity, according to the systems of the Holy Alliances and Leagues of Nations based on these fatal discriminations.[1]

Although such criticism undoubtedly masked Pacelli's anti-Soviet propaganda, viewed 60 years later it appears fair comment.

With Roosevelt's death and the increasing inroads of communism, the Holy See's criticism intensified. In its 1945 declaration *Between War and Peace* the United States episcopate stated:

> We must face the facts. There are profound divergences of thought and political aims between Russia and the Western democracies; Russia has acted unilaterally in many

important decisions ... There is a clash of ideologies. Frank recognition of these divergences must precede any sincere effort for realistic world co-operation for peace.[2]

Using the American Bishops – or even *L'Osservatore Romano* – to express his position by proxy ensured that Pacelli could retain his role of superordinate peacekeeper, above national or international politics. In his *Pacifying Impartiality* Christmas message of 1947, he stated:

> Our position between the two opposing camps is exempt from any prejudice, from any preference for this or that people, for this or that bloc of nations, as it is foreign to any sort of temporal consideration. *To be with Christ or against Christ: that is the whole question.* [Italics added][3]

However, such seeming equivocation only served to mask a more trenchant attack on communism. In the same message, Pacelli decried as

> a deserter and traitor anyone who lends his material support, his services, his talents, aid or vote to parties and to forces that deny God, that put might in place of right, and threats and terror in place of liberty, that make lying, opposition, and incitement of the masses to revolt so many weapons of their policy, thus rendering national and international peace impossible.[4]

In the late 1940s Pacelli's barbs against communism became ever sharper. Even after Stalin's death in 1953, he still continued to resist *détente* with the USSR. His great fear was that Italy – and, indeed, Europe – would succumb to Russian-inspired communism. The alternative seemed to be American-inspired capitalism. Pacelli strove for a third way: a Spanish model of Church aligned with state, a *civitas christiana*. It is no coincidence that his latter concordats were all with Fascist and, indeed, totalitarian regimes: Salazar's Portugal (1940), Franco's Spain (1953) and Trujillo's Dominican Republic (1954).

For Pacelli, democracy was vulnerable both to mindless materialism (which has happened), or socialism – and thus communism by the back door. Yugoslavia, with its 'benevolent' communism, was just across the Adriatic close to Albania, whose communism was the very reverse of benevolent. Pacelli feared a communist takeover of Italy and the extinction of the Church. It is important to stress that such a view was by no means unreasonable at the time. In the late 1940s and early 1950s, many Europeans were nervously anticipating another world war with Russia – one where atomic weapons would almost certainly be used. The Cold War was intensifying. The USSR was committed to a programme of world-wide destabilization. The enforced partition of Germany created a police state of sickening viciousness.

Pacelli called the 1948 Italian election, between Christian Democrats and communists/socialists, a battle for Christian civilization. With a total absence of his former neutrality toward Fascism, he poured 100 million lire into anti-communist measures. He told Catholics that it was their 'civic duty' to vote. The slogan was 'Rome or Moscow'.[5] Tisserant stated that neither communists nor socialists could receive the sacraments or Christian burial. Mass violence, even civil war, was feared. Pacelli declared: 'My post is in Rome and, if it be the will of the Divine Master, I am ready to be martyred for Him in Rome.'[6]

As it happened, the Christian Democrats won convincingly. But the communists were far from finished. They called a general strike. The US poured money into Italy to combat the menace. If Italy fell to communism, the prospects for all Europe were bleak. *Civiltà Cattolica* suggested that the Communist Party should be banned. Pacelli riposted: 'To take such action would encourage a revolution and would be inconceivable in the light of democratic procedures.'[7] Nevertheless, he issued a decree which stated that it was not lawful for Catholics to be members of the Communist Party. The message was clear: one could be a Catholic or a communist – not both. The battle lines were starkly drawn.

Although democracy prevailed in Italy, the formerly Catholic countries of Poland, Hungary and Czechoslovakia were now well-nigh lost to communism. Bishop Mindszenty of Hungary had been imprisoned for his resistance to the Nazis. Pacelli brought him to Rome and made him a cardinal. Both men knew what the outcome would be. 'You will be the first to suffer the martyrdom whose symbol this red colour is', Pacelli told him.[8] In late 1948 Mindszenty was arrested on trumped-up charges and made to endure the indignity of a show trial, before being condemned to life imprisonment. The Western world was shocked.

Pacelli roundly condemned the proceedings. For him, no deals could be struck with communism, there was no appurtenance of neutrality. In the event Mindszenty spent seven years in prison, followed by 15 years of what amounted to house arrest.

The Church was threatened by communism from without; it was simultaneously threatened by corruption from within. One night in the late 1940s, a letter was pushed under Pasqualina's office door. It claimed that Church clergy in Sicily were working with the Mafia to subvert law and order. Even the sacred trust of the confessional was allegedly being used to garner information for criminal use.

It was well known that Pasqualina, the *virgo potens* (powerful virgin) of the Vatican, was the most effective conduit to Pacelli; she also acted as gatekeeper for the incessant demands aimed at him. At first she said nothing about the allegations. But as time passed, more and more information came her way. Finally, in January 1947, she told Pacelli. At first he fobbed it off: 'Mother Pasqualina! How could one as brilliant as you be so easily taken in? Do you really believe that our dear, devoted clergy would take to sin and crime?' Then his psychological denial hardened. 'I am tired', he told her brusquely. 'I am going to get some rest.'[9]

When Pacelli had had time to get over his initial denial, he summoned Cardinal Ruffini of Sicily to a papal audience. Formerly, Ruffini had been the Cardinal most favoured by Pacelli. Accustomed as she was to the power politics of the Curia, this time even Pasqualina felt that she was getting out of her depth. She went to the only person she knew who would have the answers – her mortal enemy, Tisserant.

Tisserant's judgement was damning:

147

Ruffini is a powerful man in Sicily. Even Vizzini, who runs the Mafia there, bows to him. Vizzini not only kisses the ring of the Archbishop of Palermo, but he kisses his ass as well. Pius is afraid to take action. Afraid that any stand the papacy might take would lead to widespread governmental investigations and prosecutions. With our clergy involved, the publicity alone could wreck the Church. Besides, Ruffini is too powerful for Pius to tackle.[10]

Tisserant burst into cynical laughter at this linkage of the Church and the Mafia. 'How do you suppose Pius's hypocritical papacy can wriggle out of this dilemma, dear Mother Pasqualina?' he taunted, thrusting his bearded face up against hers.[11]

After Ruffini had been to the Vatican, Pasqualina ventured to ask Pacelli if they had discussed the situation. 'It is none of your business!' he snapped. 'Tend to your own affairs and whatever work remains to be done!'[12]

To Pasqualina, Pacelli was making exactly the same mistake that he had made in World War Two, when he failed to face up to the Nazis. If he failed to face up to the Mafia links, she feared that the Church would be damaged irrevocably in the eyes of the world.

Shortly afterwards a septuagenarian native of Sicily, a Signore Cannada, came to the Vatican to attempt an audience with the Pope. He told Pasqualina a horrifying tale. Not only was the Church aligned with the Mafia in Sicily, but for decades Franciscan friars had been terrorizing the countryside. Shockingly, Cannada swore that he had actually seen a priest cut off the head of his own abbot on a refectory table. At his wit's end, he begged for a papal investigation. When Pasqualina told Pacelli, the pontiff regarded Cannada's story as ludicrous. But four days after Cannada returned to Sicily, he was murdered.

'Holiness, how can you justify your place as Holy Father when people cry out for help, and you do nothing?' Pasqualina furiously exploded. 'When are you going to rid yourself of your *appeasement mentality* and stand strong and brave for what is right?' [Italics added][13]

Pacelli recalled Ruffini to Rome once again and, in the presence of Pasqualina, quizzed him on the alleged crimes of the Franciscans. Ruffini pointed out the number of Franciscans in the Church. The implied threat was clear: they were too strong for even a pope to attack. But this time, Pacelli was undeterred. 'If there are further crimes in your diocese and any of our clergy are accused, I will hold you, Ruffini, personally responsible!'[14]

As Ruffini came out of the Pope's office, Pasqualina, the perennial eavesdropper, rushed in. 'Holiness, I am so very proud of you!'[15]

'I should have acted sooner in this instance', Pacelli gravely replied. It was clear that Cannada's murder preyed on his conscience.

'Only a great Pontiff has the strength to admit his mistakes', Pasqualina told him.

'A true Pontiff of Christ rectifies his past mistakes', Pacelli told her. 'He does so by taking affirmative action in the future.'[16]

Subsequently, Pasqualina herself went to Sicily to investigate. At that time, Ruffini's home town of Palermo was the murder capital of the world, with 50 people killed in 50 days. Vast quantities of heroin were being brought in from the Middle East, *en route* to the US and other countries. Tales of Franciscan crimes were legion. In the words of an honest and brave man, Signore Di Stefano, the police chief of Mazzarino:

> The Franciscans were clever operators. They were the shrewdest of businessmen, and many carried loaded guns; some even had sub-machine guns for protection. Their interests ranged from loan sharking to pornography. Their personal wealth was enormous. Even though they had taken vows of poverty, most of the priests and monks had millions of lire stashed in various banks throughout Italy.[17]

Pasqualina continued working with the Sicilian police to gather evidence. Yet when it looked as though the Franciscans would finally be brought to trial Pacelli, typically, became frightened by the power of adverse world opinion of the Church. Despite Pasqualina's persistent entreaties, the Pope strove to delay prosecutions.

As Archbishop Cushing of the US noted sadly of Pacelli's stance toward Pasqualina:

> Her hands were tied in many ways. Even though Pasqualina was very close to the Pope for most of her life, she was still looked upon as a mere nun at times, even by Pius himself. On any issue as explosive as the Franciscan crimes in Sicily, church clergy maintain an inbred, prejudiced mentality, which is entirely convinced that the male mind is right, in the final analysis, and must never yield to female pressure. Pius was certainly a Pope with that kind of intellect.[18]

Cushing also viewed his former mentor, Cardinal Spellman, as instrumental in blocking prosecution of the Franciscans. 'Spellman saw the Catholic mind, especially in the US, as exceedingly fragile in matters of faith', Cushing commented.[19] Doubtless Spellman had an eye on the rich donations of wealthy Americans, who would be scandalized by public revelations of the Franciscans' shocking crimes. And, as we have seen previously, Spellman had his own links with the Mafia.

Throughout Pacelli's papacy, the Franciscans continued to evade prosecution. During the papacy of Pope John XXIII, they were finally brought to trial – and found innocent. A year later, in 1963, a further court hearing overturned the verdict and the Franciscans received 13 years apiece in prison. Pasqualina had waited 17 years for justice; the downtrodden Sicilians had waited even longer.

Looking back on the whole distressing episode, many years later, Pasqualina had the following comments to make. They are most revealing in casting light on Pacelli's tortured ratiocinations:

> At times, Holiness would be fully dedicated to a cause, as he first was in his desire to end crime by the clergy in Sicily. *Frequently, he would then procrastinate; he would dwell upon the harm that might result from some bold stand on his part. Sadly, he would often alter his whole course of action.* Pius was a holy man but unfortunately, like so many of us, he, too, was misguided on occasion. [Italics added][20]

Chapter 17

The Great Design

In 1944, Cardinal Maglione died. After his burial, Pacelli mentioned to Pasqualina that he had a shortlist for the vacant position of Secretary of State. Pasqualina shook her head. 'Holiness,' she said, 'you spend so much time convincing others, far less astute than yourself, to do your bidding. Why not simply be your own secretary of state?'[1]

Henceforth, the two most powerful positions in the Catholic Church were concentrated in one man. Pacelli's Great Design, his vision of a monolithic Church with absolute power concentrated at the apex, was coming to fruition. Pasqualina successfully nominated Pacelli's two nephews, the Princes Carlo and Giulio Pacelli, to a 'kitchen sink' cabinet.

Their financial expertise was put to use in the rapidly expanding Vatican Bank. Pacelli's inner circle included another nephew, Prince Marcantonio Pacelli, and papal Count Enrico Galeazzi, the Vatican's architect and Spellman's close friend and mentor.

Pasqualina shielded Pacelli from those she deemed 'unnecessary wasters of the Holy Father's valuable time'.[2] Unfortunately this included many of his cardinals. Even Tisserant, the Dean of Cardinals, was kept waiting for up to two months for an audience with Pacelli. Naturally this increased the Frenchman's loathing for the stony-faced Bavarian nun. At times her Vatican nickname, 'the German General', seemed well earned.

To add insult to injury, Pasqualina would freely allow members of the public audiences with Pacelli – but only if they passed muster with her. She was particularly partial to movie stars. Once, during the war, she had kept Bishop Roncalli, the future Pope John XXIII, waiting for nearly two hours while Clark Gable spent time with the pontiff.

Pasqualina's policy of protecting Pacelli had several unhelpful consequences. The diocesan bishops, ignored by the Pope and humiliated by the Curia, were thoroughly demotivated. More adroit figures in the Curia were free to play their political games. Once Monsignor Tardini, Pro-Secretary of State, confided his frustration to Cardinal Ottaviani, the Head of the Curia. At first, the wise Ottaviani exhorted Tardini to obedience: 'We are old soldiers, my dear compatriot, who must serve the Church blindly.' Tardini shook his head in dismay, whereupon Ottaviani put his arm around his shoulder, in avuncular fashion. 'Popes pass but the Curia lives on.'[3]

The simplest way of negating Pacelli's will was for the Curia to operate with bureaucratic, maddening slowness. Thus Pacelli's autocratic management style became self-defeating. However, the collective antagonism, although hidden from the public, was leaving a bitter legacy within the Church. On a personal basis, Pasqualina was making unforgiving enemies. And, perhaps most worrying of all, the supposedly omnipotent Pacelli was becoming increasingly confirmed in his isolation.

In the triumphalist Holy Year of 1950, when millions of pilgrims flocked to Rome, Pacelli issued the encyclical *Humani generis* (Of the Human Race). 'Error and discord is only to be expected outside the fold of Christ with, for instance, the communist credo that the "world is in continual evolution".' These errors cannot be 'properly treated unless they are rightly diagnosed'. There was a 'reprehensible desire for novelty' even in the Church.[4]

The Pope's solution derived from his Code of Canon Law. 'It is incumbent to flee also those errors which more or less approach heresy and accordingly "to keep also the constitutions and decrees by which such evil opinions are proscribed and forbidden by the Holy See."'[5] Papal encyclicals hitherto regarded as 'ordinary teaching authority' (i.e. not infallible) must, Pacelli asserted, henceforth be accepted without any argument when they are intended to be definitive by the Pope.

The First Vatican Council had decreed that only 'solemn definitions', i.e. dogmas made *ex cathedra*, were infallible. But now:

> If the Supreme Pontiffs, in their official documents, purposely pass judgment on a matter up to that time under dispute, it is obvious that that matter, according to the mind and will of the same Pontiffs, cannot be any longer considered a question open to discussion among theologians.[6]

Not every encyclical was to be regarded as absolute. However, Pacelli was making it quite clear that when the Pope was settling an argument, his absolute authority must be deferred to by all – laymen and specialists alike. Thus was the Church subjugated to 'creeping infallibility'.[7]

At the beginning of the twentieth century, during Pacelli's early years in the Vatican, vicious anti-Modernist witch-hunts had stamped the Church with orthodoxy. Now, once more, Pacelli was stamping the Church with orthodoxy. Undoubtedly he felt that intellectual openness would bring a dangerous lack of control which would be ruthlessly exploited by socialism and its cruel sister, communism. The Jesuits and Dominicans were severely disciplined. The famous theologian Teilhard de Chardin was given a stark choice of exile or what amounted to house arrest. He chose exile to New York.

In France, a 'worker-priest' movement had grown up. Its antecedents were the forced conscriptions of clergy by the Germans in the war. Cardinal Suhard had written in 1946: '...when I go out into the factory areas, my heart is torn apart with sorrow ... A wall separates the Church from the masses.'[8] The worker-priest movement reached out to the masses; Pacelli's intolerance of change closed it down.

If a further sign of Pacelli's unrelenting orthodoxy was needed, it came when he proposed the anti-Modernist Pius X for beatification. The messages were clear. Pluralism was not acceptable in the Church. Creativity was not wanted.

To present-day commentators, such a position seems deplorable. But Pacelli's 'benevolent paternalism' was merely the religious equivalent of similar attitudes which pervaded industry and public sector organizations throughout the Western world. The rulers of the 1950s were men who had endured the horrors of two world wars. They were terrified of another world war, bringing nuclear weapons and the demise of the human race. It was an era of well-meaning conservativism, with an ethos of 'We know what is best for you'.

For many, socialism seemed the obvious pathway to a better world. But the 1950s rulers were worldly enough to believe that socialism, however seemingly fair, would have led inexorably to the evils of communism. Undoubtedly communism was one of the greatest victors of World War Two. The Berlin wall was a loathsome symbol of partition. Eastern Europe came under Soviet control. With the fall of Shanghai in 1949, Chinese domination of the Far East was almost complete. Now, most of the world was communist.

In the West, France and Italy boasted particularly vigorous communist parties. The post-war desire for a better world encouraged widespread political activism, almost unimaginable only 60 years later, in these times of political apathy. As with Catholicism, communism presented itself as a 'total solution' to the human condition. But unlike 2,000-year-old Catholicism, communism was relatively new, and therefore exciting and potent. Inspired by the desire for a better world, many of the best minds, the most altruistic and highly motivated people, flocked to communism. Sadly, when confronted with communist thuggery in Hungary, in 1956, and in Czechoslovakia, in 1968, most proponents of communism developed selective amnesia.

While the communist dream was promoted in the West by well-meaning intellectuals ('useful idiots', in Lenin's supremely contemptuous term), in the East the sinister gulags testified to its brutal reality. Meanwhile, the USSR was implementing a programme of world-wide destabilization.

Pluralism gave an open door, first to dialogue, then subversion, intellectual and otherwise. Of course, the ultimate irony was that communism itself was anything but pluralist.

The situation of the Church in Romania, from 1945 to 1953, gives a chilling illustration of the reality of communism. All 12 bishops and archbishops were imprisoned, condemned or deported. Three of them died in prison. The clergy were reduced from 3,331 to 1,405. Some 55 were killed, and 250 were dead or missing. Two hundred had been sent to forced labour camps. An equal number languished in prison.[9]

In 1949, the Holy Office decreed that it was unlawful:

1. to join or show favour to the Communist Party;

2. to publish, distribute, read or write in periodicals which supported communist teaching or action.

Offenders could not receive the sacraments (apart from matrimony). Promoters of communism faced excommunication. In 1956, Pacelli said bluntly:

> You know what is at stake. It is your eternal salvation and the salvation of your children and neighbours. Today, because of the ever-growing curse of atheism, this is placed in the gravest peril.[10]

Viewed in its historical context, Pacelli's 1950s rejection of communism, while undoubtedly an expression of his personal political view, arguably contributed to prudent stewardship of the Church. But rejection of communism was merely one aspect of his rejection of pluralism *per se*. The growing triumphalism of Pacelli's Church simply left no room for dialogue with dissenters. All communists were excluded. So were Freemasons and anti-clerical Irish Republicans. And so too were Jews, Protestants and Eastern Orthodox Christians. External exclusion was mirrored by rigidly enforced internal conformity. Unfortunately, however, stifling creativity and freedom of expression tends to turn healthy debate into unhealthy conflict. It was inevitable that the intellectuals whom Pacelli suppressed would, one day, have their say. The 1960s Second Vatican Council would be the world stage on which their ideas would be comprehensively expressed. Pacelli's anti-Modernism would have a spectacular backlash.

If Pacelli vigorously opposed the Soviet model of atheistic communism, he also renounced the US model of rampant materialism. Today, in fact, Pacelli's criticism of post-war bureaucratic society seems prescient. In the early 1950s, the Pope was denouncing 'the demon of organization which invades and tyrannizes the human spirit'. He pointed out that 'in some countries, the modern state is becoming a gigantic administrative machine'. He wrote trenchantly of the alienation of the individual, who is 'the origin and end of society':

> Here may be recognized the origin and source of that phenomenon which is engulfing modern man under its tide of anguish: the despoiling him of his personality. In large measure, his identity and name have been taken from him; in many of the more important activities of life, he has been reduced to a chattel of society, while society itself has been transformed into an impersonal system and into a cold organisation of force.[11]

Having rejected Soviet communism and American materialism, Pacelli looked to a distinctively European style of government. He found this in General Franco's Spanish model of alignment of Church with state. The 1950s saw the flexing of political muscles by the superpowers. In 1953, the Russians made their first hydrogen bomb tests. The threat of a nuclear war seemed ever-closer. Was a third – and final – world war the fabled Third Secret of Fátima?

The appearance of Our Lady at Fátima, in 1917, on the very day that Pacelli had been made an archbishop, seemed to be a sign that disaster could be averted only by prayer to the Mother of God. In 1954, General Franco spoke thus to the Spanish people about the insidious threat of nuclear annihilation: 'With the hope that his hour does not come, we confide ourselves in full faith to the protection, which cannot fail us, of our holy patron and the intercession of the Immaculate Heart of Mary.'[12] The year 1954 was declared a Marian Year, for special devotion to Our Lady.

Four years previously, in the Holy Year of 1950, Pacelli announced to a million people thronged around St Peter's Square: 'The Immaculate Mother of God, Mary, ever a Virgin, when the course of her life was run, was assumed in body and soul to heavenly glory.' In the decree *Munificentissimus Deus* (God the Most Generous), published shortly afterwards, the Pope declared as 'absolute doctrine of Holy Mother Church' that Mary's body did not corrupt and die to await the Resurrection. Instead, it was taken in glory into heaven.[13]

Pacelli's issue of the Assumption as decree inspired a new wave of devotion to the Virgin Mary. It perfectly demonstrated the Pope's power to issue dogma which must henceforth be regarded as absolute truth. And it dovetailed neatly with General Franco's long-standing use of the cult of the Assumption as a 'hearts and minds' bulwark against communism. But it divided the Church. It seemed to make theologians redundant. And it smothered moves toward unity between Catholics and other Christians.

Pacelli's dogma of the Assumption was made more poignant by his account of personal mystical experiences. He reported that while walking in the gardens of the Vatican, he witnessed the phenomenon of the spinning sun, as related by the original children of Fátima. He claimed that it was as though the sun spiralled downward to the horizon; then, like a celestial firework display, it swung straight back up again. At the same time the Blessed Virgin Mary appeared before him, as she had done on two previous occasions.

For many, Pacelli the canon lawyer, bureaucrat and diplomat seemed the most unlikely person to be having mystical experiences, let alone reporting them. Yet, as Pasqualina always averred, he had the soul of a mystic. To him, the Great Design was not merely a construct of this world; it was also a bridge to heaven.

For her many enemies, any oddness in Pacelli could be blamed on Pasqualina. 'That woman is fanatical on some matters of faith', Cardinal Valeri complained. 'She puts almost as much belief in Mary as some Catholics place in Christ. She's behind most of this.'[14]

Pasqualina had a swift retort to such charges:

> The Assumption of the Blessed Virgin Mary has been a long-held belief of Popes and prelates, since the earliest days of Holy Mother Church. In creating a new dogma, Holiness was confirming more than 1,500 years of Catholic belief that the Holy Mother was taken up, body and soul, to be with Jesus in heaven.[15]

Some critics felt that Pacelli was putting the Blessed Virgin Mary almost on the same level as Christ. Others questioned papal infallibility. And some people scoffed that the Pope was becoming senile. Matters were not helped by the Pope's plan to declare Our Lady 'Mediatrix of All Graces'. He simultaneously intended to declare her 'Co-Redemptrix with Jesus Christ'. Opposition to such a contentious proposition was rife among the theological confraternity in Rome. Throughout 1954, it was a constant source of anxious conversation in such circles. I was a student at the time in Rome's Pontifical Beda College where one of my follow students was Thomas Murray, the translator of the life of Pope Pius X. I mention this because that pope was canonized in 1954, when the controversy about the plan to create Our Lady Mediatrix of All Graces was at its height.

To have done this, according to conventional theological opinion, would have been tantamount to ascribing divine powers to the Blessed Virgin and it was therefore deemed dangerously heterodox. Pius, it was thought, never finally gave up his ambitions in this direction, but they waned as time passed. Although they were extinguished by his death in 1958, they did not entirely perish. Exaggerated devotion to the Mother of Jesus has, since time immemorial, been a prominent feature of Catholic history.

Mariology has often given way to Mariolatry; in other words, legitimate and reasonable veneration of Our Lady has occasionally been supplanted by something akin to worship of her, as of a deity. Some modern self-styled 'traditionalists' have fallen into this trap; they include extreme opponents of the Second Vatican Council.

Devotion to Our Lady greatly increased after she was declared to be the *Theotokos*, or Mother of God, by the fifth-century Council of Ephesus, and St Thomas Aquinas (1225–74) formulated the doctrine of the 'hyperdulia' proper to Mary. This, though infinitely inferior to the 'latria' (worship or adoration) due to her divine Son, surpasses that befitting angels and saints.

Ever loyal to Pacelli, Pasqualina pointed out:

> There is an extraordinary misconception as to the infallibility of the Pope. According to the tenets of Holy Mother Church, the Holy Father can be as mistaken as anyone in most matters, and it is no sin to disagree with him. It is only when the Supreme Pontiff solemnly speaks, *ex cathedra*, on faith and morals that he is held to be infallible. Holiness, a master of theology himself, had instructed his ecclesiastical scholars to examine all the evidence in every minute way, and to interpret it for him. In proclaiming the dogma of Assumption, Holiness was officially confirming a belief long held by officials of Holy Mother Church.[16]

And Pasqualina was similarly matter-of-fact concerning the matter of Pacelli's reputed visions: 'I believe with all my heart and soul in the power of our Holy Mother. If she chose to appear before Holiness, I am sure she did.'[17]

In addition to his Marian devotion, Pacelli instigated an extensive series of excavations beneath St Peter's Basilica for the tomb of St Peter. His old colleague from the 1930s, Monsignor Kass, was put in charge of this project. Professional opinion did, indeed, seem to suggest that the tomb of the first pope was in this place of such fundamental importance to the Church. Pacelli took a close personal interest in the excavations. It was as though, with St Peter as with Mary the mother of God, he was determined to buttress the Church with imperishable spiritual foundations.

In retrospect, the 1950s appears as a golden age of Catholicism. At the time though, the communist menace was acute; there was certainly no sense of complacency. Yet from the Holy Year of 1950 onwards, there was a new triumphalism about the Church. The 1870 loss of temporal power and the dreary decades of papal self-imprisonment in the Vatican were forgotten. Pacelli's 1930s international visits and the increasing use of mass media had put the Catholic Church on an immeasurably more assured footing. Understandably, the war had overshadowed these developments. But as the post-war turmoil of Europe finally began to subside, Rome began to emerge as a kind of spiritual superpower. The Vatican and its surroundings increasingly resembled a stage where adoring audiences were seduced by pomp and majesty. One wonders what St Francis of Assisi or St Catherine of Siena would have thought of such ostentation.

Always ready to make money out of a trend, the cinema of the time testifies to the commercialization of religious fervour. Films such as *La mia Via* (My Way), *Le Campane di Santa Maria* (The Bells of St Mary's) and *Città dei Ragazzi* (Boys' Town) were immensely successful. Doubtless their success increased not only the prestige of the Church but also its bank accounts. As previously noted, after the Pacelli-inspired financial *volte-face* of the Lateran Treaty, the Church had shown an increasing propensity for making money, not only from film-making but from virtually every other profitable industry.

In 1942 Pacelli had founded the Vatican's first bank, under the curiously bland title of *Instituto per le Opere di Religione* (Institute for Religious Works). In fact the name was Pasqualina's suggestion, and probably reflected her intention of using money for charitable causes. Undoubtedly Vatican money was well used in funding the vast wartime and post-war relief programmes, even though at times investment was anything but 'ethical'. For instance, during World War Two the Vatican placed investments with both the Axis and Allied powers. Pacelli claimed that this was a form of neutrality! However, when America entered the war and it began to become clear that Germany and Japan were ultimately doomed, the Vatican wasted no time in making massive investments in US armament plants. To some, this seemed dangerously akin to profiteering from war.

As wartime austerity faded and the subsequent economic miracle gathered force throughout Europe, increasing Vatican wealth was followed firstly by ostentation, then, inevitably, by corruption. Ironically Nogara, the mysterious financier, the man with the Midas touch, seemed utterly honest and loyal in his business dealings. In an ironic contrast to the bloated bureaucracies around him, with a staff of only two – a bookkeeper and a secretary – he made untold millions for the Church. He invested in Riviera casinos, Perrier water, Miller beer – wherever there was money to be made. At one time, it was claimed that up to 20 per cent of shares traded on the Italian stock exchange were owned by the Vatican.

Nogara's investments brought new levels of affluence to the lives of Vatican supremos. The still-impoverished inhabitants of Rome grew accustomed to seeing big black limousines sweeping by, with the telltale SCV (*Stato Città Vaticano*, i.e. Vatican City State) number plates. Cynical wags suggested that SCV really meant '*Se Cristo Vedesse!*' ('If Christ could only see this!')

One day in autumn 1949 Tisserant burst into Pasqualina's office, puffing on a cigar, with Monsignor Tardini, the Pro-Secretary of State, trailing nervously in his wake. 'Woman, give us the balance sheet!' he shouted at her. 'The Sacred College demands the information!'[18]

Pasqualina had heard on the Vatican grapevine that the College of Cardinals had been seeking a full financial statement of papal funds. Traditionally this was secret information, which no pope had ever been known to divulge. Although surprised that the request should have come about in such a brash manner, she stood her ground before Tisserant and his accomplice. Exasperated by her icy stare, Tisserant banged his fist on her desk. 'Either you give us the report, woman, or we'll get it from the Pope himself!' he ranted. 'It's not the Pope we don't trust. It's you!'[19]

Mortally insulted, Pasqualina calmly reached for the telephone. 'Send the Swiss Guards immediately!' she commanded. Seconds later, the papal soldiers rushed to the doorway. 'Remove these intruders at once!' Pasqualina coldly demanded, pointing to the miscreants.[20] The Swiss Guards were as shocked as Tisserant and Tardini. The tiny nun looked every bit 'the German General'.

Tisserant's eyes blazed with rage. 'We will leave of our own accord', he told her. As proud as Pasqualina, his haughty demeanour defied any servant of the Vatican to lay a finger upon him. His parting shot was laden with menace. 'Woman, may God have mercy on you, from now on!'[21]

Pasqualina was entirely unrepentant about the episode. No financial statements were issued to anyone. 'We held to papal tradition', she later asserted. 'One responsibility of the Holy Father is to make certain that sufficient resources are always on hand to perpetuate the charities and the religious work of the Holy See, for the welfare of all Catholics. To divide His Holiness's supreme authority with any source would open the doors to the likely dissipation of the great holy and charitable work of Holy Mother Church.'[22]

Tisserant, for one, was notably unconvinced by any such rhetoric. 'It was bad enough in the early days, when the woman still took her orders from Pius', he bitterly reflected. 'But now she wields such power that many of the hierarchy have come to deride her as *La Popessa*.'[23]

At least the transparently honest Pasqualina was using her power for worthy motives. Spellman had perfected the prestigious Knights of Malta society as a fundraiser *par excellence* for the Church. Wealthy, status-hungry Americans were paying up to 200,000 dollars for their 'knighthoods'. Of these vast sums, only 1,000 dollars per donation was reaching Rome.

Spellman was using the remainder as he saw fit. Given his penchant for construction projects, it was not difficult to envisage large-scale corruption. At that time, the US construction industry was notorious for its links with organized crime – particularly in New York. Spellman, of course, had long-time contacts with the Mafia, which had proved so helpful to the Allies in World War Two.

The French branch of the Knights of Malta had an additional, even more embarrassing problem. Bishop Roncalli (later Pope John XXIII) had appointed a close friend, Baron Marsaudon, as head of the organization. Unfortunately the Baron happened to be a thirty-third-degree Freemason – the highest rank possible. Church law specifically forbade Catholics from being Freemasons or practising Freemasonry. The sanction was excommunication.

Cardinal Canali, one of the most powerful figures in the Sacred College, lobbied hard to be put in charge of the entire Knights of Malta society. Conversely, Pasqualina wanted an investigation. Pacelli eventually gave in to her demands – but not without some rancour. 'Cardinals have the privilege of being above suspicion', he curtly informed her. 'Mother Pasqualina, you must learn to have more respect for the purple.'[24]

The following day, Pacelli told her that he was appointing Tisserant as head of the tribunal to investigate the alleged improprieties. Pasqualina's response was immediate: 'Holiness, you are making a terrible mistake! Eminence Tisserant will do nothing constructive, but will use the trial to his own advantage!'

'Tisserant is a Frenchman, and the French branch of the society is involved', Pacelli loftily retorted. To Pasqualina, this was a ludicrous justification.[25]

Tisserant invited four other cardinals to the tribunal; one of them was none other than Canali, the very man who had expressed such a personal interest in the Knights of Malta. Canali was a close friend of Tisserant's. For Pasqualina, this amounted to nothing more than a 'kangaroo court'. She braced herself for the inevitable outcome.

'The purple is above suspicion!' Tisserant proudly boasted to Pacelli. A furious Pasqualina yearned to reply: 'The purple is in mourning for the sins of its wearers, cardinals like yourself, Tisserant!'[26] Only the presence of the Pope made her hold her tongue.

Inevitably, further corruption occurred. The Cippico and Giuffrè affairs are, today, mere historical footnotes, but the telling phrase 'God's Banker', which emerged from the latter scandal, would subsequently be applied to Roberto Calvi, found hanging under Blackfriars Bridge in London in 1982. And the tragically short reign of Pope John Paul I in 1978 – a mere 33 days – inspired rumours that he had intended to clean the Augean stables at the Vatican Bank.

Back in the 1950s the Vatican Bank augmented its activities by large-scale currency smuggling using specially trained clergy, the fabled *uomini di fiducia* ('men of trust'). Perhaps the most notorious of these was Cardinal Spellman of New York. Spellman's biographer, Father Robert Gannon, describes him becoming 'as slick and skilled in transporting vast amounts in cash and securities as the most celebrated and daring of international smugglers.'[27] With his clerical garb and cherubic smile, Spellman spirited millions of dollars across national frontiers without ever being searched. On one occasion, on arriving at the Vatican, he was welcomed by Tisserant, on characteristic form. 'Greetings, Excellency Spellman! How is our chief undercover agent doing these days?'[28]

Although Pasqualina had lost the battle over the Knights of Malta, she was more determined than ever to win the war. The inner circle became even more restricted. Nogara was eased into semi-retirement, as Pacelli's nephews took over the day-to-day running of the Vatican finances. None of them was a member of the clergy; neither was Enrico Galeazzi, the Vatican Governor-General. But all four men were trusted by Pasqualina with the Vatican's finances. Spellman was the only member of the hierarchy to continue to receive both Pasqualina's blessing and ready access to Pacelli. Even Pacelli's sister Elisabetta, his cherished childhood companion, struggled to gain admittance to her brother.

Pasqualina disapproved of Elisabetta because of her habit of concealing a bottle of rare wine under her heavy skirts. When Pasqualina's back was turned, the elderly lady would whip out the bottle of wine and start pouring measures for her brother and herself.

'Elisabetta, don't you dare give Holiness another drink!' Pasqualina chided, having found the pair decidedly the worse for wear on one occasion. 'It's wonderful hearing you two reminisce about the past, but must you both toast every milestone in your lives? Holiness is not a well man, Elisabetta.'[29]

'For heaven's sakes, Pasqualina. Eugenio is no longer a baby! And you are not quite that old to be sounding like such a fuddy-duddy. Now leave us alone and stop listening at the door!'[30]

More than any other man, Pacelli was responsible for increasing the financial strength and public image of the Church. In the context of a fight to the death with communism, both achievements are greatly to his credit. But his excessively centralized 1950s management style, with its tiny circle of decision-makers, laid the Church open to abuse – financial and otherwise.

Half a billion people, a quarter of the population of the world, were Catholic; Pacelli was their undisputed master. His Great Design, begun with the enormous compilation of Canon Law in the early years of the twentieth century, had finally come to fruition. The Church was a codified hierarchy with Pacelli, a mystical symbol of holiness, at its apex. Its conservatism was institutionalized. The Church had become a totalitarian regime, a spiritual correlate of the 'benevolent' Fascist states of Spain and Portugal.

The public image of the Church was triumphant, omnipotent. The private reality was cold and authoritarian. It was as though the Church was suffering from spiritual exhaustion. And Pacelli too was exhausted. He was utterly worn out from the rigours of two world wars, and the ceaseless struggle against communism. The once charming diplomat had grown old and querulous. Like Ratti he had become authoritarian, making senior figures in the Church kneel before him for long periods – embarrassing, both for them and Pasqualina. And, unlike the down-to-earth Ratti, Pacelli had an intellectual arrogance that was increasingly being displayed.

'Holiness was such a hard, efficient and precise worker himself, he could not accept slackness, delays or the mistakes or others', Pasqualina recalled. 'When he found someone in the wrong, no matter of what position in the Holy See, Holiness let the offender have a piece of his mind, without any mincing of words.'[31] Having appointed Bishop Roncalli as French nuncio, Pacelli became incensed when he could never manage to speak with him. In the end, he shouted down the phone: 'From now on, Bishop Roncalli, you are not to leave the nunciature without my permission! You understand!'[32] Roncalli subsequently became Pacelli's successor as Pope John XXIII.

In his 29-year reign, Pacelli created cardinals on only two occasions: 18 February 1946 and 12 January 1953. At the first consistory, Spellman was made a cardinal. His old boss, Cardinal O'Connell of Boston, had died in 1944, spitefully lobbying Rome to the very end against giving Spellman a red hat. With O'Connell out of the way, however, Spellman's loyalty to the Church – and to Pacelli personally – could be aptly rewarded. Predictably, this caused outrage in the Vatican.

That first consistory marked a break with tradition; cardinals were created on a more world-wide basis than had ever occurred before. On one level, this illustrated Pacelli's growing internationalization of the Church. But on another level, it meant that the Italian power bloc was eclipsed by the greater number of non-Italians – with ominous implications for future conclaves.

'Holiness, the Italians are now in a minority', an anxious Pasqualina pointed out. 'Have you considered the consequences in reversing tradition?'

'Indeed I have!' Pacelli replied. 'It means that I as Holy Father can have a foreign successor.'[33] Given that Pacelli was Italian, Roman and a member of a family of 'Vatican insiders' going back to 1870, this was a mortal insult to the College of Cardinals.

With Spellman's red hat and the eclipsing of the Italian cartel, Pasqualina believed that Pacelli was paving the way for Spellman to become his successor. But the sidelining of the Italians could also bring benefits for one notable contender – her deadly enemy, Tisserant. 'It then occurred to me why Eminence Tisserant had remained so calm throughout the consistory', Pasqualina reflected, many years later. 'Indeed, he appeared to be quite genuinely delighted, an attitude he had never before shown since Holiness became the Holy Father.'[34]

The first consistory, Pacelli's disregard of the Curia, his Marian dogma, and his mystical experiences all contributed to an increasing enmity between the hierarchy and the Pope. Yet outward appearances were maintained by both sides, with steely resolution. Archbishop Cushing noted: 'One would never think that Pius XII and those of the Sacred College ever held anything but love for each other in their hearts.'[35]

However, Pacelli's second consistory, in 1953, threatened to make the rift public. The Pope announced that once again, as part of his internationalization policy, he was going to appoint a significant number of Cardinals from far-flung countries. Pasqualina, a fellow advocate of internationalization, nevertheless had her doubts. 'Holiness, you realize that all the pressure from the Romans will descend upon your head', she cautioned. 'But you are right. If Holy Mother Church is to thrive throughout the world, we know that people everywhere must have representation.'[36]

'Dear Mother Pasqualina, I am not overly concerned about the Italian membership', Pacelli wryly replied. 'I am the Holy Father of all Catholics everywhere, and, furthermore, I am an old man now. What can anyone do, particularly when I am behaving in the best interests of the Holy See?' Pacelli paused and smiled gently. 'What is there to fear when I have a good friend and warrior like you to do battle for me?'[37]

At the second consistory, Pacelli made 24 new cardinals. With some 70 cardinals drawn from 27 nations, the Italians comprised just over a third. In only two consistories, they had been relegated to a pitiful minority. Pacelli justified his decision thus: 'We want the largest possible number of peoples and backgrounds to be represented, so that the Sacred College of Cardinals may be a living image of the Church's universality.'[38]

New cardinals came from North and South America – 13 – and also from Armenia, Australia, China, India, Hungary and Poland. The cardinals from the latter two countries received their red hats in absentia. Communist states rightly saw the appointment of local cardinals as a threat. Sanctions varied from Cardinal Stepinac's house arrest in relatively benign Yugoslavia to Cardinal Mindszenty's sentence of life imprisonment in far from benign Hungary.

Monsignor Tardini, the Vatican Pro-Secretary of State, viewed Pacelli's refusal to make him a cardinal, after so many years of devoted service, as a personal insult. The day after the consistory he stormed, Tisserant-style, into Pasqualina's office. 'You're to blame!' he shouted, stabbing the air with an accusing finger. 'I'm going to write a book about the politics of Pius XII's reign!'[39] Then, in emulation of the master, he theatrically stormed out. True to his word, he wrote his book some years later.

By contrast Monsignor Montini, an aspirant for the papacy, reacted quite differently to Pacelli's refusal to make him a cardinal. Montini too was a Vatican Pro-Secretary of State, with much loyal service. But the quiet, reserved Montini contented himself with sending Pasqualina to Coventry. 'He merely sulked for weeks afterward', Pasqualina remembered. 'I don't believe he even said hello to me for a long while.'[40]

Bishop Roncalli, the future Pope John XXIII, was one of the very few Italians to receive his red hat. The amiable Roncalli made a surprise visit to Pasqualina's office bearing gifts of a pet goldfinch for the Pope and a pair of hand-carved rosary beads for her. Pasqualina was touched by Roncalli's thoughtfulness. Nevertheless, she felt highly embarrassed; the easygoing Roncalli had often felt the sharp bite of her tongue. Honesty compelled her to confess, 'But, Eminence, I had nothing to do with your appointment.'

'You are so wrong, Mother Pasqualina', Roncalli told her, with a knowing smile and a courtly bow. 'Your failure to oppose me was what turned the trick.'[41]

Archbishop Cushing summed up the prevailing situation:

> The cardinals believed that Pius was systematically depriving them of all authority. He was the kind of Pope who was accustomed to doing everything possible by himself. He also realized that over half of the Italians in the Sacred College of Cardinals were either so old or in such ill health that they could not carry out their duties with the type of efficiency that Pius demanded.[42]

Three factors inhibited the discomfited Italian cardinals – and aspirant cardinals

– from making their thoughts known to an ever more inquisitive press. Pacelli's internationalization of the Church was widely viewed as equitable and laudable, and Italian complaints would smack of sour grapes. Nor would it be wise to challenge a pope so generally beloved – particularly one in ailing health, who was not likely to reign for very much longer. The last factor was particularly ironic: any such challenge would incur the wrath of an extremely powerful and most unusual supporter of the Pacelli policy. This was none other than Tisserant, the Dean of the Sacred College and a fierce contender for the papacy himself. Each appointment of a non-Italian cardinal subtly increased Tisserant's chances. Consequently, the wily Frenchman 'had nothing but praise for the internationalisation of the cardinalate'.[43]

Chapter 18

The Church of Silence

Pacelli had always been neurotic about his health. To Pasqualina's horror, he had the utmost confidence in Dr Riccardo Galeazzi-Lisi – an eye specialist rather than a general medical practioner – and believed that the latter possessed the training and expertise to treat all illnesses. On one occasion, when Pacelli had come down with a severe cold and Pasqualina feared the onset of pneumonia, she finally spoke her mind about Galeazzi-Lisi.

'Holiness, that alleged doctor hasn't the ability to treat even your pet birds', she told the Pope, as she disgustedly spoon-fed him a potion that Galeazzi-Lisi had prescribed and in which she had no belief. Pacelli pulled a face at the sour taste of the medicine. 'You see everything wrong in every one of the few friends I have left. You're jealous of everyone who is close to me.'

'That's utterly preposterous!' Pasqualina exclaimed. 'I'm trying my best to look after your health, and you accuse me of selfish motives!'

She placed the bottle and spoon on the table by his bed and carried on tidying his room – saying nothing, but looking deeply hurt. Pacelli kept stealing nervous glances across at her, hoping for a smile of forgiveness, which didn't come. Instead, when Pasqualina had finished, she said stiffly, 'Holiness, your room is in order now. Call me when you need further care and I will be pleased to phone your doctor. Perhaps the next time he'll try to cure you by dancing about the bed.'[1] Without further ado, she bowed dutifully and stalked out of the room.

In the early 1950s, Pacelli was in his mid-seventies; Pasqualina was in her mid-fifties. Sometimes she wondered where her life had gone. What had happened to that sprightly girl from the little farm at Ebersberg, with such dreams and determination to make the world a better place? And the young novitiate at Altötting – a misty figure from a bygone age...?

Both Pacelli and Pasqualina were prodigious workers. On the rare occasions when anyone dared to ask Pasqualina when she found time for relaxation, or – heaven forbid – fun, they always received the stock answer: 'I could never imagine myself being anything but a nun, buried in work and prayer.'[2]

In addition to her unremitting work and prayer, Pasqualina shouldered huge burdens of responsibility. Although she had little formal authority, in reality she was the second most powerful person in the vast, monolithic Catholic Church. The rapidly ageing Pacelli was increasingly leaving the reins of government in her hands. From the lowest position imaginable, that of humble novitiate, she had risen to a pinnacle of eminence that no other woman has reached in the

Church, before or since. To millions of Catholic worshippers, the lofty cardinals seemed godlike, ethereal figures; the battle-hardened Pasqualina knew them for the vain, pompous and politically avaricious creatures that so many were.

Pasqualina had given her life to Pacelli. Now, he was increasingly becoming a shadow of his former self. Had she made the right choice? During her many nights of loneliness, only her rosary beads and her unrelenting faith in Jesus Christ carried her through to dawn and the onset of another back-breaking day.

> I placed everything in the hands of Our Saviour. Before I ever made a decision or took a stand, I asked myself, 'How would dear Jesus and the Blessed Mother decide and act?' When I was never more than a nun, I would not allow anyone, even though he be priest or prelate, to dishonour Our Lord. When I spoke my mind for what was ethical and honourable, I became hated for it. There was great sadness in my heart, for no one wants to be disliked. Yet, at no time were there regrets on my part. *Only the mistakes of Holiness himself brought tears to my eyes; in my mind, he remained a great and holy man, no matter what his human errors.* [Italics added][3]

One morning in August 1954, when Pacelli had just finished saying Mass, Pasqualina took him to one side and whispered to him that she was almost 60. 'Holiness looked shocked at my forwardness', she later ruefully reflected. With a blank look, he marched off. She felt that he was irritated with her for 'being silly enough to bring up such a trite matter'. Bitterly she reproached herself: 'I felt that I should have known better. All his life, Holiness was so attached to religion and work that any thought of sentimentality appeared as a waste of time to him.'[4]

And yet it seems that Pasqualina misjudged Pacelli. On her 60th birthday, 25 August 1954, he called her to his study. 'Happy Birthday, Mother Pasqualina!' he exclaimed as she entered.[5] Despite failing health, his voice was vibrant with emotion. Gleefully, like a little boy, the absolute master of the Catholic Church pointed to a table by his desk; on it was placed a small, white cake with a little figure of a nun in black robes. The candles were lit.

Pasqualina, who had steeled herself to expect nothing on her 60th birthday, was overwhelmed. 'But Holiness,' she ventured a little sadly, 'there are only 16 candles and I am 60!'

Pacelli came towards her, his aged eyes misty with tears. He took both her hands in his. 'Mother Pasqualina, you will always be 16 to me', he said tenderly, bending to kiss her on the forehead.[6]

Pasqualina and Pacelli spent the summer of 1954 at Castel Gandolfo. Pasqualina had tried to get him to go earlier, in hopes that the peaceful setting would be good for his health. But Pacelli was having none of it; and he set such a punishing pace on his supposed holiday that, to the dismayed Pasqualina, they might as well have stayed at the Vatican.

When Pasqualina complained to Pacelli's confessor that the Pope was 'ruining his health', word got back to him. A furious Pacelli rounded on her and denounced her 'nagging behaviour': 'If you do not stop telling me, the Holy

Father, what I am to do, I will send you back to the Stella Maris retreat house!' he stormed.

Pasqualina had been carrying in a tray of coffee and fruit for Pacelli's mid-afternoon snack. Startled by his outburst, she stopped dead in her tracks. As she felt her own anger flare up within her, she banged the tray down on the floor.

'I will leave in the morning!' she threatened, her eyes flashing with anger. 'It will be a long time before you find another nun who is as good to you!'[7]

By her refusal to address him as 'Holiness', Pacelli realized how distraught she was. But when he failed to show any sign of repentance she turned and fled, too angry for tears.

Within the hour, Pacelli ordered her to come back. He was the Pope; she was a mere nun. Her vow of obedience compelled her to return.

'Mother Pasqualina, I am so sorry!' he contritely apologized. Pasqualina sank to her knees and obediently kissed his Fisherman's Ring. Her heart was pounding with joy. 'Mother Pasqualina, you know that I cannot go on without you', Pacelli confided. His voice trembled slightly, as he led her to a chair beside him. 'But is it wise that you soon consider leaving the Vatican? We both know that I am not going to live much longer. It would be better for you to be away from Rome when the end comes.'[8]

Pasqualina tried to interject – but Pacelli motioned her to silence. 'You must allow me to find you a peaceful haven', he ruminated. 'A place where you can spend your remaining days after I am no longer the Holy Father.'

'Holiness, I cannot find it in my heart to leave you', Pasqualina begged him. 'No matter what the future holds, I shall always remain at your side.'[9]

Pacelli made no reply. Instead, he slowly rose and crossed to the window, seemingly gazing out across Rome. But Pasqualina knew that he was trying to mask his tears. 'You have been such a good and loyal friend', he whispered. 'And yet you have received so little in return.' Pacelli turned to her, his face drawn and sad. 'Mother Pasqualina, you may remain as long as you desire. But I want you to think of yourself for a change.'[10]

By the early 1950s, Pacelli's well-being had visibly declined. He was becoming enfeebled and shockingly emaciated. Indeed, by 1954 he was at death's door. At the end of the year, however, he was reported to have been the recipient of a miraculous cure and to have been vouchsafed a heavenly vision. What most people did not know, and few know even now, was the strange story of what had actually been happening that year.

The vision and miraculous cure were reported to have occurred on 1–2 December, 1954. The aged pontiff had been through a year of serious illness and suffering. The faithful were often bracing themselves to be told the worst. In early December, he was sitting up in bed greeting his visiting doctors with a robust 'Good morning, gentlemen!', ready for a day of hard work. And yet during the preceding month he had lain almost lifeless, a pitiful skin-and-bones spectacle, with death expected at any moment. Now, suddenly, he appeared to be a very new man. He was to live for four more years. How and when had this amazing recovery occurred? The story behind it is strange indeed.

The well-known German musician, Wilhelm Furtwängler, came to Rome to direct a Wagner Festival. The Pope happened to be listening to a broadcast of the first concert, and granted the musician a private audience. Furtwängler was struck by the expertness of the Pope's musical knowledge. Pacelli explained that he often listened to music at night because he had difficulty sleeping. He normally only slept for four to six hours a night, in any case. However, due to his anxieties this had deteriorated to little more than an hour.

Furtwängler said he too had once suffered badly from insomnia but had by chance been given refuge, just before the end of the war, at the home of a Swiss friend. The latter was also a surgeon, and his home doubled as a clinic. Furtwängler stayed for a year and a half and underwent a revolutionary course of treatment, in which his friend was a pioneering expert. The friend's name was Paul Niehans. His treatment consisted of cellular rejuvenation by injecting serum which was specially prepared, after being extracted from the foetuses of still-live pregnant ewes. The Pope expressed keen interest, and Niehans was invited to the Vatican.

His first private audience was on 14 October 1953. No official record was kept of this audience, which was also the case with all future activity by Dr Niehans on behalf of the Pope. The original audience was quickly followed by a second one, at which Dr Galeazzi-Lizzi was present.

Niehans diagnosed fatigue and nervous exhaustion. But his requirement of total rest for a week, before any treatment could begin, was deemed impossible, such were the demands of Pacelli's self-imposed workload.

No further meetings took place until, in February 1954, an alarmed telephone call from Castel Gandolfo, the Pope's country residence outside Rome, reached Niehans, telling him that the Pope was struggling against death. When Niehans arrived, Pacelli, his transparent skin stretched over his face, now a mere frame of bone, was vomiting blood and being attacked by horrendous convulsions of hiccups which had been going on from some considerable time. Niehans diagnosed haemorrhagic gastritis. He massaged the Pope's stomach and, having turned him on his right side, managed to make him swallow two spoonfuls of iced water.

The hiccups became less frequent. The Pope was kept on his side and given further massage, after which the hiccups stopped. Two days later cellular injections began, the new cells having probably been taken from a pregnant ewe on the papal farm, part of the pontifical estate. (Some reports say the cells were Niehans's famous lyophilized, i.e. vacuum-frozen, version, which he had brought with him.)

Niehans remained at Castel Gandolfo for eight weeks after which the Pope's cure, for which the entire Catholic world had been praying, was announced. A further course of injections was advised and administered in July, this time at the Vatican itself. The Pope then returned to Castel Gandolfo, with all Rome buzzing about his miraculous recovery. The Niehans treatment was never officially recorded.

The Pope suffered a terrible relapse in November and, this time, was thought to be on the point of death. By chance, Niehans happened to be in Rome. The

Pope was still at Castel Gandolfo and Niehans was called. Italy's most famous surgeon, Dr Paolucci, was also summoned. The Pope was groaning in agony and seemed likely to choke to death.

Diaphragmatic hernia was diagnosed; Paolucci advised an immediate operation, which Niehans opposed, much to Paolucci's indignation. After acrimonious conversation with the other doctors in attendance (and with the German nuns praying beside the apparently dying Pope), reluctant agreement was given to Niehans' proposal. This was to anaesthetize the patient's phrenetic nerves with Novocain (local anaesthetic) to relax the diaphragm. Once that was achieved, it would be necessary somehow to free the portion of the stomach which was momentarily strangulated. Niehans recommended that the Pope should swallow some mashed potatoes.

The regular doctors were furious. But this course of treatment was adopted, and an x-ray revealed sufficient reduction of the hernia to make recovery possible. Paolucci had stormy interviews with the Pope's powerful nephew, Prince Carlo Pacelli, as well as with Mgrs Montini (later Pope Paul VI) and Dell'Acqua. But the Pope's apparently mortal illness had definitely receded. This was officially recognized, although no official mention was ever made of the part played by Niehans. Instead, a very different and even more remarkable story emerged. On 1 December, when Pacelli had lain on what had seemed his deathbed and troubled crowds gathered in St Peter's Square, Pasqualina slipped into the papal chapel where Pacelli had said Mass every morning for years. 'Dear Jesus, be merciful to Holiness', she prayed. 'He is a good man. Forgive him for whatever he may have done wrong, for Eugenio Pacelli never sinned intentionally.'[11]

When she returned to his bedside, Pacelli had changed. Although as weak as ever, his mind had recovered its former clarity. 'Mother Pasqualina,' he told her, 'I want to be left alone tonight. No doctors, no one, not even you! I am expecting a vision.'

'Holiness, you are too ill to be left alone!' Pasqualina protested.

Pacelli struggled to raise himself in the bed. 'Mother, do as I say!' he sternly told her.[12] Distraught, she backed out of his bedroom, leaving him on his own.

In the early hours of 2 December, Pacelli woke alone. Dreadfully weak, he was certain that he was going to die. He began his favourite prayer, *Anima Christi* (Soul of Christ). When he came to the fateful words '*in hora mortis, meae voca me*' ('in the hour of my death, call Thou me'), the Pope said later that he had beheld none other than Jesus Christ Himself, standing by the bedside. '*O bone Jesu!*' Pacelli joyfully exclaimed. '*O bone Jesu! Voca me; iube me venire ad Te!*' ('Oh, good Jesus! Oh, good Jesus! Call Thou me; order me to come to Thee!') Yet Christ had not come to summon Pacelli; instead He had given comfort. 'And, after a little while,' Pacelli wistfully recalled, 'he went away.'[13]

When Pascalina fearfully entered Pacelli's room at 6.25 a.m. she found the pontiff out of bed and on his feet. To her astonishment, he greeted her with a cheerful 'Good morning, Mother Pasqualina! I am happy to see you!' Joyfully, he blurted out: 'This morning, I saw Our Lord ... silent in all His eloquent majesty!'[14]

Pacelli told Pasqualina what had happened. As she put it, he added that the day before he had heard 'a very clear voice announce, quite distinctly, that he would have a vision'. As he was speaking, a host of doctors entered the room; they were as amazed as Pasqualina. Later, Dr Galeazzi-Lisi also stressed Pacelli's vastly recovered state of health:

> The entire story was told by the Holy Father with remarkable presence and clarity of mind ... It should also be pointed out that, precisely on that same morning of December 2nd, the Holy Father, having briefly described what had happened, turned to current business and, among other things, made his final revision of his speech to the Catholic lawyers, the text of which was read to their convention on the following day.[15]

Pacelli was the first pope in almost 2,000 years to have claimed to have seen Christ. He was the *only* pope – apart from Saint Peter – who had made such a claim. Had this experience preceded or accompanied the final, highly unconventional, cure initiated by Niehans? Certainly the pontiff seemed to have made a miraculous recovery on 2 December.

Just over three weeks later, after having ostensibly been on his deathbed, Pacelli had composed his Christmas message and read it on Vatican Radio. It was hailed as one of the Pope's finest speeches. Few people had expected the Pope to survive 1954. Yet as the year drew to an end, Pacelli's recovery continued apace. And as 1955 began, Pasqualina knew that the pontiff was back to his old form when she heard him bellowing, in familiar fashion: 'Mother Pasqualina, come here at once! I don't know what I've done with my eyeglasses!'

However, when Pacelli told her that he intended to make public his vision of Christ, Pasqualina's joy turned to unease. 'I want everyone to hear of the miracle that Our Dear Saviour has performed, in order to increase their faith in Almighty God', Pacelli affirmed.[16]

Previously, Pasqualina had cautioned: 'Nobody should hear of this. The doctors are under Hippocratic oath and will not say anything if you so order them.' Now she diplomatically reminded him that he had appeared to be on his deathbed at the time: 'Holiness, people are such sceptics. The critics of Holy Mother Church will howl with ridicule. They will point to your age and illness and....'.[17]

'Some will say that I am senile', Pacelli finished for her. 'But, for each one who doubts, thousands will believe. For that is what belief in Almighty God is all about. One must have faith to believe.' Taking her hand in his, Pacelli looked at her. 'Mother Pasqualina, you did not doubt the visions of our Holy Mother. Why do you doubt now?'[18]

'You were not on the threshold of death, at that time', Pasqualina replied, as gently as possible.

'How, then, can you explain my miraculous recovery from almost certain death?' Pacelli asked. 'Especially when Our Dear Saviour told me that my time had not yet come?' The Pope paused. When he continued, it was obvious that he too was trying to avoid any slight or insult. And yet his words pierced her terribly. 'Mother Pasqualina, where is your faith in Almighty God?'[19]

Mindful of the still delicate state of Pacelli's health, Pasqualina did not want to upset him further. 'Holiness, forgive me if I have offended you', she apologized. 'We shall not speak further of this matter, at this time. Later, perhaps, but, for now, you must get your rest.'[20] She pulled the Pope's blanket over his arms, gave him a loving smile, and left.

While Pacelli slept, Pasqualina telephoned Spellman in New York. In strictest confidence, she told him of Pacelli's latest vision and his desire to proclaim it to the world. 'Eminence, I am afraid of the consequences', she concluded.[21] Spellman agreed. He assured her that he would catch the first available flight to Rome. In the meantime, Pasqualina would ensure that not a word leaked out from any source.

But while the steely and formidable 'German General' exerted iron control over many members of the Vatican, there was one man whom even she could not contain. By the time Spellman arrived, the news had leaked out – from none other than Pacelli himself. It appears that he told several people; for instance, he gave graphic details to his trusted friend, the German Cardinal Bea. Somehow, a reporter named Luigi Cavicchioli came to hear of the episode; he wrote an account for the popular Italian magazine, *Oggi*. Inevitably, this created a furore all around the globe.

The Vatican press office was bombarded with requests for the story to be confirmed; knowing nothing themselves, however, they were caught flat-footed. At first they issued an outright denial; then they hid behind the anodyne 'No comment.'[22] Finally Pacelli, reluctant to have the unfortunate Cavicchioli further derided, told the Vatican press director to confirm the story.

The news of Pacelli's vision of Christ inspired a range of emotions, from ridicule to adoration. To some, this showed how ludicrous religion was. For others, it aligned with their portrait of a senile Pope, whose usefulness had long passed. And yet for many other people, it was a confirmation of their faith in Almighty God and His servant, Eugenio Pacelli. Their beloved Pope had been visited by God Himself; Jesus Christ had personally appeared, to snatch His earthly Vicar from the jaws of death. From then on, there could be no stopping the process of mythologizing and deifying Pope Pius XII. At the Pope's next public audience, thousands cried: '*Viva il santo Papa! Viva il santo Papa!*'[23]

However great the popular appeal, at the Vatican feelings ran high, while in the Sacred College of Cardinals the mood was explosive. The Pope, it was held, had plunged the Church into unwonted controversy. Yet if anyone spoke out publicly, it would be tantamount to fuelling the controversy. After much discussion, it was agreed that the most sensible option was for the Sacred College to retain a dignified silence.

Tempers snapped, however, when it was revealed that Pasqualina had known all along of the Pope's intention of going public with his vision, and that she had asked for Spellman's help rather than alerting the Sacred College. The outraged Cardinals bided their time until Pacelli was giving one of his famous special interest group talks. Then, led by Tisserant, they marched into Pasqualina's office.

'Woman, are these stories true?' Tisserant furiously demanded.[24] Seated at her desk, Pasqualina looked up at him. Accustomed as she was to his volatility, she had never before seen him so animated. Sweat dripped from his forehead into his thick beard; he was flanked by his fellow cardinals, staring icily at her.

Thousands of years previously, the Chinese military genius Sun Tzu warned of the folly of engaging in futile battle. It is doubtful whether Pasqualina had ever read Sun Tzu. Nevertheless, she instinctively acted in a way which would have drawn approval from probably the greatest military strategist ever. Knowing that she was outnumbered and outmanoeuvred, she refused to engage in battle; instead, she nimbly sidestepped it. Her *snellezza* (mental agility) and *scaltrissima* (extreme cunning) were as strong as always.

Calmly yet defiantly, the 'German General' retorted: 'Eminences, if you have any complaints, speak with the Holy Father!' At this, Tisserant grew livid.

'Woman, your days are numbered!' he thundered.[25]

The tiny Bavarian nun stood her ground. It may be that her stony silence and the impatient tapping of her fingers on the desk aroused uncomfortable childhood memories of stern Mother Superiors for these august Fathers of the Church. Beaten, Tisserant's henchman slunk away, until only their ringmaster remained. Finally, he too yielded to her natural authority. He followed his departed cardinals, shaking his head in baffled anger.

When Pacelli returned to the Vatican, he received the full measure of Pasqualina's wrath. 'Holiness, I had warned you not to speak of the vision!' she snapped at him. 'Yet you went ahead without saying a word to me. Now look at what this embarrassment has caused! If you wanted to let the world know of the vision, why didn't you make a formal announcement yourself?' Her voice almost breaking with emotion, she lambasted him: 'Why didn't you dignify the vision the right way?'[26]

Pacelli was shocked by her words. He asked her what had elicited this 'explosion of temper'. She told him. Immediately he picked up the telephone and contacted Tisserant. 'Pacelli speaking! You are to come to my office now, Tisserant! You are to bring the others with you!'[27]

With that, he hung up. His commands were delivered in tones of frigid severity.

Within minutes the miscreants were at the Pope's feet, kissing his Fisherman's Ring in obedience. 'Arise!' he told them. Pointing to Pasqualina, standing to one side, he ordered the cardinals to apologize to her. 'Tell good Mother Pasqualina of your repentance', he sternly commanded.[28]

The cardinals had no choice but to bow to Pasqualina and beg her forgiveness. Thus was quelled the uprising from the College of Cardinals. Pasqualina knew that she was safe from further attacks – at least for the time being.

Pacelli's miraculous recovery in 1954, undoubtedly inspired by Niehans, extended his life and reign for almost another four years. Yet in many ways, they were melancholy ones. Slowly his new-found vitality began to ebb away from him again and, more and more, Pasqualina had to endure his cry: '*Quotidie morior!*' ('Every day I die a little!')[29]

Throughout the entire first half of the twentieth century, Pacelli had assiduously striven to create his Grand Design. Finally, he had triumphantly completed it. The Church was a vast, totalitarian monolith, with ultimate authority concentrated in the person of the Pope. And yet it seemed that the lonely, frail Pacelli had become a prisoner of his Grand Design. Powerful figures in the Curia blocked his imperious dictates, by the simple expedient of prolonging delay. Pacelli, the formerly consummate bureaucrat, was becoming defeated by his own bureaucracy.

And sadly, Pacelli the once charming diplomat had become disdainful and viciously rude. His many enemies were conducting whispering campaigns against him. His reign was being described as 'a disaster for the Church'. Pope and Church, it was claimed, were 'settling into a childish, devotional dotage'. Tisserant, his arch-critic, was sneering that 'the Church appears to be dying with him'.[30] Tardini regarded Pacelli as a 'weak Pope' with a 'lack of trust in others' and an 'incapability of working with the hierarchy' which he frequently ignored.[31] Tardini regarded Pacelli's failings as due to an 'inability to open his spirit and confide with the clergy'.[32] Alas, it was too late for that.

One morning, early in 1955, when Pasqualina, inquisitive as ever, was tidying up Pacelli's desk, she unearthed a bombshell. The Pope had made two lists: one list advancing reasons for his resignation, and the other giving reasons for remaining in office, at least for the time being.

Clutching the incriminating lists, a shocked Pasqualina ran into the study where Pacelli was quietly reading his breviary. 'Holiness!' she burst out, 'You cannot be seriously contemplating resignation?'[33] The Pope struggled to his feet, to comfort her. 'Mother Pasqualina, the time has long been at hand for Pacelli – tired old man that I have become – to consider stepping down. I remain at my post only because the doctors have assured me that I shall be as strong as I was before.'[34]

'Holiness, your strength must be conserved for ecclesiastical affairs!' Pasqualina instinctively replied. 'Too much energy is lost on temporal matters. Holiness, you must be relieved of many of your temporal duties. Holiness, I will help you. I will take charge of your temporal responsibilities.'[35]

Shafts of sunlight filtered through the stained-glass windows of the Pope's study as Pacelli silently paced the room, pondering Pasqualina's words. Her offer had no precedent in the history of the Church. As a female and a nun, Pasqualina's official status in the eyes of the hierarchy was little more than that of a chattel. No sufficiently senior authority could ever be invested in her. But could she really take over the day-to-day running of the Church from the frail hands of a pope who exercised absolute authority in theory, but faltering control in practice?

Typically, Pacelli's decision was not to make a decision – either for or against Pasqualina's proposal. After almost 40 years, however, she could read him like a book. She simply took his lack of a veto as a signal of assent. This suited his character and hers. *Always, Pasqualina's nature was to assume power, not to sit and wait for it to be given to her.*

From then on, Pasqualina acted not merely as an adviser to Pacelli but also as a conduit, deciding what issues deserved his attention, which papers he should ignore and which he should sign, who would be allowed to see him and who would not. The latter dictate was rigidly enforced by the radical expedient of placing the Pope effectively under armed guard.

Summoning the officers of the Vatican security staff to a special meeting, Pasqualina sternly told them: 'The Holy Father requires that the palace guard stand duty directly outside these quarters! You are to admit no one to the papal apartment, regardless of position, without my specific order. That includes all cardinals and other prelates. And the palace guard is to remain on duty at all times, twenty-four hours a day, with no exceptions!'[36]

The Swiss Guard was the second line of defence around Pacelli; Pasqualina remained the first. With his immense experience of international diplomacy Pacelli enjoyed the company of politicians, although he continued to deplore the long-dead Hitler, Mussolini and Roosevelt as 'architects of war'. But with rare, favoured exceptions, politicians received short shrift from Pasqualina. 'In almost every instance, I knew they were out to use the Holy Father, usually for their own personal gain', she caustically adjudged.[37]

Once Pasqualina's 'iron curtain' had dropped into place, Pacelli became almost entirely remote from the daily life of the Curia. Increasingly he spent his time becoming an amateur authority on a bewildering variety of topics. It became his habit to accumulate a wide variety of books and papers on specialist subjects, and to digest them into lectures. Typically these lectures were given in French and Italian, although some were delivered in German, Latin, Spanish or English. His bizarre compendium of lecture subjects included accountancy, aeronautics, agriculture, animal slaughter, business, cinema, communication, dentistry, economics, education, footwear, gymnastics, gynaecology, genetics, heart attacks, history, international affairs, mineral extraction, newscasting, nuclear physics, ophthalmology, outer space, penal law, pharmacy, plastic surgery, psychiatry, psychology, philosophy, sociology, sport, statistics, surgery, tourism and urology. In addition Pacelli gave solemn pronouncements on then current topics such as Chinese schoolchildren, Ethiopian boy scouts, the Harlem Globetrotters, Irish pipers and Tibetan lamas.

One day in the summer of 1958 at Castel Gandolfo, Cardinal Tardini came upon the Pope with a huge pile of reading matter. Pacelli commented, 'You know, all those books are about gas.'[38] On 28 September, he gave an address to a congress of the gas industry. Since he had less than two weeks to live, this begs the question of whether the Pope was making the best use of his time. Significantly, Pacelli's talks rarely dealt with pure religion. Today we would regard such diversions as 'displacement activities'.

This habit of the Pope in his later years, of spending so much time preparing and memorizing speeches and allocutions on trivial, non-spiritual subjects, is very significant; but his complex motivation is unknowable. Was it a subconscious guilty conscience about his past failures, and a desire to blot out unwanted memories by feverish activity of a diverting kind? Or did it become more obsessive when turning, as it did, into a sort of game played out almost every evening by Pius and Pasqualina?

They would spend many happy hours immersing themselves in the textbooks, reference books, lexicons and encyclopaedias necessary for that particular subject of enquiry, be it dentistry, ophthalmology, gases, internal combustion engines, or whatever. They revelled in trying to outdo each other in discovering the right word or expression required to illuminate some point, and each would cry out exultantly like an excited child at any such triumph, at the expense of the other. It was, indeed, curious to think of an aged pontiff spending several hours of every day in such trivial pursuits. The crowds, moreover, who listened to the resulting discourses, two or three a week sometimes, were equally bemused by such performances and invariably came away from them bewildered and disappointed.

Pacelli continued with his radio broadcasts, especially his Christmas messages, which had achieved wide audiences in wartime and remained extremely popular. Typically these dealt with the post-war reconstruction of Europe. And he made regular public speaking appearances, though he was never a natural orator, his mode of delivery being stiff and wooden.

Clearly his *modus operandi* was to memorize his speeches, word for word. When his normally excellent memory occasionally failed, long pauses could be highly embarrassing, both for himself and his audience. Such caveats aside, in 1955, under Pasqualina's 'iron curtain' regime, he made an extremely impressive series of major speeches, more than 60 in all, appearing before nearly 400,000 people in total.[39] His work ethic was extreme. Even on his deathbed, he called out: 'To work! Files! Documents! To work!'

If Pacelli 'felt thrice blessed with his able nun in charge', Pasqualina's 'iron curtain' was deemed 'tyrannical and humiliating to the hierarchy' at the Vatican.[40] In addition to '*virgo potens*' (the powerful virgin) and 'the German General', a new nickname had been coined for her – '*La Popessa*' – 'the Female Pope'.[41] She felt surrounded by enemies – Tisserant, of course, who had never pretended otherwise – and Tardini, with his criticism of Pacelli, which to Pasqualina was sheer disloyalty.

Despite his long years of service and friendship, the once favoured Monsignor Giovanni Montini was, by the early 1950s, being belittled repeatedly by Pacelli. Rumours abounded that Montini had made embarrassing discoveries at the Vatican Bank, run by Pacelli's nephews, and that he was growing over-tolerant of socialism. The Pope's refusal to elevate him to the cardinalate, in the 1953 consistory, had rankled deeply.

As staunch clerical conservatives and political anti-communists, both Pacelli and Pasqualina were suspicious of Montini's liberal tendencies. As a cardinal, Montini would be well placed to mount a challenge in the next conclave. Pacelli bluntly told Pasqualina that he felt Montini was 'too progressive in his social and political outlook to be considered a reliable successor'.[42] 'Holiness furthermore felt that Monsignor Montini did not possess the stature to be Holy Father', Pasqualina confided to Spellman.[43] Montini's habit of carrying a portable altar and associated kit in a large briefcase, and bringing Mass to the peasant streets of Italy, found acute disfavour with the aloof pontiff, who airily dismissed such innovations as 'theatrics'.

In 1954 Pacelli mentioned to Pasqualina that he was considering giving Montini the vacant post of Secretary of State, to appease him for his disappointment at not having being named a cardinal. Pasqualina lost no time in informing Spellman, on one of his visits to Rome. Spellman, another archconservative, lobbied Pacelli. 'Holiness, Montini must not be in a position to command voters at the next conclave', he firmly stated.[44] He clinched the argument by putting into Pacelli's mind the dreadful thought that if Montini became Pope, Pasqualina would be banished.

Within the week Pacelli had removed Montini as Pro-Secretary of State and made him Archbishop of Milan, in theory a promotion, but in reality an exile from the power centre of Rome to the Church's equivalent of Siberia. His poignant leave-taking was typical of the heartlessness of the Vatican. On a cold, drizzling morning in January 1955, a devastated Montini, clutching a single suitcase, got into a battered old lorry, famously loaded with 90 boxes of books. Despite his decades of loyal service, not a single figure from the Vatican hierarchy, nor any colleague, turned out to say goodbye. On that dreary, desperately lonely morning, it must have seemed impossible that he would ever become a cardinal. And yet, in one of those fascinating reverses of history, the brutally discarded Montini became not only a cardinal but also the successor to Pope John XXIII as Pope Paul VI. Long before then, however, Pasqualina would make a similarly sad exit from a Vatican which no longer had any use for her.

As Pacelli passed his 80th birthday, the public façade of unity was wearing perilously thin. Guiselle Dalla Torre, a former editor of *L'Osservatore Romano*, published a piece which noted that the Pope was 'separating himself from direct contact with life'.[45] Elsewhere, Pacelli was viewed as a 'commander increasingly divorced from reality'.[46] Even the notoriously autocratic Pasqualina winced when Pacelli ordered senior Vatican officials on their knees to address him, and made them walk backwards when exiting from his presence. Pacelli's few meetings with his staff were becoming increasingly threadbare, and almost pointless for either them or him.

Pacelli's interest in his 'displacement activities' continued unabated. He would dictate lengthy articles to reporters from *L'Osservatore Romano*, who were also commanded to kneel at his feet. His only respite from ceaseless, almost neurotic work came with his afternoon walks in the papal gardens. Even then, Pasqualina had to nag him to take them. Solitude was so important to him that he ordered the gardens closed to the public while he sauntered through them, reading his breviary. The gardeners had to hide, sometimes in ludicrous positions, while he passed by.

As ever Pacelli continued to eat his meals, either alone or with Pasqualina. Typically, he would request her presence at the last minute. Apart from his nephews, who were regular visitors, family contact was restricted to a once-a-year audience, usually for two or three hours only, on Christmas afternoon. Pasqualina had always adored Christmas, and Pacelli allowed her to have a small tree in a corner of the papal apartments. Toward the end, he started to grumble at even this simple pleasure, asserting that he valued the traditional Nativity rather than the Nordic import of a Christmas tree. However, Pasqualina's little symbol of joy, a reminder of an impoverished yet carefree childhood, was too important to her. Pacelli dared not gainsay her.

For four years after his miraculous recovery, Pasqualina struggled to help Pacelli maintain the appurtenance of normality. The public image of poised serenity was sharply at odds with the private reality of a man in severe decline. Pasqualina wore herself out tending to him. And she was filled with foreboding for the future. 'It was the mounting political drumbeat of the hierarchy that sounded fear throughout Pasqualina', Archbishop Cushing noted. 'She knew they were waiting anxiously to take control of Pius's throne and to besmirch his beliefs and standards.'[47]

Schooled from her earliest days in restraint and obedience, Pasqualina was equally committed to Pacelli's Great Design, a Catholic Church of undisputed authority governing almost every aspect of human existence. 'There will be a great falling away from Holy Mother Church, if the bars of morality and ethics are let down', she predicted.[48]

In 1958, Pasqualina turned 64. As a girl, she had given up her family for the Church. As a young woman, she had devoted her life to Pacelli. She had endured his selfishness for the sake of his greatness. Although she had asked for almost nothing for herself, the thought of her uncertain future was daunting. The Vatican was filled with powerful men who loathed 'La Popessa' and were biding their time, waiting impatiently for their chance to strike.

Sometimes, glancing at Pacelli, a mere ghost of the dashing figure who had once enthralled the world, Pasqualina would whisper: 'It's not the same any more. Nothing is the same.'[49] But she could not let him catch her looking sorrowful. Always she put on a brave face.

In the autumn of 1958, at Castel Gandolfo, Pacelli had a terrible bout of hiccups. Despite the ministrations of his doctors, nothing seemed to work. Pasqualina telephoned Spellman, in Naples, and asked him to come at once.

'Holiness will not recover this time', Pasqualina told Spellman. 'He's very weak.'[50] Now that it was too late to save Pacelli, Pasqualina was concerned to do all in her power to preserve the legacy of his papacy.

The teachings of Christ, she told Spellman, were being 'subjugated by the politics of personal greed' – in the Vatican, no less. To Pasqualina, it was deplorable that the hierarchy had taken such umbrage at the 'eccentricities of an old man'. For her, it was 'tragic for good men of God, influential leaders of the most powerful religion on earth, to have allowed such a disaster to happen'.[51]

'They will choose someone his exact opposite, mainly to discredit Pius's papacy', Pasqualina told Spellman. 'Holiness is that much resented by some. As you are aware, Eminence, there are those who cry out for liberalization, but freedom without strong leadership will only lead to disaster for the Church. It is to be hoped that those who steer the Holy See will not find out too late.'[52]

The German nun and the American Cardinal spoke of the likely successor to Pacelli. Pasqualina dreaded Tisserant but Spellman, a consummate politician, allayed her fears. 'Even with the present internationalisation of the Sacred College, Tisserant will never make it. He's made too many enemies.'[53] Spellman was more concerned with the Montini faction of liberals in the Church. He hinted that his first vote would be for a fellow arch-conservative, Cardinal Ruffini, Archbishop of Palermo. Pasqualina was astounded. Spellman knew full well of Ruffini's association with the Mafia in Sicily. She looked at Spellman with new eyes. Was her old and cherished friend really all that he seemed?

When the conversation turned to Cardinal Roncalli, Pasqualina noted something very interesting indeed about Spellman. Formerly he had scoffed at Roncalli as a 'harmless soul', with no more intellect than a 'simple banana man peddling his fruit'.[54] But now, significantly, Spellman had stopped criticizing Roncalli. Was it possible that he was being proposed as a compromise candidate between the conservative and liberal factions within the Church?

To Pasqualina, Roncalli had been the 'poorest of dark horses'.[55] Pacelli had given him almost no powers of decision-making, and kept him on a notoriously tight rein. It certainly seemed unlikely that Roncalli would defend Pacelli's papacy or continue with his Great Design.

Pasqualina's disapproval was not personal. She found Roncalli 'a good soul . . . a well-adjusted, agreeable old Cardinal'. But to her the 77-year-old patriarch, little younger than Pacelli, was 'an easy mark and on the threshold of eternity'. With her instinctive distrust of the Vatican hierarchy, she feared that powerful figures would 'twist him around their fingers', and that Pacelli's lifetime's work would be undone.[56]

On 9 October 1958 Eugenio Pacelli, Pope Pius XII, died. For almost 60 years, he had given his life to the service of the Church. For over 40 years, Pasqualina had devoted herself to the welfare of this strange and difficult man of genius. Theirs was a love affair possibly unique in the history of the world, all the more precious for its platonic nature.

When Pacelli died Tisserant, as *Camerlengo*, wasted no time in getting rid of Pasqualina. She left the Vatican penniless, with all her worldly belongings in a tiny suitcase. An old priest, crossing St Peter's Square, saw her struggle into a taxi with some cages of Pacelli's favourite pet birds. The priest admitted he was ashamed that no member of the Holy See had turned out to say goodbye to this nun who had given her life to Pacelli and to Pius XII's papacy.

The taxi drove away and Pasqualina disappeared, as though she had never existed. Nobody in the Vatican seemed to know or care where she had gone. She was an embarrassment, a painful memory, to be airbrushed from official Church history.

Chapter 19

Casa Pastor Angelicus

'Loneliness is not simply a matter of being alone', Pasqualina sombrely reflected. 'Loneliness is the feeling that nobody else truly cares what happens to you.'[1]

In a secluded convent in Switzerland, the other nuns kept their distance from her, doubtless intimidated by her daunting reputation. Pasqualina's grief consumed her. She was enveloped in desolation. 'I did not sleep for three weeks after Holiness passed away', she confided many years later. 'And I ate precious little.'[2] For more than 40 years, almost every waking minute had been taken up with Pacelli's endless needs. A dozen times a day, especially in the final years, she had scurried toward the querulous cry: 'Mother Pasqualina, come here at once! . . . I need this . . . I need that . . . I NEED YOU!'[3] Now Pacelli was gone. Now, nobody would ever again say to her, in such a way, 'I NEED YOU!'

Pasqualina's own health, both physical and psychological, had been severely impaired by the terrible burden of so many years of struggle, culminating in the shock of Pacelli's death. She asked permission to go back to the little farm in Ebersberg and recuperate in the company of what remained of her family. Coldly and cruelly, the Church refused her request.

For hour after hour Pasqualina sat ramrod-straight in her chair, lost in meditation, praying to a God with whom she had always kept faith.

Dull years of exile passed. In all that time, Pasqualina had only one visitor – Cardinal Spellman. For all his politicking, for all his love of luxury, for all his vanity, in the end Spellman proved to be her one true friend. One day they sat together, holding hands in the Stella Maris retreat house in Switzerland, where she had met Pacelli nearly half a century before.

Pasqualina poured out her heart to Spellman. Pacelli's Great Design was crumbling; the Church was falling into decay. The genie of liberalism, now released from the bottle, was spreading deadly viruses.

'Stop pitying yourself, Mother Pasqualina! You've always been the staunchest activist in support of the teachings of Christ. If you believe that the Holy See is failing these days to show proper example, what are you showing?'[4] The normally amiable Spellman was being deliberately harsh, in order to snap her out of her depression.

'There are millions in the same predicament as you', Spellman continued, warming to his theme. 'You are such a great force of strength for women everywhere to look to and call upon in their declining years. Gather together as many as you can. Build them a home. Give them new hope and new life.'[5]

With inspired wisdom, Spellman had given Pasqualina the perfect sense of purpose, one arising naturally from the trauma of her own life. From then on, she had a mission – to build a sanctuary for old and lonely women. First though, she needed the blessing of the new pontiff, the formerly disregarded Roncalli, now Pope John XXIII. Although he had made no contact with her during the weary years of exile, to Pasqualina's surprise 'he did not deny me an audience, or keep me waiting as I had kept him, during Pius's papacy'.[6]

And so Pasqualina returned to the Vatican, a forlorn figure standing in a thronged anteroom, waiting her turn. 'How different everything seems', she thought, looking around her at the crowd, remembering a time when she had allowed so very few to come near the Pope's inner sanctum.[7]

Suddenly Roncalli was standing in the doorway. Although he had not known of her presence, his eyes went straight to her and his face lit up. 'Mother Pasqualina!' he exclaimed. 'How nice of you to visit me! And you've brought me a gift!' he smiled.[8] Playfully he snatched up Pasqualina's bag, which contained a quilt she had made for him.

Sadly, Pasqualina was too stiff and reserved for Roncalli's easy informality. Instead of lobbying for her women's sanctuary, she began to tell him everything which, in her view, was wrong with the present Church. Of course, every liberal tendency had been inspired by the very person sitting opposite. Their meeting was a fatal clash of personalities and beliefs. 'Opening the windows of the Church to the world will create an ecclesiastical tragedy', Pasqualina told Roncalli with typical bluntness. 'People look to the Holy See for strong leadership.'[9]

Unconsciously Pasqualina was lecturing the Pope, as she had so often lectured Pacelli. 'If you repudiate Rome's authoritarian heritage, if you deprive the human spirit of authoritarian direction, man's moral and ethical judgments will be overwhelmed. Sin and crime, then decadence, will too often seize control.'[10]

Another pope might have told Pasqualina, a mere nun, to hold her tongue; but that was not Roncalli's way. He would not embarrass her. And, familiar as he was with her indomitable spirit, he well knew the futility of arguing. Instead he smiled. 'Mother Pasqualina, you are always thinking and brooding. A beautiful woman like you should stop worrying about the world. Think of yourself for once. Enjoy life. Let change take care of the future.'[11] Although Pope John's words were kindly meant, Pasqualina bristled inwardly at what she took to be chauvinism and condescension. But already she could see that the papal assistant had entered the room and assumed the severe stance that she had so often taken with guests who outstayed their welcome.

Pasqualina had ruined her chances of getting papal permission for her sanctuary during Pope John's reign. Although she subsequently wrote to him, he never replied.

Pasqualina was left with no option but to wait for the next pope. Unfortunately Pope Paul VI was none other than her former enemy, Giovanni Montini, who had been banished to Milan courtesy of Pacelli, Spellman and herself. Pope John had rescued Montini from oblivion and made him a cardinal, to pave the way for a liberal successor. 'In my young days, he [Montini] seemed like such a poke', Pasqualina laughingly recalled. 'I used to love to torment him. If I saw that he was in a hurry, I'd deliberately rush ahead of him to the mimeograph machine. He'd be furious. The worst he ever dared to say to me was that he'd pray for the salvation of my wicked soul. I knew he meant what he said when he blessed himself afterward.'[12]

As a lobbyist of popes, Pasqualina was incorrigible. At 70 she still carried herself ramrod-straight, whereas to her Montini seemed old and withered. 'I hope I don't look as ancient as you!' she shamelessly blurted out. After his initial shock, the Pope replied: 'I see my prayers have not been answered. Pasqualina, you are as wicked as ever!'[13] The pair of them broke out in unexpected laughter.

To Pasqualina, the former animosity between Montini and herself was unimportant compared to her present mission. She had learned a bitter lesson from her disastrous meeting with Pope John. This time, she didn't waste a second. During the decades with Pacelli, and even long before that, as a child in the little farm at Ebersberg, Pasqualina argued for what she wanted with utter fervour.

'Mother Pasqualina, you are a good nun', Pope Paul told her.[14] He gently touched her forehead with his Fisherman's Ring as she knelt for his blessing. This time, she instinctively knew that all would be well. Somehow, their long history of enmity had been superseded by the spirit of love.

And so Casa Pastor Angelicus came into being. Pasqualina's sanctuary was set on a hill overlooking the Tyrrhenian Sea. It was rumoured that the donor was Count Enrico Galeazzi, former governor-general of the Vatican, a rare figure who was trusted by two very different popes, Pacelli and Montini.

Unlike Galeazzi however, Spellman, the long standing confidant of Pacelli, incurred acute disfavour from Montini because of his exile to Milan. The relationship between the two men worsened over the 1960s war in Vietnam. The papacy called for an end to the conflict, whereas the arch-conservative Spellman was a hawk who sided publicly with the US administration in what it saw as an anti-communist war.

During Pacelli's papacy, Spellman had made a fortune for the Church and had been applauded for it. But Spellman, like many a financier before and since, was not above resorting to dubious methods. Pacelli had consistently turned a blind eye. But Montini saw Spellman in a very different light. There were too many questions to be asked about where the money was coming from, and where it was going. For Spellman, these questions amounted to 'ingratitude' after all he had achieved for the Church.[15] Aged 75, and about to celebrate his 50th anniversary as a priest, he angrily tendered his resignation. Montini considered this for a full month, while Spellman's remaining friends in the Vatican pressured the pontiff to reject it. Eventually he did. Spellman publicly stated: 'I accept this decision of His Holiness as God's will for me.'[16]

Two years later, in 1967, Spellman died. Pasqualina greeted the news of her dear friend's passing with equanimity. 'He is happier with Jesus', she said. 'Cardinal Spellman's spirit had been broken.'[17] It was a terribly sad ending for a man who had achieved so much for the Church, albeit by questionable means. And it was another tart reminder of the impermanence of Pacelli's legacy.

During the social and political turbulence of the 1960s, Pasqualina saw the Church she loved torn apart. Attendance at Sunday Mass dropped by a half. Donations to the Church dropped by a half. Nearly 90 per cent of married couples were using banned forms of contraception. Seminaries were half-empty. A quarter of priests asked in vain for permission to marry. Thousands of priests and nuns, and millions of Catholics, abandoned the Church.

Pasqualina's forebodings had been deadly accurate. She took no pleasure in being proved right. She wearily concluded: 'The well-disciplined, cohesive, mystical Church of Pius was severely compromised by those who followed him and, most especially, by the Second Vatican Council.'[18]

Pasqualina believed that Pacelli's Great Design was 'the centrepiece in a model of Church life ... Pius spurned ecumenism and feared the increasing demo-cratisation of ecclesiastical decision-making'.[19] To Pasqualina 'the vernacular Mass, the growing role of the laity in Church policies, and the rising debate over the Holy See's sexual ethics' were 'signs of decadence and profanation of Catholic heritage'.[20]

'Those who doubt Pius's beliefs have only to look at the present record of the Church to see the disaster that has come about', she sorrowfully concluded. 'I pray that, one day, Pius will be canonised a saint. Holiness set the example for what is important in life. Catholics during Pius's papacy felt God's reward of peace in their hearts and souls. What greater gift can anyone ask?'[21]

Pasqualina ended her days amid the tranquillity of *Casa Pastor Angelicus*, her memorial to Pacelli. From her peaceful hillside, she could look across toward Rome and remember the days of his greatness. Even in her late eighties she continued giving unstintingly of herself, working from five o'clock in the morning until late at night. Recalling how Spellman had roused her from grief, she strove to rouse others from the grief of their fractured lives: 'We have no time for "down-in-the-mouth" ladies who sit around pitying themselves. We live by the teachings of Christ; that means good common sense and moderation in everything in life. With that philosophy, how can one not be happy?'[22]

Pasqualina lived for 25 years after the death of Pacelli. She died on 13 November 1983, at the age of 89.

What can we possibly make of this extraordinary woman? She was vilified by the College of Cardinals, and the memory of Pasqualina remains a severe embarrassment to the Vatican. She loved the Church, she loved Christ, and she loved Pacelli, His Vicar on earth. Always Pasqualina strove to strengthen a man who fatally doubted himself. Certainly in the latter years, the pupil had grown to surpass the master. It is fascinating to speculate how this papal adviser might have fared, had she been Pope herself. From her account of her exchanges with Pacelli, it is almost certain that she would have protested much more robustly against the Nazi regime. Pacelli consistently adopted an appeasement stance of 'damage limitation', not only with Fascism but also with the Mafia in Sicily and with corruption within the Church. Undoubtedly he thereby suffered terrible torment. Only with communism, where appeasement was futile, did he show unremitting resistance.

Appeasement was utterly alien to Pasqualina's character. Hitler, who remarked of the British Queen Mother 'she is a dangerous woman', might have met his match in this tiny Bavarian nun, as a snake transfixed by a mongoose. It is probable that Pasqualina possessed the character to have become one of the very greatest of popes. Sadly, this is one of those tantalizing riddles of history to which we shall never know the answer.

Chapter 20

The Verdicts of History

When Pope Pius XII died, the world was full of praise for him. But within a few years his Great Design had faded, as though it too had never existed. The Second Vatican Council of Pope John XXIII was Catholicism's 'Second Spring' for many, a desperately needed modernization of a Church which had been in a state of permanent defence since the Reformation. But, as with the 1968 'Prague Spring' of Czechoslovakia, its time was fleeting. Ever since Pacelli's death, the forces of anti-Modernism have held sway. The rationale behind his Great Design underpins so much of the Church today – from the iconic papal image to the centralization of control.

If the 1950s were Catholicism's golden age, the 1960s were its *anni horribili*. The role of religion in society decayed dramatically. In its place came the rampant materialism which Pacelli despised. Searches for meaning transcending this world became increasingly meretricious. While many of the later New Age proponents were sincere, some of their dogma strains credulity.

Jewish judgement on Pacelli has, by and large, been surprisingly magnanimous. In 1945, the World Jewish Congress donated two million lire to the Vatican in gratitude for its wartime aid programme. It is estimated that the relief programme initiated by Pacelli and Pasqualina saved some 860,000 Jews, more than every other such initiative, both governmental and international, put together.[1] Although the deportation of Jews from Rome was a terrible affair, one estimate has it that some 7,000 lives were saved, via pressure put by Pacelli on the occupying forces.[2]

Golda Meir, Israeli Foreign Minister at the time of Pacelli's death, sent the following telegram to the Vatican:

> We share in the grief of humanity at the passing away of His Holiness, Pope Pius XII. In a generation affected by wars and discords, he upheld the highest ideals of peace and compassion. When fearful martyrdom came to our people in the decade of Nazi terror, the voice of the Pope was raised for the victims. The life of our times was enriched by a voice speaking out on the great moral truths, above the tumult of daily conflict. We mourn a great servant of peace.[3]

A most poignant footnote comes from the noted author Michael O'Carroll, about his meeting with the Pope in 1957. After offering the benign greetings of Dr Isaac Herzog, Chief Rabbi of Israel, O'Carroll ventured: 'I think Jews everywhere are grateful for what you did for them during the war.' Pacelli's reply is replete with sadness and regret: *'I wish I could have done more'* [Italics added].[4]

In 1963, Rolf Hochhuth's play *The Representative* excoriated Pacelli. Although the accusations were repudiated by authorities such as the Jewish historian Jeno Levai, and Hochhuth's shortcomings were later brutally exposed by the television interviewer David Frost, nevertheless a floodgate of criticism was opened. The Holy See did not help matters by suggesting, initially, that Pacelli may have been ignorant of the true horror. The argument of ignorance quickly proved untenable. It seems that the Holy See had been kept extremely well-informed of wartime atrocities, particularly in Poland and Croatia. On 30 May, Pacelli had written to the Polish Cardinal Primate, Hlond: 'We are fully aware, and grievously feel the repercussions, of the present deplorable situation of Poland, stricken by so many terrible misfortunes.'[5]

Throughout the war, Pacelli's Christmas broadcasts had deplored inhumanity, albeit in characteristically elliptical terms which failed to identify the Nazis. His Christmas 1942 broadcast had been more blunt; yet, for the President of Poland, it was not blunt enough. On 2 January 1943 he appealed to Pacelli:

Holy Father, divine laws trampled upon, human dignity humiliated, hundreds of thousands of men murdered without trial, families separated, churches profaned and closed, religion forced into the catacombs – this is the picture of Poland as shown in the reports we receive from the country.

In this tragic moment, my people are fighting not only for their existence, but for everything they hold sacred. They do not want vengeance but justice, they do not ask for material or diplomatic aid – for they know that such aid cannot reach them, except on the very smallest scale – but *they implore a voice which will clearly and definitely indicate the evil and condemn those who collaborate in it.* I am convinced that, if the people can be strengthened in their belief that divine law knows no compromise and is above all human considerations of the present, the Polish people will find the strength to resist...

In the past, in Poland's times of difficulty, though times less fraught with tears and blood than the present, Your Holiness's great predecessors addressed fatherly words to the Poles. Today, when in the greater part of our country, men can neither preach nor pray in Polish, *the silence must be broken by a voice from the Apostolic See, and those who die with the consolation of religion, defending their faith and their traditions, must be able to count on the blessing of the Vicar of Christ.* [Italics added][6]

No appeal could have been more sincere or more pitiful; and yet it was in vain.

At the Nuremberg trials after the end of World War Two, Albrecht von Kessel, the Vatican diplomat and aide to von Weizsäcker, had testified on the particular issue of the Jews of Rome:

I am convinced, therefore, that his Holiness, the Pope, did, day and night, think of a manner in which he could help the unfortunate Jews in Rome. If he did not lodge a protest, then it was not done because he thought, justifiably, that if he protested, Hitler would go crazy and that would not help the Jews at all, that would give one the justified fear that they would be killed even more quickly. Apart from that, the SS would probably have been instructed to penetrate into the Vatican and lay hands on the person of the Pope.[7]

In 1963, commenting on the Hochhuth play, von Kessel wrote of the wider issue:

> We were convinced that a fiery protest by Pius XII against the persecution of the Jews would have, in all probability, put the Pope himself and the Curia into extreme danger, but ... would certainly not have saved the life of a single Jew. Hitler, like a trapped beast, would react to any menace that he felt directed at him, with cruel violence.[8]

Tisserant's famous 1940 letter to Cardinal Suhard has endlessly been cited as fatal criticism of Pacelli. Tisserant had caustically noted: 'I fear that history will reproach the Holy See for having practised a policy of selfish convenience and little else.' But the volatile Tisserant was perfectly capable of making utterances in anger. The tone of his letter may well reflect his frustration at not being allowed to play a more proactive role with France. Later on in the war, when Pacelli released the cardinals from their vows, Pasqualina reported that the doughty Tisserant was visibly moved and was among the first to offer his allegiance to Pacelli.

Certainly, toward the end of his life even the fiery Tisserant seemed to find magnanimity. In a 1964 interview, he had this to say:

> '[Pacelli] could guide the Church with invincible strength ... I could not have dealt with the tragedy which was yet to unfold [the Holocaust].'
> The Pope's attitude was beyond discussion. My remarks [in the 1940 letter to Cardinal Suhard] did not involve his person but certain members of the Curia. In the dramatic period of the war, and what a dramatic period that was, Pope Pius XII was able to guide the Church with invincible strength ... If the consequences [of a protest] were to fall on himself alone, Pius XII would not have been in the slightest way concerned. Everyone knows that he was ready to go to a concentration camp. But he weighted before all else the mortal risks to which the victims of Nazism could be exposed in the case of a protest which would have been fruitless in regard to the concrete rescue action being effected, on the Pope's orders, throughout the Church.[9]

Of protest against the Nazis, the author Pierre Lapide has this to say:

> The saddest and most thought-provoking conclusion is that, whilst the Catholic clergy of Holland protested more loudly, expressly and frequently against Jewish persecutions than the religious hierarchy of any other Nazi-occupied country, more Jews – some 110,000 or 79 per cent of the total – were deported from Holland to death camps; more than anywhere in the West.[10]

One of the victims was the noted philosopher, Edith Stein. Mgr Bernard, Bishop of Luxemburg, has given this chilling account of the effect of papal protest on the treatment meted out to the inmates of Dachau:

> The detained priests trembled every time news reached us of some protest by a religious authority, but particularly by the Vatican. We all had the impression that our warders made us atone heavily for the fury these protests evoked ... whenever the way we were treated became more brutal, the Protestant pastors among the prisoners used

to vent their indignation on the Catholic priests: 'Again your big *naïve* Pope and those simpletons, your bishops, are shooting their mouths off . . . why don't they get the idea, once for all, and shut up. They play the heroes and we have to pay the bill.[11]

When Fr Scavizzi, an Italian chaplain, told of conditions in the concentration camps, Pacelli broke down in tears.

> Please tell everyone, everyone you can, that the Pope suffers agony on their behalf . . . Perhaps my solemn protest would have earned me praise from the civilized world, but it would also have brought more implacable persecution of the Jews . . . I love the Jews.[12]

Yet in Poland, it had bitterly been asked 'if the Pope, about whom they [the Poles] had been told and preached to when things were going well, had forgotten them now that they were in such great need'.[13] And again:

> The Catholic population of the Wartheland is constantly raising the question if the Pope cannot help and why he is keeping silent. It eagerly awaits a declaration from your Holiness in the misery of our religious situation. And even if it were not now possible to pronounce in public a word of this kind, the Catholics of the Wartheland still believe that a vigorous protest by your Holiness to the Reich government, against the harassment which borders on oppression and against the restrictive regulations imposed on Church life by governmental, especially police authorities, would have some good result.[14]

On 10 June 1942, Hitler had banned official representation by the Holy See in the religious affairs of Poland. The nuncio had fled to Romania with the government. Ironically, Pacelli's refusal to accept the German invasion hindered diplomatic initiatives. Clearly none of this cut any ice whatsoever with the Poles, who constantly infuriated Hitler with their unremitting opposition to Nazism.

The exiled Bishop Radonski of Wladislava bluntly wrote thus to Cardinal Maglione on the Nazi propaganda value of papal silence:

> All this time, the Germans cry aloud that everything is being done in the sight and with the knowledge of the Sovereign Pontiff and with his consent. And, as no denial is issued, simple, honest people end by believing it, according to the maxim: he who does not speak, consents.[15]

Karol Jozef Wojtyla, later Pope John Paul II, had this to say:

> I shall never forget the profound impression which I felt when I saw him [Pacelli] close-up for the first time. It was during an audience which he granted to the young priests and seminarists of the Belgian College. Pius came to each one and, when he reached me, the College Rector told him that I came from Poland. The Pope stopped for a while and repeated with evident emotion 'from Poland'; then he said, in Polish, 'Praised be Jesus Christ.' This was in the first months of the year 1947, less than two years after the end of the Second World War, which had been a terrible trial for Europe, especially for Poland.[16]

Cardinal Tardini noted:

> Pius was, by natural temperament, meek and rather timid. He was not born with the

temper of a fighter. In this, he differed from his great predecessor, Pius XI, who rejoiced, at least visibly, in the contest. Pius XII visibly suffered.[17]

However, Cardinal Tardini also noted:

Yes. Pius XII was strong; he did not fear criticisms, opposition, lamentation, accusation. We saw him advance, calm and sure, along the way opened to him by God and his conscience.[18]

Tardini also noted that Pacelli's capacity for work surpassed anything he had ever encountered. Pacelli's erstwhile colleagues, Pius XI and Gasparri, had been exceptional. But with Pacelli, the work was 'Ceaseless, Ceaseless'.[19] Eighteen-hour days were a regular occurrence.

Pope Paul VI commented:

The frail and gentle exterior of Pius XII and the sustained refinement and moderation of his language concealed – if they did not rather reveal – a noble and virile character capable of taking very firm decisions and of adopting fearlessly positions that entailed considerable risk.[20]

Even critics of Pacelli have praised his exemplary character:

His whole career is characterized by a rigid sense of ascetic piety and exemplary morality. A fine figure of a priest, imbued with a sense of his mission and the holiness of his office, Eugenio Pacelli cannot but arouse honest and sympathetic admiration for the dignified moral figure he presents and his proud composure as a prelate ... He is undoubtedly one of the most eminent figures among the Roman clergy of the past 50 years. His personal piety, his exemplary apostolic zeal, the religious sensibility of his temperament, are all qualities that commend him to universal respect and consideration.[21]

And yet Carlo Falconi's shrewd estimation has an uncanny resonance:

At bottom he was an intellectual, a man interested in systems and abstract ideas, indeed a utopian in the best sense of the term – but not a man of action. A man of action and a statesman is someone who can recognise his peers, for better or worse, and make use of them for his own ends, exploiting their gifts and abilities – not a man who draws back from contacts with them and fears their reactions. *But Pius XII was paralysed by his fear of contact with other men: their cleverness and shrewdness disarmed him, their vanity and passions bewildered him.* [Italics added][22]

Always the wily Hitler feared Pacelli's power; and yet always Pacelli acted as though Hitler held all the power and he held none.

Ultimately, who would know a man better than his confessor? Cardinal Bea, who was Pacelli's confessor for ten years in Rome, has given us this estimation of his character:

As his confessor, I can, of course, say nothing, but fortunately my relations with Pius XII began more than 20 years before I became his confessor, that is, they go back to the time when he was nuncio in Munich, in 1921. In addition, even when I was his confessor, I was also in touch with him on matters which had nothing to do with confession. So I can speak of him with an easy mind...

189

Pius XII was clearly a man of different stamp [from Pope John XXIII who, the cardinal said, had great esteem for him] and perhaps fundamentally *a lonely man in his greatness and in his keen sense of responsibility*, and in this way, too, he was lonely in his personal austerity and life. It should perhaps be added that *it will be many years, if not centuries*, before the immense work of this Pope and his enduring influence on the Church and even on the history of humanity can be properly evaluated. In the midst of a terrible and catastrophic war and during the period of reconstruction which followed it, *his help was solicited from all sides as was no other man's*. [Italics added][23]

Undoubtedly the public image of Pacelli has suffered from comparison with that of his successor. Archbishop Cushing of Boston's comparison of the two men is thought-provoking:

[Pope] John had a far more effective way of dealing with the news media than Pius. In many ways, John was the shrewder of the two. His humble, rather beguiling manner won people over far more effectively than Pius's cold and direct authoritarian words . . . Misguided liberals, especially those of the news media, hated Pius for his silence on the Nazis' persecutions of the Jews. They looked upon Pius as a devil, while they were quick to make John a saint, often simply because he seemed just the opposite to Pius. They were wrong in both instances. Neither Pope was as good nor as bad as he was painted. In many ways, they differed only slightly, except in style. But the liberal news media could not see this.[24]

Malachi Martin has pointed out how supporters and detractors of both Pacelli and Roncalli have fallen easy prey to temptingly convenient images. Pacelli is the *Pastor Angelicus*, or he is an 'image of neo-Roman imperialism'. (In fact, he was both.) Roncalli was 'a simple peasant searching for love' who wanted 'to update the Church' and 'open windows on the world' to 'undo the authoritarian grip of the Vatican'. Alternatively, he did not know what he was doing by unleashing the chaos of 'individual thought and allowing masses of people to participate in reforming' the Church.[25]

Certainly Montini, who knew both men well, was able to respect their individual contributions to the Church. On 18 November 1965, as the recently elected Pope Paul VI, he announced the Cause of Canonization of both his predecessors, Pope John XXIII and Pope Pius XII.

And what of Pasqualina – the woman who loved Pacelli for more than 40 years. What was her estimation of his character?

Almost every day, throughout all the years of the war, the Holy Father, as the spiritual head of more than 350 million Catholics, was the recipient of confidential information. Often it was some horrible news or devastating statistic. I will never forget when His Holiness was told that, in Poland alone, 2,647 priests were taken to concentration camps and either gassed to death or shot. As horrible as that news was, there were times when the revelations were even more terrifying.

When His Holiness was told of their demise [the deaths of first Mussolini, then Hitler], he said nothing, holding to the Catholic teaching that one does not speak unkindly of the deceased. But I could tell from the grim expression on his face that he could never bring himself to forgive them for their crimes and sins. Yet he went to the papal chapel, on both occasions, and said silent prayers for the repose of the souls of

Mussolini and Hitler. I joined him in those prayers.

Relations between His Holiness and President Roosevelt became distinctly cooler after the bombardment of Rome in 1943. He never really trusted any of the world leaders after that. To Pius, the Allies' plan for a Grand Alliance after World War Two, that included communist Russia, was a sellout of the free nations of Europe, Poland, and others. Think now how right His Holiness was! [Pasqualina's comments were made before the collapse of communism.]

People ask, 'Why did Pius XII remain silent?' It is easy enough for anyone to ask such a question. But, when the lives of millions of people were at stake, the Holy Father was obliged to use discretion. At one point, Hitler threatened to exterminate many thousands of additional priests and others of the clergy, if His Holiness were to speak out in condemnation. Perhaps when one considers that terrible price upon human lives, one might understand the reasons for Pius's silence.[26]

In the course of an interview with Paul Murphy, author of *La Popessa*, Pasqualina made the following comment:

I would like to show you a respected historian's view of who was the more honourable – the Allies or the papacy – when it came to helping Jews and others during World War Two.[27] [She then gave the following quote from John Toland's biography of Hitler.]

The Church, under the Pope's guidance, had already saved the lives of more Jews than all other churches, religious institutions and rescue organizations combined, and was presently hiding thousands of Jews in monasteries, convents and Vatican City itself. The record of the Allies was far more shameful. The British and Americans, despite lofty pronouncements, had not only avoided taking any meaningful action but gave sanctuary to few persecuted Jews. The Moscow Declaration of that year – signed by Roosevelt, Churchill and Stalin – methodically listed Hitler's victims as Polish, Italian, French, Dutch, Belgian, Norwegian, Soviet and Cretan. The curious omission of Jews (a policy emulated by the US Office of War Information) was protested, vehemently but uselessly, by the World Jewish Congress. By the simple expedient of converting the Jews of Poland into Poles, and so on, the Final Solution was lost in the Big Three's general classification of Nazi terrorism.[28]

A tearful Pasqualina concluded:

How unfair that His Holiness was forced to suffer so much of the blame. The self-righteous Allies – particularly Roosevelt, who would accept nothing short of uncon-ditional surrender, even though it meant prolonging the Holocaust – were devious enough to shift responsibility. *The Allies blamed Pius for his so-called 'silence', to escape the world's criticism for their disgraceful hypocrisy.* [Italics added][29]

Chapter 21

Pope Pius XII: An Apologia

Use of the word 'apologia' in relation to Pope Pius XII must be explained. It is meant to designate a defence of this Pope's activities – particularly his most controversial ones – in terms that have not been described before in quite such a way. For they principally involve the interaction of psychological factors with political ones. It is thus a defence, primarily, of the man as an individual rather than as a Pope. It explains rather than excuses his actions, and presupposes an understanding of the state of papal affairs which he inherited with his first involvement during the years preceding the First World War. Then, as Assistant Secretary of State, Pacelli had been the principal architect of the Vatican's concordat with Serbia, which contributed so significantly to the outbreak of war. He was swept forward by this momentum, although ultimately his direction was primarily dictated by his personal character.

The political aspect of Pope Pius XII's reign, and his outlook in general, date back to the days of Pius IX, the latter part of whose long pontificate was dedicated to an unremitting struggle against enlightenment, liberalism and democracy. The struggle was continued in a slightly different but, in some ways, even more vehement form during the anti-Modernist campaign of the next Pope but one, Pius X (1903–1914). There was some mitigation of this campaign during the reign of Benedict XV (1914–1922), but in the reign of Pius XI (1922–1939) it gained a new lease of life, although in a different form.

The Roman Church now entered what has been called its 'Fascist phase', the first chapter of which was the concordat with Mussolini's Italy and the Lateran Treaty of 1929, establishing Vatican City. This re acquisition of some sort of 'sovereignty' by the Holy See had been the chief preoccupation of all the Popes since the 1870 demise of the Papal States.

During this period the popes had become almost morbidly concerned with what came to be called the 'Roman Question', involving the 'imprisonment' of the Pope in a no-man's-land in a Rome that was, for the first time for centuries, an entirely secular city and the capital of a united Italy.

Pius XI's *rapprochement* with Mussolini has been called a pact with the devil. It did indeed have dire consequences. The Holy See, obsessed by its fear of communism, made alliances on all sides with the Fascist countries – Spain, Hungary, Portugal, Italy and Germany being the most important.

For Pius XI's Secretary of State, Cardinal Eugenio Pacelli, later Pius XII

(1939–1958), the power and authority of the Roman Catholic Church were the most important things that existed. They were forces to be strengthened and defended, for the spiritual salvation of the world. He thus sought the supremacy of the Church, at the expense of any other consideration, because nothing short of that could ensure the success of God's plan for the world as entrusted to His Earthly Vicar – himself.

A part of the sacrifice necessary for this was the disappearance of all Catholic political parties, so that all power could be centralized from Rome. Pacelli therefore arranged for the self-destruction of the Catholic ('Centre') party in Germany, thus removing the last obstacle to the assumption of power by Hitler. Pacelli's attitude toward Hitler was the most controversial aspect of his pontificate.

A more detailed consideration of what has been said above would be a highly desirable introduction to this overall assessment of Pope Pius XII. It would go a long way to explaining why, almost despite himself, he was led into the line of action toward Nazi Germany for which he has been condemned by so many historians. Such a line of action on his part had horrendous consequences for millions of people, particularly the Jews.

But is it correct to call him, for example, 'Hitler's Pope?' Almost certainly not.

One can see reasons, in the final analysis, for so sensational a description, but it is a misleading one. The real reasons why Pius, as Pope, could not escape from the momentum of papal – pro-Fascist – policy lay ultimately within himself; in his character and in the beliefs that motivated his actions.

We thus come to the consideration proper of *Pius the man*. Given his political inheritance, could he have broken the mould and initiated an entirely different strategy for the Holy See in his time? The answer is yes – but only if he had been a man of very different psychological make-up from what he was. It was the combination of papal outlook, as inherited from the late nineteenth century, with the personal character of Pope Pius XII, which determined the course of history during this period. Had either of these elements been different, the whole pattern of events would have developed otherwise. It was their interaction that made what happened virtually inevitable.

Let us, at this point, go straight to the 'jugular' and outline in a few, possibly very harsh, words the hard core of Pacelli's personality (in contrast to previous assessments).

The earliest biographies of Pope Pius XII – almost all virtual hagiographies – depicted him as a saint. This he certainly was not, except in a particular 'technical' and traditionally Roman Catholic sense, beloved of devotees of the canonization process. A saint, in the real meaning of the word, would not have let millions die, which is what in effect he did, since he knew about such deaths without engaging in any activity on the victims' behalf. The result of his activity in this regard, such as it was, was indirect. His accompanying outlook was convoluted, tortured and agonized, being based on his own particular theory of how the Roman Church should react to this situation, coupled with his love for political and diplomatic intrigue.

194

Later biographies, on the other hand, particularly the most recent of all, have depicted him as little less than a monster. This, equally, he was not. He was no deliberate and sardonic murderer-by-default. He was a man of considerable compassion, despite his aloofness and grim but, to him, logical mode of proceeding. But, to go back to the 'jugular'...

As time went on Pacelli, monumentally conscious of his position as a man sent by God to save a deeply troubled world, came gradually but increasingly to inhabit a fantasy world. More and more, he feasted upon the image of himself as a demigod; a man above other men, the supreme arbiter of events. He was a sort of spiritual megalomaniac, and he was ever supremely conscious of himself as a man of destiny.

How can all this possibly contribute to an 'apologia'? The answer is that Pacelli took his every action with the purest and loftiest of intentions. He was at no moment aware of himself as other than the divinely appointed guardian of the world's most precious heritage, being sometimes forced into terrible, heart-rending decisions for the greater good.

This last principle had a venerable tradition in Catholic theology, as Pacelli was well aware. This, coupled with his own vivid awareness of the *unlimited* extent of papal power over all men, not just Catholic or even Christian, made him the last great pontifical despot – a sovereign of unimaginably immense power and authority. (Or so, at least, he personally thought.)

If he was ever in danger, however improbably, of being assailed by doubts as to the plenitude of his powers, there were many well-established precedents on which he could rely. He was, moreover, steeped in the details of all these and what they implied for him. He was thus the inheritor of a vast accumulation of gradually increased and enhanced papal power, ever since the time of that 'first rich father' who derived his power from what came to be called 'The Curse of Constantine'. Dante thus immortalized the situation:

'Alas! Constantine! What evil you bore into the world
Not by your conversion, but that dowry
Which the first rich father took from you!'

Pacelli, as mentioned, was inordinately conscious of his inheritance of what, from the time of Constantine onwards, gradually become the most powerful and far-reaching dictatorship the world has ever known. The Church virtually replaced the western Roman Empire, becoming a police state to enforce membership of official Christianity. Popes became emperors, imperial titles such as Pontifex Maximus being taken by the Bishop of Rome, starting with Leo the Great (440–461). He it was who stated that St Peter, through his successors as bishops of Rome, 'rightly rules all who are vested in the first instance by Christ'. Others took such claims much further, notably Gregory the Great (590–604). In the eighth century, the Holy See suddenly produced a document appearing to show that Constantine had made an extensive grant of territory to the papacy in the person of Sylvester I. It purported to give the popes 'imperial power' over Rome and 'all the provinces, localities and towns in Italy and the Western

Hemisphere' (amounting roughly to the entire extent of the western Roman Empire), a stupendous claim known as the 'Donation of Constantine'. After that the Roman Church soon became the most powerful monarchical power in history, with a head who claimed unlimited power of life and death *in this world and the next* over all peoples. No single man in modern times has had such power over humanity.

In 1302, Boniface VIII asserted that 'because of the need for salvation, every human creature is subject to the Roman Pontiff'.[1]

The Renaissance popes can be compared in a certain sense – though the analogy may come as a shock – to the larger-than-life characters who are the typical 'baddies' in James Bond films. These popes presided, after all, over a system whereby, particularly in the Albigensian Crusade, thousands were sought out and slaughtered for opposing the master plan (for men's salvation) of the Roman Church. The Inquisition, the favourite weapon of such popes, was a machinery of death. Its victims were not only 'heretics' but also 'witches'.

The whole drama, moreover, was not without its kinky sexual content. Officials of the Inquisition (mostly Dominican friars) were charged with extirpating the vile evil of witchcraft. Thousands of (in fact, perfectly innocent) women were brought before the Inquisition, stripped and flogged to expel the devil from their wicked bodies. All this was done 'for their sake', for the sake of their souls. Their bodies were fit only for burning.

The Pope, though himself in no way wicked, ruled the world as no Bond villain has succeeded in doing. He held all in thrall. He had the power to release sinners, by granting pardon for the guilt due to their sins, from punishment in this world and in the next. Indulgences, a likely source of revenue, were the instruments to quench the fires of purgatory and hell, in which men were encouraged to believe.

Strong words, I admit, from a Roman Catholic, but necessary to explain how popes could do such evil things and think they were doing good. One of them, Pius V, was officially declared to be a saint. Pius also held passionately to the conviction that all that ultimately mattered was the good of God's Church.

In the fifteenth century, the so-called 'Donation of Constantine' was discovered to have been a forgery but, by this time, the staggering acquisition of papal power had gone too far and was too strong to be held back. Even after the Reformation, Pope Pius V, in excommunicating Queen Elizabeth I, made triumphalist claims for 'This one ruler [the Pope] whom God established as prince over all nations and kingdoms, to root up, destroy, dissipate, scatter, plant and build, so that the Holy Spirit might bind together a faithful people ... and present it, safe and sound to the Saviour.'[2]

It is no exaggeration to say that Pope Pius XII applied this principle to himself and to his own time. Hence the possibility of summarizing his 'apologia' – albeit with drastic compression – as follows: such was the might and importance of the mandate he had personally been given by God that it was his duty to put the safety of the Roman Church above all other causes, however worthy. Coupled with his strict understanding of traditional Roman Catholic theology (to be discussed below), this made it, for him, an inevitable piece of inescapable logic, however harsh, that even so terrible a fate as the slaughter of millions of Jews was not so great an evil as would have been the fatal weakening of the one, true, Roman Catholic and Apostolic Church, of which he was guardian.

And it was just such a fatal weakening which, as long as Hitler was alive, he used to fear and dread, daily and nightly. From his own words, it is clear that he considered the appeasement of the Nazis to be vital for the avoidance of a possibly fatal crisis for the Church in Germany, representing, as it did at that time, Catholicism's strongest bastion in Europe.

In other words, much as he agonized over the fate of the Jews (and other Nazi victims), he was forced, by this view of affairs, to put their fate second to that of his Church. Its weakening or demise would be the greatest possible disaster for the world. This brings us to the point made about traditional Roman Catholic theology.

Cardinal Newman once said that, according to Catholic theology, no human tragedy, however extensive or terrible (such as wholesale death by, for example, famine, flood, earthquake or war), could be as great an evil as even one single venial (minor) sin.[3] Pacelli believed this fully, in his own way. In a private audience after the war with Father Martin D'Arcy SJ (who told me the story himself), Pacelli employed almost the exact words used by Newman to express his own philosophy, based as it was on the age-old Catholic belief that even the slightest deliberate offence against God's omnipotent majesty was a more reprehensible and evil phenomenon than any purely 'natural' disaster or instance of man's inhumanity against man. The latter, as part of God's providential (if inscrutable) plan and overall salvific will, must be preferred to any actual sin. To help men in their fight against sin, and to bring them to ultimate salvation, He had sent his only Son into the world. He, in turn, had founded a Church with a visible head on earth whose legitimate successor was the Pope.

When Eugenio Pacelli, as Pope Pius XII, viewed this Church as being in mortal danger, he conceived it as his duty to stop at nothing, however heart-breaking or heavy the cost, to steer the 'Ark of the Covenant' (his favourite name for the Church) into calm and safe waters.

Pacelli, in other words, was no monster. He was a man of distinct compassion and intense sensibility, whose very 'strength' (in the sense used by conventional promoters of sainthood by canonization) was his determination to crush all the devil's temptations to desert his post as guardian of God's Church, the one and only 'Gate of Heaven' for humanity, by currying human favour or by expressing humane/human reaction to an evil such as the Holocaust.

Thus he acted as he did toward Nazi Germany, *making superhuman efforts at all times to give shelter to Nazi victims and save Jewish lives.* Such were his convictions as conditioned so largely by his strange and complex personality that he could never permit humanitarian considerations, however shocking and painful, to depose his conception of the Church. The terrible logic of his heroic defence of the principles in which he so deeply believed made him, in some peoples' eyes, an accessory to murder and monstrous human suffering. It is an unjust charge, but one can easily see how it has come to be made.

Was Pacelli pro-German? Certainly he had a long-standing relationship with that troubled country. He had been nuncio for eight years in Munich and five years in Berlin. His leaving of Berlin had inspired a sense of almost national loss. His Bavarian and Reich concordats had been hailed as diplomatic coups. His close inner circle – Pasqualina and her sister nuns, together with Jesuits such as Leiber and Bea – were German. He spoke fluent German with them. And his life was a model of Teutonic discipline. So, culturally, Pacelli was greatly influenced by Germany.

But the suggestion that Pacelli was pro-Nazi is laughably wide of the mark. And, lest further investigation be called for, it is only necessary to look at the character of Pasqualina, Bavarian-born, German to the core, yet passionately anti-Hitler and anti-Nazi.

Was Pacelli anti-Semitic? Almost certainly not, in the normal sense of the term. He loved Jews; he loved all peoples. But, from the earliest age, he had certainly been exposed to anti-Semitic sentiments. We recall that his childhood teacher, Signor Marchi, had waxed eloquent about the supposed 'hard-heartedness' of the Jews.

Perhaps a more pernicious element in the Church has been the perception that, because the Jews were guilty of deicide in being party to Christ's cruci-fixion, they are in some mysterious way damned throughout all of history. This 'historical fatalism' goes far beyond being utterly depressing and lacking in humanity. It leads to deadly outcomes. Those Christians whose world views are neatly buttressed by this 'historical fatalism' might do well to reflect that Christ Himself was a Jew, and that Christianity purports to be a religion of love. What would Christ have to say about historical fatalism? And what would He have to say about anti-Semitism, its bastard offspring?

The Christian community was originally Jewish. However, as it became subsumed into the early Church, an anti-Semitic theological response to deicide became enshrined in the prevailing ethos. This theological anti-Semitism became evident in anti-Jewish regulations. The result is that, for almost two millennia, the Jews have been treated by the Church as, at best, second-rate members of the human race. At worst, the Church has persecuted the Jews and condoned those who have persecuted them. Thus a monster such as Hitler could blithely declare that he was finishing the work that the Church had started.

While the Church has stated that it 'deplores' anti-Semitism, it has stopped short of condemning it. And while it has exonerated Jews from the guilt of Christ's crucifixion, it has failed to exonerate them from deicide. The Holy See long refused to give diplomatic recognition to the state of Israel. The stated objection was that Israel remained in a state of war, with its boundaries in dispute. Much the same objection could have been made about the Republic of Ireland, which of course was diplomatically recognized.

With such equivocation on the part of the Church, is it any surprise that large numbers of Catholics remain anti-Semitic – whether explicitly or implicitly? The struggles between Israel and her neighbours have spawned an anti-Zionism which is often informed by anti-Semitism. Such anti-Semitism in the Catholic Church always was, and always will be, utterly repugnant.

Any catalogue of anti-Judaic pronouncements by prominent Catholics in homilies and dissertations is made all the more disturbing if we remember the part played by preachers in the early Church. In the modern age of theatre, cinema and television, we find it hard to imagine a world in which there was virtually no entertainment of any kind. This void was filled by the small army of itinerant preachers who moved from community to community attracting hundreds, even thousands, to their sermons. Such sermons were not brief discourses but lengthy tirades, lasting two or three hours and delivered at least twice a day, like modern matinée and evening theatrical performances.

The preachers roused themselves and their audiences into a fever of excitement, their recurrent theme being the evil of sin and the horror of the punishment that it might incur in the next world. Inevitably there were the favourite 'baddies', as in modern melodramas; and these, of course, were the Jews. From about the third century onwards, they became the familiar figures whom Christians loved to hate as the accursed murderers of their beloved Lord and God. The impression grew into a monstrous caricature, and is still with us.

It is, in fact, worth citing at this point an interesting and surprising example of the largely subconscious image Catholics instinctively continue to have of Jews. It comes from what is easily the leading place of pilgrimage in the Catholic world, namely Lourdes in southern France. The example reflects no criticism on the author's part of that town or its religious activities. I have often been there, and find it most interesting in devotional, theological and historical terms.

Adjacent, however, to the main 'grotto' area is a small, rounded hill on which are depicted, in a series of larger-than-life tableaux, the Stations of the Cross. These are for the devotional act wherein pious Catholics move between fourteen 'stations' depicting scenes in Our Lord's progress toward His crucifixion on Mount Calvary. The Roman soldiers are depicted as well-disciplined protectors of Jesus from the snarls and lewd gestures of members of the rabble in the background. The latter appear as Jews of the most hideous aspect, like something from a gruesome, illuminated medieval text, with gaping mouths, hooked noses and gnarled accusing fingers. Our Lord meanwhile, a Jew himself, is the central figure, being depicted as a god-like Aryan figure, resembling nothing so much as a Hollywood star like Robert Redford.

The significant aspect of this travesty is that its incongruity is scarcely ever, if at all, noticed by the hundreds and thousands of pilgrims who faithfully trudge up one side and down the other of this long hill, stopping to pray at each station. In a post-Conciliar Catholic world, where anti-Judaism has been anathematized, these particular and offensive stations should be removed. They probably would be, were it not for a fear of the outcry that would arise in Catholic circles if such a restitution of justice were attempted. It took years, after all, for the objectionable anti-Jewish features of the famous Oberammergau Passion Play to be removed, in the face of self-righteous Catholic protest. Something similar would almost certainly happen at Lourdes.

One of the crucial tests of Catholicism in the twenty-first century must be its willingness to cleanse the Augean stables of its troubled history with the Jewish community world-wide. Repairing a schism which has endured for almost 2,000 years would be an act of love very much in keeping with the character of the founder of the Catholic Church – Himself a Jew.

Rightly or wrongly, Pacelli's name will always be linked with Hitler's persecution of the Jews. And yet it may be argued that to ask why Pacelli was silent about the Holocaust is to ask the wrong question. A better question may be to ask why Pacelli remained silent on virtually every atrocity throughout the 1930s and 1940s. (Indeed, as we have seen, he maintained a relative silence on distressing post-war subjects such as financial corruption within the Church and the dreadful behaviour of certain of the clergy in Sicily.) Certainly Pacelli's silence regarding the Croatian genocide prefigures his silence on the Holocaust. Always he felt that he was working for the greater good. Always he chose to believe that *détente* would preclude retribution and operate in the best interests of the victims. Of course, in retrospect we can see that Hitler played Pacelli with consummate expertise. Pacelli's belief that some accommodation – however distasteful – with Fascism might be possible, was ultimately a delusion. Hitler, by his own admission, intended to crush the Church beneath his heel, when the time was right.

In retrospect, we can also see that Pacelli's much-vaunted neutrality was a façade. Certainly his complicity in the plot to overthrow Hitler (almost certainly by assassination) exposed the Church to a shocking risk and made a mockery of neutrality.

In contrast to his 'appeasement mentality' with Fascism, Pacelli was uncompromising and unrelenting in his long-standing campaign against communism. Here, there was no accommodation, no delusion, no façade. If communism triumphed, the Church would thereby perish. For the sake of all humanity, it must not prevail.

Pacelli's character is endlessly intriguing. Certainly, aspects of his character are closely connected with the most controversial areas of his life. We know that he was neurotic, particularly in matters of health. In various descriptions and at various times, he has been described as arrogant and vain. His arrogance was like that of many a pope before him: being aware of possessing a supreme, almost mystical superiority over all other human beings and consequently exuding an inevitable aura of effortless triumphalism and self-exaltation. As to his vanity, it was that of an actor at the height of his powers, anxious that his every word should have its maximum impact on the world through – in the case of Pacelli – his incessant stream of discourses.

In June 1945, in a condemnation of unprecedented ferocity, Pope Pius XII stated that Nazism was 'a satanic spectre ... the arrogant apostasy from Jesus Christ, the denial of his doctrine and work of redemption, the cult of violence, the idolatry of race and blood, the overthrow of human liberty and dignity'. The reason for his not uttering such a condemnation earlier is implicit in the above account.

On one particularly fraught occasion, Pasqualina noted the resemblance to Shakespearean tragedy. In many ways, Pacelli's whole life was such a tragedy. He was a man of great goodness, facing terrible evil. His epitaph is the haunting refrain: '*I wish I could have done more.*'

Acknowledgements

A source of invaluable information was Archbishop Canisius van Lierde, papal sacristan. This information came indirectly, as van Lierde was a great friend of Fr John Flynn, a fellow Augustinian, whom he met frequently and to whom he told much of significance about the Pope. I came to know John Flynn well; he was a mine of helpful expertise and insight.

Another valuable source (again indirectly) was Cardinal Giuseppe Pizzardo, a close confidant of Pius XII. My connection with this interesting, somewhat bird-like cardinal came about through my friendship with three remarkable American sisters who went to live in Rome after World War Two. These were Estelle, Carola and Francesca MacMurrough – never married, very rich, thoroughly Catholic and greatly enamoured of Rome.

I had previously known the MacMurrough sisters during my schooldays in the USA during the war. They were great friends of my sister; I often met them while on visits to New York. Their nickname was 'the Holy Women', a title given liturgically to a class of female saint, honoured by a special feast in the Roman Missal.

Knowing that the MacMurrough sisters were in Rome, I looked them up when I was at the Beda College. They had an apartment in the piazza on the former courtyard, or *cortile*, behind the Church of Santa Cecilia in Trastevore, an ancient and extremely interesting church on the south (Vatican) side of the River Tiber. It was the titular parish church of Cardinal Pizzardo, who lived on the opposite side of the *cortile* from the MacMurrough sisters. They had known him for quite a long time and took over the entire running of his household, for which he was immensely grateful.

They saw him often, at least once a week, and had many conversations with him about the Pope, a great hero to Pizzardo and the 'Holy Women'. On my various visits to the MacMurroughs, conversation often turned to the subject of Pius XII; and I learned a great deal from this source, even though I only actually met Pizzardo once. The latter knew Pius well and sympathized with his 'Great Design'. He once said, regarding Pius XII's behaviour in relation to Nazi Germany: 'He could act in no other way.'

Another person whom I came to know well, as he was an old friend of my mother's, was a certain William Babington Macaulay. He was at one time the Irish Ambassador to the Holy See and had been married to the extremely rich American lady, Countess Brady (Macaulay). She, in turn, had been married to an influential American Catholic who had been created a papal count by the Holy See in return for his 'services' (mostly monetary) to the Vatican. The Brady home, which I have visited, was called Inisfada, near Manhasset, Long Island, New York. It is now a Jesuit retreat and study centre. It was here that Pacelli stayed during his visit to the USA in 1936. Bill Macaulay, with this background, was immensely informative on the subject of Pacelli.

Count Henri de Maillardoz was also an old friend of my mother's. He worked in the Special Administration of the Holy See, a part of the Vatican financial department, and was very interesting indeed in his comments about Pius XII.

Last but not least is Cardinal Augustin Bea himself, Malachi Martin's superior, and Pope Pius's confessor and confidant. I translated his *The Way to Unity after the Council*, which taught me much about his mode of thought although, being German, his Italian tended to be heavy and opaque. My translation of his work provided a valuable opportunity for meeting him. Although we never talked about the Pope, our meeting was enough to convince me that Cardinal Bea thought very highly of Malachi Martin. They had evidently formed a relationship conducive to the exchange of much otherwise confidential information.

The sources mentioned above may indicate the rather unusual approach to my treatment of Pacelli. The information received from these sources was extremely varied. Each individual item of information, though important, was incomplete and inconclusive in itself. It was only by putting all the pieces together, against the background of the known facts of Pacelli's career, that it has been possible to present this entirely new interpretation of the life and career of Pope Pius XII.

Others who directly or indirectly supplied information, during my time in Rome or through later contacts, were: Mgr Charles Duchemin, Rector of the Beda College; Mgr Giovanni Battista Montini, afterwards Pope Paul VI, Patron of Beda College (later Pope Paul VI); Brother Walsh, Office of the Maestro di Camera; Mgr Domenico Tardini, Pro-Secretary of State, Mgr Charles Burns, Secret Archives of the Vatican; Don Berti, Secretary, Vicariate of Rome, and Archbishop (later Cardinal) Benelli.

Others who provided information, directly and indirectly, arising from personal acquaintance, include:

Rabbi Israel (afterwards Eugenio) Zolli;

Stanley Morrison, a patient of Dr Niehans who treated Pacelli with cellular rejuvenation;

Mgr Peter Whitty, Vice-Rector, Beda College, Rome;

Fr Jean-Marie Charles-Roux, son of the former French Ambassador to the Holy See;

Signora Compitelli, widow of a sergeant in the Swiss Guard, who had been in charge of security outside the papal apartments in Pius XII's time;

Alan McElwain and Michael Wilson, Rome correspondents of the *Catholic Herald* (1952–68);

Princess Doria, Mgr Hemmick and Mgr (afterwards Archbishop) Carew, secretaries to successive popes; and many others.

Others from whom I garnered valuable information about Pacelli include: Archbishop Eugenio Cardinale, a Curial official at the time of Pius XII and later Apostolic Delegate in Great Britain and papal nuncio in Brussels; Peter Bander van Duren; Cardinal John Wright; and Monsignor Charles Duchemin.

The foregoing will, it is hoped, give some idea of what I have called 'the quarry', from which I have excavated over the years much valuable knowledge about Pacelli the man, and Pius the Pope.

To begin with, there was no one whom the Fuhrer feared more than Pacelli. All was changed by the Concordat. Though, to the very end, Pacelli remained the 'Hound of Hitler', this role was gradually eroded by the Great Design. The panoply of paradoxes ended in Greek tragedy.

Bibliographical Notes

Each chapter is referenced as appropriate; thus the reader can source the evidence as it is assembled. In addition, the Acknowledgements above show other, more personal sources. However, it would be remiss not to pay a particular debt of thanks to *Hitler's Pope: The Secret History of Pius XII* (London, 1999) by the noted academic John Cornwell. In some sections of this book I tread common ground with Mr Cornwell. Although we come to rather different conclusions about Pope Pius XII, I would like to take this opportunity to pay tribute to his most scholarly and fascinating exposition.

Another book to which I owe a particular intellectual debt is *La Popessa* (New York, 1983), by Paul I. Murphy with R. René Arlington. Thirty-five years elapsed between Mr Murphy's first writing about the Church and this excellent biography of Pasqualina. It is therefore something of a labour of love. Pasqualina was a character of great interest in her own right. (She may well have been 'the greatest Pope that never was'.) And 'the Pasqualina factor' sheds much-needed light on Pacelli the man, that brave, vulnerable figure enshrined as the omniscient and numinous Pope Pius XII.

I am particularly grateful to Mr Murphy's book for Pasqualina's dialogue with such key characters as Pacelli and Tisserant. This was garnered from some 30 hours of tape recordings, spanning a period of almost 90 years. Mr Murphy makes the valuable point that, with the passage of so much time, it was not always possible to be certain of the exact words spoken. Thus, Pasqualina's dialogue with Pacelli had to be reconstructed to some degree. The important point is that such reconstruction captured the essence of her indomitable and loving spirit.

Gilles Lambert, *Conquest of Age: The Extraordinary Story of Dr Paul Niehans* (New York/Toronto, 1959) gives a comprehensive exposition of Dr Niehans' novel approach to rejuvenation. Again, the contribution of Dr Niehans is rarely mentioned in accounts of the life of Pope Pius XII. The Furtwängler connection is a fascinating historical footnote.

Chapter One
1. Quoted in J. Cornwell, *Hitler's Pope: The Secret History of Pius XII*, Viking (London, 1999), p. 17.
2. N. Padellaro, *Portrait of Pius XII*, Eng. trans. (London, 1956), p. 10.
3. Ibid., pp. 10–11.
4. Quoted in P. Lehnert, *Ich durfte ihm dienen: Erinnerungen an Papst Pius XII* (Würzburg, 1982), p. 9ff.

5. Quoted in I. Konopatzki, *Eugenio Pacelli: Kindheit und Jugend in Dokumente* (Munich, 1978), p. 34.
6. Quoted in *Hitler's Pope: The Secret History of Pius XII*, p. 20.
7. Quoted in C. Falconi, *The Popes in the Twentieth Century* (London, 1967), p. 295.
8. See *Articoli per il processo* (Rome, 1967), p. 16; I. Girodani, *Pio XII: Un Grande Papa* (Turin, 1961), pp. 31–2.
9. Quoted in *Hitler's Pope: The Secret History of Pius XII*, p. 32.
10. Ibid, p. 33.
11. Ibid.

Chapter Two

1. *Codex Juris Canonici* (Rome, 1917), Canon 218.
2. Ibid., Canon 1324.
3. T. Lincoln Bouscarew, SJ and Adam C. Ellis, SJ, *Canon Law: A Text and Commentary* (Milwaukee, 1951), p. 743.
4. Ibid.
5. *Codex Juris Canonici* (Rome, 1917), Canon 1325.
6. Quoted in *Hitler's Pope: The Secret History of Pius XII*, p. 53.

Chapter Three

1. Paul I. Murphy with R. René Arlington, *La Popessa* (New York, 1983), p. 23.
2. Ibid., p. 26.
3. Ibid., p. 27.
4. Ibid., p. 28.
5. Ibid., p. 29.
6. Ibid., p. 6.
7. Ibid., p. 38.
8. Ibid., p. 39.
9. Ibid., p. 39.
10. M. O'Carroll, *Pius XII: Greatness Dishonoured* (Dublin, 1980), p. 27.
11. Ibid.
12. *Vatican SRS, Guerra Europa, 1914–18*, I, viii, 17, Vol. III, folio 62.
13. *Hitler's Pope: The Secret History of Pius XII*, p. 65.
14. Ibid., p. 66.
15. Quoted ibid., p. 68.
16. Ibid.
17. Ibid.
18. *Pius XII: Greatness Dishonoured*, p. 29.
19. *Portrait of Pius XII*, p. 41.
20. Quoted in *Hitler's Pope: The Secret History of Pius XII*, p. 72.
21. Ibid., p. 69.
22. Ibid., p. 71.

Chapter Four

1. *La Popessa*, p. 43.
2. Ibid., p. 44.
3. Ibid., p. 45.
4. Ibid.
5. Ibid., p. 47.
6. *Vatican SRS*, Bavaria letter from Pacelli to Gasparri, 18 April 1919, folio 37.
7. Quoted in *Hitler's Pope: The Secret History of Pius XII*, p. 77.
8. Ibid.
9. Ibid.
10. *La Popessa*, p. 51.
11. Ibid., p. 52.
12. Ibid.

Chapter Five

1. Quoted in E. R. Huber and W. Huber, *Staat und Kirche*, Vol. 2 (Berlin, 1976), p. 540.
2. Quoted in *Hitler's Pope: The Secret History of Pius XII*, p. 83.

3. Ibid.
4. *Vatican SRS*, Germania, 1919, Fasc. 885, folio 11.
5. Quoted in Klaus Scholder, *The Churches and the Third Reich*, Vol. 1 (London, 1987, 1988), p. 61.
6. Quoted in *Hitler's Pope: The Secret History of Pius XII*, p. 92.
7. *The Churches and the Third Reich*, pp. 62, 249.
8. Ibid., p. 62.
9. *Vatican SRS*, Germania, 1921, Fasc. 902, folios 20ff.
10. Foreign Office Papers, 371/43869/21 (Kew Public Record Office).
11. Quoted in *Hitler's Pope: The Secret History of Pius XII*, p. 98.
12. Quoted in A. Hatch and S. Walshe, *Crown of Glory: The Life of Pope Pius XII* (London, 1957), p. 83.
13. *La Popessa*, p. 60.
14. Ibid., p. 62.
15. Ibid., p. 67.
16. Ibid., p. 69.
17. Quoted in *Hitler's Pope: The Secret History of Pius XII*, p. 114.
18. Quoted in J. D. Holmes, *The Papacy in the Modern World* (London, 1981), p. 80.
19. Quoted in *Hitler's Pope: The Secret History of Pius XII*, p. 115.
20. Ibid.
21. Ibid.

Chapter Six
1. *La Popessa*, p. 70.
2. Quoted in *Pius XII: Greatness Dishonoured*, pp. 33–4.
3. *La Popessa*, p. 70.
4. *The Popes in the Twentieth Century*, p. 293.
5. Ibid., p. 292.
6. *La Popessa*, p. 75.
7. Quoted in *Hitler's Pope: The Secret History of Pius XII*, p. 111.
8. Quoted ibid., p. 94.
9. Ibid.
10. Stehlin, Stewart A., *Weimar and the Vatican, 1919–1933: German-Vatican Diplomatic Relations in the Interwar Years* (Princeton, 1983), p. 69.
11. A. Hitler, *Mein Kampf*, translated by Ralph Manheim (London, 1992), pp. 105–7.
12. *Hitler's Pope: The Secret History of Pius XII*, p. 107.
13. *The Churches and the Third Reich*, pp. 132–3.
14. Quoted in *Hitler's Pope: The Secret History of Pius XII*, p. 109.
15. Quoted in *The Churches and the Third Reich*, p. 134.
16. Quoted in *Hitler's Pope: The Secret History of Pius XII*, p. 110.
17. Ibid.
18. *La Popessa*, p. 99.
19. Ibid, p. 100.
20. Ibid, p. 102.
21. Ibid, p. 103.
22. Ibid, p. 104.
23. Ibid, p. 106.
24. *Hitler's Pope: The Secret History of Pius XII*, p. 116.
25. Ibid, p. 118.
26. Ibid, p. 121.
27. Ibid, p. 124.
28. Heinrich Brüning, *Memoiren, 1918–1934* (Stuttgart, 1970), p. 360.
29. Quoted in *The Churches and the Third Reich*, p. 153.
30. Ibid., p. 157.
31. Ludwig Kass, 'Der Konkordatstyp des faschistischen Italien', *Zeitschrift für ausländisches öffentliches Recht und Völkerrecht*, III.I, 1933, pp. 488–522.

Chapter Seven
1. Quoted in *Hitler's Pope: The Secret History of Pius XII*, p. 134.
2. Quoted in E. C. Helmreich, *The German Churches under Hitler* (Detroit, 1979), p. 237.
3. Quoted in *Hitler's Pope: The Secret History of Pius XII*, p. 135.

4. Quoted in *The Churches and the Third Reich*, p. 299.
5. O. Chadwick, *Britain and the Vatican during the Second World War* (Cambridge, 1986), p. 86.
6. Quoted in *The German Churches under Hitler*, p. 239.
7. Quoted in *The Churches and the Third Reich*, p. 253.
8. Quoted in W. L. Patch, Jr, *Heinrich Bruning and the Dissolution of the Weimar Republic* (Cambridge, 1998), p. 301.
9. Quoted in *The Churches and the Third Reich*, p. 253.
10. S. Friedländer, *Nazi Germany and the Jews, Vol. 1: The Years of Persecution, 1933–39* (London, 1997), p. 42.
11. Quoted in *Hitler's Pope: The Secret History of Pius XII*, p. 140.
12. Quoted ibid., p. 141.
13. Quoted ibid., p. 142.
14. Quoted ibid., pp. 142–3.
15. Quoted ibid., p. 143.
16. Quoted in *The Churches and the Third Reich*, p. 388.
17. Quoted in *Hitler's Pope: The Secret History of Pius XII*, p. 145.
18. Quoted in ibid., p. 147.
19. Quoted in *The Churches and the Third Reich*, p. 398.
20. Quoted in L. Volk, *Kirchliche Akten über die Reichskonkordatsverhandlungen*, 1933 (Mainz, 1975), pp. 82–5.
21. Quoted in *Hitler's Pope: The Secret History of Pius XII*, p. 148.
22. *Heinrich Bruning and the Dissolution of the Weimar Republic*, pp. 302–3.
23. R. Leiber, 'Reichskonkordat und Ende der Zentrumspartei', *Stimmen der Zeit*, 167, 1960–61, p. 220.
24. Quoted in *The Churches and the Third Reich*, p. 404.
25. Ibid.
26. Ibid., p. 404.
27. Count Harry Kessler of Brüning, quoted in J.-G. Vaillancourt, *Papal Power* (Berkeley, 1980), p. 191.
28. DBFP 1919–1939, Second series, Vol. V, 1933 (London, 1956), p. 524.
29. Ibid., p. 525.
30. *Pius XII: Greatness Dishonoured*, p. 39.
31. DBFP 1919–1939, Second series, Vol. V, 1933, p. 525.
32. *The Churches and the Third Reich*, p. 411.
33. Quoted in *Hitler's Pope: The Secret History of Pius XII*, p. 160.
34. Ibid., p. 161.
35. Ibid., pp. 162–3.
36. Quoted in *The German Churches under Hitler*, p. 262. See also *The Churches and the Third Reich*, p. 515.

Chapter Eight

1. Quoted in D. Tardini, *Pio XII* (Rome, 1959), p. 105.
2. Quoted in *Pius XII: Greatness Dishonoured*.
3. Quoted in *Hitler's Pope: The Secret History of Pius XII*, p. 167.
4. Quoted ibid., p. 168.
5. Quoted in *Portrait of Pius XII*, p. 117.
6. *Crown of Glory*, p. 109.
7. Quoted in *The Popes in the Twentieth Century*, p. 246.
8. Quoted in *Hitler's Pope: The Secret History of Pius XII*, p. 173.
9. Quoted in *La Popessa*, p. 114.
10. Ibid., p. 115.
11. Ibid., p. 117.
12. Quoted ibid., p. 124.
13. Ibid, p. 133.
14. Ibid, p. 136.
15. Ibid.
16. Ibid.
17. Quoted ibid., p. 136.

Chapter Nine
1. Quoted in *La Popessa*, p. 139.
2. Quoted ibid.
3. Quoted ibid., p. 140.
4. Quoted ibid.
5. Quoted ibid.
6. Ibid, p. 141.
7. Ibid.
8. Ibid, p. 142.
9. Ibid.
10. Ibid., p. 143.
11. Quoted ibid.
12. Ibid.
13. Ibid.
14. Ibid., pp. 143–4.
15. Quoted in *The German Churches under Hitler*, p. 279.
16. *The Popes in the Twentieth Century*, p. 228.
17. Quoted in *Hitler's Pope: The Secret History of Pius XII*, p. 182.
18. Quoted ibid.
19. Quoted in *The German Churches under Hitler*, p. 280.
20. Quoted ibid., p. 282.
21. Quoted ibid.
22. *L'Osservatore Romano*, 19–20 July 1937.
23. Bergen to Berlin, 23 July 1937, *DGFP 1918–1945*, Series D, Vol.1, pp. 990–92, quoted in S. Friedländer, *Pius XII*, p. 7.
24. K. Scholder, *A Requiem for Hitler* (London, 1989), p. 160.
25. Quoted in *Portrait of Pius XII*, p. 128.
26. Quoted in *Hitler's Pope: The Secret History of Pius XII*, p. 185.
27. Quoted ibid., pp. 185–6.
28. M. Y. Herczl, *Christianity and the Holocaust of Hungarian Jewry* (Eng. trans. New York, 1993), p. 94.
29. Quoted in G. Noel, *The Anatomy of The Catholic Church* (London, 1994), p. 30.
30. *Nazi Germany and the Jews*, p. 277.
31. Quoted in *Portrait of Pius XII*, p. 129.
32. Quoted in *Hitler's Pope: The Secret History of Pius XII*, p. 191.
33. Quoted ibid, p. 190.
34. Quoted ibid, p. 191.
35. See *Portrait of Pius XII*, p. 133.
36. Quoted in *Hitler's Pope: The Secret History of Pius XII*, p. 203.

Chapter Ten
1. Quoted in *Hitler's Pope: The Secret History of Pius XII*, p. 204.
2. Quoted ibid.
3. N. Lo Bello, *Vatican Papers* (London, 1982), p. 70.
4. Quoted in *Britain and the Vatican*, p. 34.
5. Quoted ibid., p. 42.
6. Quoted ibid., p. 43.
7. *La Popessa*, p. 145.
8. Ibid, p. 146.
9. Ibid.
10. Ibid, p. 147.
11. Ibid.
12. Ibid.
13. Ibid., p. 148.
14. Ibid., p. 149.
15. Ibid., p. 157.
16. G. Zizola, *Quale Papa?* (Rome, 1977), pp. 145–47, cited in Chadwick, *Britain and the Vatican*, p. 47.
17. *Portrait of Pius XII*, p. 147; A. Spinosa, *L'Ultimo Papa* (Milan, 1994), p. 141.

18. F. Charles-Roux, *Huit ans au Vatican, 1932–1940* (Paris, 1947), p. 267.
19. *Portrait of Pius XII*, p. 147.
20. *La Popessa*, p. 153.
21. Ibid., p. 154.
22. Ibid.
23. Ibid.
24. Ibid., p. 155.
25. H. Belloc, letter, 22 March 1939, quoted in A. N. Wilson, *Hilaire Belloc* (London, 1984), p. 358.
26. T. Driberg, *Ruling Passions* (London, 1977), p. 111.
27. Quoted in *Hitler's Pope: The Secret History of Pius XII*, p. 212.
28. Quoted ibid., p. 213.
29. Quoted ibid., p. 214.
30. Ibid.
31. Ibid., p. 160.
32. Ibid., p. 159.
33. Ibid., p. 160.
34. Ibid.
35. Ibid, pp. 160–1.
36. Ibid., p. 161.
37. Ibid.
38. Ibid.
39. Quoted in *Britain and the Vatican*, p. 47.
40. Quoted in *Hitler's Pope: The Secret History of Pius XII*, p. 218.
41. Quoted in *Britain and the Vatican*, p. 47.
42. Ibid.

Chapter Eleven
1. Quoted in *La Popessa*, p. 162.
2. Ibid., pp. 162–3.
3. Ibid., pp. 163–4.
4. Ibid., p. 164.
5. Ibid.
6. Ibid, p. 165.
7. Ibid.
8. Ibid.
9. Ibid.
10. Ibid., pp. 166–7.
11. Ibid., p. 167.
12. Ibid., pp. 167–8.
13. Quoted in G. Craig, *Germany 1866–1945* (Oxford, 1981), p. 709.
14. Quoted in *Hitler's Pope: The Secret History of Pius XII*, p. 226.
15. Foreign Office Papers, 371/23790/283 (Kew Public Record Office).
16. *Britain and the Vatican*, p. 74.
17. Quoted in *Hitler's Pope: The Secret History of Pius XII*, p. 230.
18. Ibid., p. 231.
19. *La Popessa*, p. 170.
20. Ibid.
21. Quoted in *The Popes in the Twentieth Century*, p. 255.
22. Foreign Office Papers, 371/23791/27 (Kew Public Record Office).
23. Quoted in *Hitler's Pope: The Secret History of Pius XII*, p. 234.
24. *Pius XII: Greatness Dishonoured*, p. 53.
25. Quoted in *Hitler's Pope: The Secret History of Pius XII*, p. 236.
26. Foreign Office Papers, 800/318/6 (Kew Public Record Office).
27. Quoted in *Hitler's Pope: The Secret History of Pius XII*, p. 237.
28. Foreign Office Papers, 800/318/7 (Kew Public Record Office).
29. Ibid. /34.
30. Ibid. /36.
31. J. S. Conway, 'The meeting between Pope Pius XII and Ribbentrop', *Historical Papers of the Canadian Historical Association*, 1968, p. 222.
32. Quoted ibid., p. 224.

33. Quoted in *Hitler's Pope: The Secret History of Pius XII*, p. 240.
34. Quoted ibid., p. 236.
35. Quoted ibid., p. 235–6.
36. *Britain and the Vatican*, pp. 98–9.

Chapter Twelve
1. *La Popessa*, pp. 175–6.
2. Ibid., p. 176.
3. Ibid.
4. Ibid., p. 178.
5. Ibid., p. 179.
6. Ibid.
7. Ibid., p. 188.
8. Ibid.
9. Ibid.
10. Ibid.
11. Ibid.
12. Ibid.
13. Ibid., p. 190.

Chapter Thirteen
1. Quoted in *Hitler's Pope: The Secret History of Pius XII*, p. 242.
2. Quoted ibid.
3. *The Popes in the Twentieth Century*, p. 252.
4. See J. F. Pollard's paper, 'The Vatican and the Wall Street Crash: Bernardino Nogara and papal finances in the early 1930s', *The Historical Journal*, Vol. 42, No. 4, Dec. 1999, pp. 1077–1091.
5. Quoted in J. Steinberg, *All or Nothing: The Axis and the Holocaust, 1941–43* (London, 1990), p. 276.
6. Quoted in *Hitler's Pope: The Secret History of Pius XII*, p. 252.
7. Quoted in *All or Nothing*, p. 181.
8. Quoted in ibid., p. 133.
9. C. Falconi, *The Silence of Pius XII* (London, 1970), p. 382.
10. Ibid., p. 388.
11. *Hitler's Pope: The Secret History of Pius XII*, p. 255.
12. Quoted in H. Butler, *The Sub-Prefect Should Have Held His Tongue*, ed. R. F. Foster (London, 1990), p. 275.
13. *Silence of Pius XII*, p. 304.
14. *Actes et Documents du Saint Siège relatifs à la Seconde Guerre Mondiale*, viii, Vatican, 1965–1981, pp. 250f.
15. *Silence of Pius XII*, p. 333.
16. Quoted in *Hitler's Pope: The Secret History of Pius XII*, p. 259.
17. *Silence of Pius XII*, pp. 344–6.
18. Ibid.
19. Quoted in *Pius XII: Greatness Dishonoured*, p. 119.
20. Ibid.
21. W. Jochmann, ed., *Adolf Hitler: Monologe im Führerhauptquartier, 1941–1944* (Hamburg, 1980), p. 41.
22. Ibid., p. 150.
23. Quoted in W. Purdy, *The Church on the Move* (London, 1965), p. 225.

Chapter Fourteen
1. *La Popessa*, p. 192.
2. Ibid., pp. 192–3.
3. Ibid., p. 193.
4. Ibid, pp. 193–4.
5. Quoted in *The Popes in the Twentieth Century*, p. 256.
6. Quoted in *La Popessa*, p. 196.
7. Quoted ibid.
8. Quoted ibid, p. 197.
9. Quoted in *Pius XII: Greatness Dishonoured* (Dublin, 1980), p. 74.

10. Quoted ibid., p. 80.
11. Quoted in L. Poliakov, *Harvest of Hate* (London, 1956), p. 17.
12. Quoted in *Pius XII: Greatness Dishonoured*, p. 80.
13. Quoted in M. Gilbert, *Final Journey* (London, 1979), p. 64.
14. Quoted in *Pius XII: Greatness Dishonoured*, p. 76.
15. Quoted in *Hitler's Pope: The Secret History of Pius XII*, p. 281.
16. Letter from Osborne to McEwan, 11 June 1942.
17. Osborne's diary, quoted in *Britain and the Vatican*, p. 206.
18. Quoted in *Hitler's Pope: The Secret History of Pius XII*, p. 283.
19. Quoted ibid.
20. Letter from Osborne to McEwan, 31 July 1942.
21. *La Popessa*, pp. 199–200.
22. Ibid., p. 201.
23. Ibid.
24. Ibid.
25. Ibid.
26. G. Lewy, *The Catholic Church and Nazi Germany* (New York, 1964), p. 303.
27. N. Stoltzfus, *Resistance of the Heart* (London, 1996), p. 147.
28. *The Catholic Church and Nazi Germany*, p. 267.
29. Quoted in *Hitler's Pope: The Secret History of Pius XII*, p. 197.

Chapter Fifteen

1. *La Popessa*, p. 212.
2. Ibid., p. 213.
3. Ibid., p. 214.
4. Ibid., p. 215.
5. Ibid., p. 218.
6. Ibid., p. 219.
7. Ibid.
8. This material appears in the Teste manuscript, pp. 831f., in the keeping of the Jesuit Curia at the Borgo Santo Spirito in Rome.
9. Ibid., pp. 836–7.
10. *La Popessa*, p. 221.
11. Ibid.
12. Ibid.
13. Ibid., pp. 202–3.
14. Ibid., p. 203.
15. Ibid., p. 204.
16. Ibid., p. 205.
17. R. Katz, *Black Sabbath* (London, 1969), p. 65.
18. Ibid., p. 87.
19. O. Hacki, *Pius XII* (New York, 1951), p. 97.
20. Quoted in *Hitler's Pope: The Secret History of Pius XII*, p. 303.
21. Blet, *Pie XII* (Paris, 1997), p. 243. Also J. Lewis, *The Silence of Pius XII*, BBC documentary, 1996.
22. Quoted in *Black Sabbath*, p. 197.
23. Quoted ibid.
24. Quoted in *Pius XII: Greatness Dishonoured*, p. 95.
25. Quoted in *Black Sabbath*, p. 198.
26. Telegram from Möllhausen to Ribbentrop, 7 October 1943 in *Inland II Geheim*, Doc. E421524 – Documents of the German Foreign Ministry, 1920-1945, in National Archives, Washington DC; quoted in *Black Sabbath*, p. 202.
27. *Actes et Documents du Saint Siège relatifs à la Seconde Guerre Mondiale*, ix, Vatican, 1965–1981, p. 506.
28. Ibid.
29. Telegram from Weizsäcker to Ribbentrop in Berlin, 17 October 1943, in *Inland II Geheim*, quoted in *Black Sabbath*, p. 215.
30. Quoted in *Pius XII: Greatness Dishonoured*, p. 97.
31. Foreign Office Papers, 371/3757/1/RI0995 (Kew Public Record Office).
32. Account in Lewis, *The Silence of Pius XII*, BBC documentary, 1996.
33. *La Popessa*, p. 220.

34. Ibid., p. 222.
35. Ibid., pp. 223–4.
36. Ibid., p. 224.
37. Ibid., pp. 224–5.
38. Ibid., p. 226.
39. Ibid.
40. Ibid., p. 227.

Chapter Sixteen
1. Quoted in *The Popes in the Twentieth Century*, p. 265.
2. Quoted ibid.
3. Quoted ibid., p. 266.
4. Quoted ibid.
5. Quoted ibid., p. 273.
6. Quoted in *Hitler's Pope: The Secret History of Pius XII*, p. 330.
7. A. Riccardi, 'The Vatican of Pius XII and the Roman Party', *Concilium* 197 (1987), p. 47.
8. J. Mindszenty, *Memoirs* (New York, 1974), p. 50.
9. *La Popessa*, p. 232.
10. Ibid., p. 234.
11. Ibid.
12. Ibid., p. 235.
13. Ibid., p. 237.
14. Ibid., p. 238.
15. Ibid.
16. Ibid., p. 239.
17. Quoted ibid., p. 240.
18. Quoted ibid., p. 241.
19. Quoted ibid., p. 242.
20. Quoted ibid., p. 243.

Chapter Seventeen
1. *La Popessa*, p. 245.
2. Ibid., p. 246.
3. Ibid., p. 251.
4. *Acta Apostolicae Sedis*, Vol. 42, 1950, pp. 561–78.
5. Ibid., p. 567.
6. Ibid., p. 568; also F. A. Sullivan, *Creative Fidelity* (Dublin, 1996), p. 22.
7. Quoted in *Hitler's Pope: The Secret History of Pius XII*, p. 339.
8. Quoted in M. Ward, ed., *France, Pagan?* (New York, 1949).
9. *Pius XII: Greatness Dishonoured*, p. 158.
10. Ibid., pp. 159–60.
11. Ibid., pp. 191–2.
12. Quoted in N. Perry and L. Echeverría, *Under the Heel of Mary* (London, 1988), p. 233.
13. *La Popessa*, p. 265.
14. Ibid., p. 266.
15. Ibid.
16. Ibid.
17. Ibid.
18. Ibid., p. 266.
19. Ibid.
20. Ibid.
21. Ibid.
22. Ibid.
23. Ibid., p. 261.
24. Ibid., p. 262.
25. Ibid.
26. Ibid.
27. Ibid., p. 254.
28. Ibid.
29. Ibid., p. 263.

30. Ibid.
31. Ibid., p. 248.
32. Ibid.
33. Ibid., p. 258.
34. Ibid.
35. Ibid., p. 268.
36. Ibid.
37. Ibid.
38. Ibid., p. 269.
39. Ibid.
40. Ibid., p. 270.
41. Ibid.
42. Ibid.
43. Ibid., p. 271.

Chapter Eighteen
1. *La Popessa*, pp. 264–5.
2. Ibid., p. 271.
3. Ibid., p. 267.
4. Ibid., p. 272.
5. Ibid.
6. Ibid.
7. Ibid., pp. 272–3.
8. Ibid., p. 273.
9. Ibid.
10. Ibid., p. 274.
11. Ibid.
12. Ibid., pp. 274–5.
13. Ibid., p. 275.
14. Ibid.
15. Ibid.
16. Ibid, 276.
17. Ibid.
18. Ibid.
19. Ibid.
20. Ibid., pp. 276–7.
21. Ibid., p. 277.
22. Ibid., p. 278.
23. Quoted ibid.
24. Ibid., p. 279.
25. Ibid.
26. Ibid., p. 280.
27. Ibid.
28. Ibid.
29. Ibid., p. 281.
30. Ibid.
31. Ibid.
32. Ibid., p. 282.
33. Ibid., p. 283.
34. Ibid.
35. Ibid., p. 284.
36. Ibid., p. 285.
37. Ibid., p. 287.
38. Quoted in *The Popes in the Twentieth Century*, p. 298.
39. *La Popessa*, p. 285.
40. Ibid.
41. Ibid.
42. Ibid., p. 286.
43. Ibid.
44. Ibid.

45. Ibid., p. 294.
46. Ibid.
47. Ibid., p. 297.
48. Ibid.
49. Ibid., p. 296.
50. Ibid., p. 297.
51. Ibid.
52. Ibid.
53. Ibid.
54. Ibid., p. 299.
55. Ibid.
56. Ibid.

Chapter Nineteen

1. *La Popessa*, p. 300.
2. Ibid, p. 301.
3. Ibid.
4. Ibid, p. 302.
5. Ibid.
6. Ibid, p. 303.
7. Ibid.
8. Ibid.
9. Ibid, p. 304.
10. Ibid.
11. Ibid.
12. Ibid, p. 305.
13. Ibid.
14. Ibid.
15. Ibid, p. 306.
16. Ibid, p. 307.
17. Ibid.
18. Ibid.
19. Ibid.
20. Ibid.
21. Ibid, p. 308.
22. Ibid.

Chapter Twenty

1. *Pius XII: Greatness Dishonoured*, p. 11. Also see P. Lapide, *The Last Three Popes and the Jews* (London, 1967).
2. *Pius XII: Greatness Dishonoured*, p. 18.
3. Telegram from Golda Meir to the Vatican, 1958.
4. *Pius XII: Greatness Dishonoured*, Foreword.
5. Quoted in *The Popes in the Twentieth Century*, p. 258.
6. Quoted in ibid., pp. 258–9.
7. *Nuremberg Transcript*, National Archives, Washington DC, Vol. 24, pp. 9518.
8. *Die Welt*, 6 April 1963.
9. Interview in *Vita*, 8 April 1964.
10. *The Last Three Popes and the Jews*, p. 202.
11. A. J. P. Taylor, *The Origins of the Second World War*, 2nd edn (London, 1963), p. 11.
12. In *La Parrochia*, 15 May 1964.
13. Letter to *The Tablet*, 28 June 1963.
14. Charles de Gaulle, *Mémoires de guerre, II: L'Unité* (Paris, 1956), p. 233.
15. *L'Osservatore Romano*, 5 February 1944.
16. *Pius XII: Greatness Dishonoured*, quote preceding Foreword.
17. *Pio XII* (Vatican Press, 1960), p. 69.
18. Ibid., p. 79.
19. *Pius XII: Greatness Dishonoured*, p. 67.
20. Letter to *The Tablet*, 28 June 1963.
21. Quoted in *The Popes in the Twentieth Century*, p. 244.

22. Ibid., pp. 295–6.
23. Quoted in *Pius XII: Greatness Dishonoured*, p. 68.
24. Quoted in *La Popessa*, p. 242.
25. Malachi Martin, *Three Popes and the Cardinal* (New York, 1972).
26. *La Popessa*, p. 228.
27. Ibid., pp. 228–9.
28. Quoted ibid., p. 229.
29. Ibid.

Chapter Twenty One

1. Encyclical *Unam Sanctum*, 18 November 1302.
2. Papal Bull *Regnans in Excelsis*, 1570.
3. Lecture VIII, 'Lectures on Anglican Difficulties', 1852.

Index